The Seattle GuideBook

Archie & Joyce Satterfield & Merle E. Dowd

The Writing Works
Division of Morse Press, Inc.
Seattle, WA

Library of Congress Cataloging in Publication Data

Satterfield, Archie.
  The Seattle guidebook.

  Includes index.
  1. Seattle (Wash.) — Description — Guide-books.
I. Satterfield, Joyce.   II. Dowd, Merle E.
III. Title.
F899.S43S27   1981   917.97'77   81-14638
ISBN 0-916076-45-8 (pbk.)   AACR2

Published by The Writing Works
              Division of Morse Press, Inc.
              417 East Pine St.
              Seattle, WA 98122

Library of Congress Catalog Card Number: 81-14638
ISBN: 0-916076-45-8   AACR2

CONTENTS

Acknowledgments

Each entry in this guide represents the cooperation of the business or agency mentioned, and to each we wish to express our appreciation. However, the authors have accepted no gratuities from any restaurant, theater, or other firm listed in the book.

Writing such a book can easily lead the authors down the thorny path to paranoia because they can become convinced that everybody waits until the guide is published before changing their address or telephone number, or going out of business entirely.

We ask that you strike a blow for the author's mental health by informing us of changes so they can be included in subsequent editions of *The Seattle GuideBook.*

About the Authors

Archie Satterfield is the author of more than a dozen books, including *Adventures in Washington* and *Elton Bennett, His Life and Art,* published by The Writing Works.

Joyce Satterfield began as a researcher on *The Seattle GuideBook's* first edition and has since done the revisions on each new edition.

Merle Dowd writes the weekly column, "Money Talk," in *The Seattle Times* and writes regularly for a number of national magazines on a variety of subjects including money. *The Seattle GuideBook* is his 10th book.

Cover Photo by Jim Larsen

Maps by Hartwig E. Petersen

INTRODUCTION

ONE of the best bits of advice we've ever heard was from a mechanic who told a customer that if his car ran, he should leave it alone. This same advice applies to writers of guide books when the time for revisions comes around. Rather than totally changing the concept—or even throwing out entire sections in favor of different material—we are sticking with what we had in the first edition back in 1975 when the book was first published.

Since that first book, which by the way was the first book published by The Writing Works and launched it as one of the area's major publishers, we have revised *The Seattle Guide Book* four times and have seen competitors come and go. Assuming that we must be doing something right, we have resisted all temptations to make radical changes.

When we decided to compile the book, we spent almost as much time discussing the tone of the book as we did the contents. We wanted it to be more than a compilation, yet not a history of the city. We felt then, as we still do, that a guide book should be a pleasure to read as compared with the Yellow Pages or a chamber of commerce publication. Otherwise, there would be no real need for the book. We hope that our enjoyment of Seattle is reflected in the way the book is written. We have tried to keep the reading light and whatever humor you may find in it not at someone's expense. Thus, we have not poked fun at anyone in the one section that everyone seems to like, Phone 'n Games. After spending many nights in strange cities watching the usual bland television shows, we have wished for a local guide book with a chuckle or two in it.

We can still boast, as we did in previous editions, that Seattle is changing for the better. When we arrived here two decades ago, it was an ordinary city in a beautiful setting. Its leadership was rather uptight, tight-fisted, and given to repeating cliches such as "Don't rock the boat." Since that time, it has undergone some of the most positive changes any American city has experienced. While it isn't so perfect that the policemen are complaining of boredom and talking about the good old days of crime waves, still nearly everyone we talk to has very positive ideas about the city.

First of all, Seattle is becoming a prettier place and directed more toward people than in the past. Our attitude toward ourselves is changing, and the city reflects that. Like a girl who decided she wasn't so homely or plain after all, we have begun dressing up a bit. Flowers appear everywhere, in boxes along the street, in windows, and along the busy sidewalks downtown. Trees are constantly being planted in areas that once were barren of everything that grows, including weeds. We have been busy revitalizing neighborhoods and small shopping areas, such as the Fremont District. For several years we seemed to think the renovation of Pioneer Square was a fluke and that it would never spread to other parts of the city. Happily, we were wrong, and many neighborhoods and business districts that were rundown and grubby now look better than they did when they were new.

The Freeway Park, a touch of greenery in a concrete jungle, is relatively new but not so new that we have learned to take it for granted. The waterfront that once was a visual and olfactory disaster has emerged as one of the most interesting waterfronts on the West Coast. The Pike Place Markets were saved from the bulldozer and the sterility bureaucrats call urban renewal. Lake Washington was returned to its natural state (the water, not the shoreline) a decade or more ago. Lake Union, a short time ago an industrial park, is now a people place, too.

In the past Seattle had a reputation of being one of the more staid—and stagnant—cities in spite of the colorful characters who have lived here. But over the past decade or two so many new people have moved here in search of life with meaning that the old order which dominated Seattle has been simply ignored. While the money and political power tend to rest in the hands of a few, the day-to-day lifestyle is in the hands of everyone else.

Seattle does not have an Establishment as a strong force any longer; it has several establishments. It is perfectly normal for its residents to move freely among the politicians, the sports figures, the cultural leaders, and other power groups with an ease and welcome not possible in other parts of the country. One not only can, but is almost expected, to follow the Kipling dictum of walking among kings without losing the common touch.

Newcomers from the Midwest and East are initially surprised at Seattle's lack of ostentation. Visit Dallas or Chicago or New York and you'll see the most magnificent homes perched on hills or on broad expanses of lawn for all to see. In Seattle, if these homes aren't in private areas such as The Highlands and Broadmoor, they are virtually hidden from view by greenery. The expression, "low profile," could have been invented here. Nor can you judge a person's success of wealth by the automobile they drive or the way they dress.

One trait of Seattle that is particularly disconcerting to newcomers is our inherent reserve. Since one's privacy is almost sacred here, an unpleasant result is that newcomers often have a difficult time making a circle of friends. "You're a tough nut to crack," one newcome said.

Consequently, there is a remarkable degree of personal freedom in the city, and the social pressures to conform and to yield the social right of way to people with proper family names exists only among those who thrive on that sort of pecking order. They are very easy to ignore, and most people are blissfully unaware of such goings on.

Far-sighted leaders in and out of government have worried more about the quality of life in Seattle than mere quantities. These were the people who urged the cleanup of Lake Washington, after it had been a sewage dump for many years. One of the nicest things we remember was going out to a seaplane harbor on Lake Washington a few years after the sewage stopped being pumped into the lake and having the pilot point down at the water and say it was the first time in his life he had seen the bottom of the lake.

These were the same people who insisted that Seattle's parks be expanded, improved and beautified. They are responsible for making Fort Lawton into a city park for all rather than a golf course for a few; for making the old Sand Point Naval Air

Station a park for all rather than an airport for a few; for turning the freeway mess downtown into a new park where before there were only overpasses and noise pollution.

So Seattle, like any other city, is a mixture of those who want to use it solely to make money (and they almost always live in the suburbs anyway), those who want it to be a decent place to live as well as work (and they're more likely to live within the city limits), those who don't really care one way or another so long as they're left alone, and those who live here because they think it is the most beautiful city in the nation—San Francisco, Honolulu, and Helena included.

Like any other city, Seattle has it odd side that keeps it from being a typical small town that simply outgrew itself. For example:

About 30 per cent of its citizens are foreign-born. Seattle is noted for its Scandinavian and Oriental populations, yet German is the most often spoken language after English.

One of the city's first ordinances was against door-to-door salesmen—not against Fuller Brush men, but Indians peddling clams.

Its very first ordinance was against public drunkenness, and the all-time record is held by a man who was checked into jail 401 times in 25 years, sentenced to 10,680 days in jail and was fined or forfeited $1,365 in bail.

A movie star can walk through town without attracting a crowd, and film makers like us because we aren't impressed with Hollywood and they can work without groupies of all ages cluttering the sets.

The color television tube was invented here, so was the electric guitar, the automobile headlight lens, and the ice cream soda. The first gas station was opened here, and the first international airmail flight was made between Seattle and Victoria, B.C. The first American to climb Mt. Everest, Jim Whittaker, is from Seattle.

The Union Gospel Mission, 318 2nd is one of Seattle's two former bordellos. The other is the Triangle Hotel, 553 1st S.

In Seattle you hear people say, "The mountains are really out today," which means that you can see them clearly. And you know you're talking to a true Seattleite when they speak of keeping more newcomers from moving in. Selfish? Yes, but a selfishness that grows from love.

Archie Satterfield

SEATTLE in Black & White

CHRISTOPHER PAUL BOLLEN, whose pen and ink sketches capture Seattle's heart from a number of viewpoints, was born here, attended the University of Washington, and now lives on Queen Anne.

In high school he began cartooning—just for fun. In Vietnam as a helicopter pilot (667 missions), he began sketching seriously. Back from Vietnam as a helicopter instructor pilot in California on weekends and evenings, he became a familiar face on the docks in the Balboa Island area as he sketched yachts, clubhouses, and boats of all kinds on commission.

At 29 and out of the Marine Corps, he returned to the Northwest. Chris bought a home on Queen Anne, and this is serving as his home and studio.

Nobody knew him as an artist here. So, he picked a residential area, sketched one of the fine old houses, framed it, and began knocking on doors. He works now in his rooftop studio where he sketches boats, houses, Mt. Rainier, barns, antique cars, railroads, and whatever catches his fancy.

Chris Bollen expounds on his own philosophy about art— "The public has been 'had.' The art community has put down the public and made them feel ignorant and inadequate.

"Music is creative art, but the public isn't concerned about whether it's 'good' or 'high quality.' They buy what they like. Strollers will walk into my studio time and time again and say, 'I like your work, but I don't know a thing about art.'

"That's crazy! They know as much about art as they need to know. Institutions and the art establishment have said to the public, 'leave art to the experts!' The art community believes—deeply believes—that the public has no taste in art. But, the public recognized Andrew Wyeth, Norman Rockwell, and others.

"My basic philosophy boils down to three principles:
- Do good art—really good, hopefully.
- Do things that the people—the public—can relate to and recognize.
- Give them a good price. I would rather make 100 people happy for $1 each than make one person happy for $100. It's that simple."

Chris Bollen's work appears throughout *The Seattle Guidebook*.

MR. LIVINGSTON,
I PRESUME...

A familiar sight in the Seattle area, the ubiquitous seagull finds many picturesque perches for sightseeing.

SIGHTSEEING

Places to Visit; Things to See

Seattle lies between salt and fresh water with two mountain ranges within sight, plus Mt. Rainier, Mt. Baker, and Mt. St. Helens looming up on clear days. It is small wonder that Seattle has the reputation of being one of the nation's most beautiful cities. Who can forget coming into town late in the day to see the low sun hitting the lakes, the Sound, and outlining the mountains? Its natural beauty alone would be enough for most people, but it also has a selection of manmade beauty spots to choose from to round out the recipe for good living. Following is a selected list of sights to see and ways to see them:

Air Activities

Airplane Rides —This is one of the best ways to see the city and its spectacular surroundings. From the elevation of a few thousand feet you will appreciate the hourglass shape of the downtown area, squeezed between Lake Washington, Lake Union, and Puget Sound. You also can appreciate the attraction of Puget Sound for residents with the scattering of islands, the fleet of pleasure boats and ships, and the closeness of the Cascades and Olympics. Most of the planes used for scenic flights are, of course, seaplanes which fly out of Lake Union and Lake Washington. A few helicopter firms also give scenic flights but cost considerably more than fixed-wing craft. Some of the scenic charter firms are:

Lake Union Air Service, 1100 Westlake N. (284-0300)

Kenmore Air Harbor, Lake Union and N. end of Lake Washington, P.O. Box 64, Kenmore (486-1257 or 364-6990)

Queen City Helicopters, 7675 Perimeter Rd. S., Boeing Field (767-0494)

Aero-Copters, 8013 Perimeter Rd. S., Boeing Field (767-2177)

Airports—Who can drive past an airport and not want to stop and watch the planes land and take off? Seattle-Tacoma International Airport with its art galleries, international shops, the computer-operated subway system that gives you a free ride down in the catacomb-like underground, and the international flavor as people depart for the Orient, the Arctic, and the South Pacific—all this makes Sea-Tac a great place to spend an afternoon. The best place for plane viewing is on the North Concourse. For smaller stuff and a more intimate atmosphere, try the little-brother airport at Boeing Field, where the smaller jets are mixed in with pleasure aircraft and helicopters. A few World War II fighter planes and trainers are found there, and you can go upstairs and watch the varied air traffic.

You'll have to go out of town for the antique-class planes. Several fly out of the Snohomish air field and others are hangared at Puyallup, Monroe, and other smaller towns where air-traffic control towers are absent.

Airshows—Some of the regional airshows are primarily static displays of vintage, W.W. II, and current military aircraft. Other shows feature aerobatics, pylon races, fly-bys, and demonstrations of military precision jet formation maneuvers by the U.S. Navy Blue Angels, U.S. Air Force Thunderbirds, and the Canadian Snowbirds in addition to static displays.

Among scheduled airshows are the following:
Thun Field Airshow
Breakfast Fly-in and Airshow at Auburn Airport
Kitsap Airport Evening Fly-in, Airshow, and Salmon Bake
International Air Fair at Paine Field, Everett
Renton Air Fair
EAA-AAA Fly-in at the Arlington Municipal Airport, featuring antique and experimental aircraft.

Sky-diving, gliders, and soaring activities are generally confined to weekends at the Seattle Sky Sports Airfield, Issaquah.

Ballooning—The Great Northwest Aerial Navigation Co., 7616 79th S.E., Mercer Island, (232-2032) offers balloon rides of 30 and 45 minutes for $45 midweek, or 90-minute rides on weekends with a brunch thrown in for $75. US Incorporated, 7342 15th N.W. (789-6702) also offers flights ranging from $180 per couple to $50 per person, the latter midweek prices.

Check with the Seattle/King County Convention and Visitors Bureau for information and specific times for airshows and events (447-7273).

Pacific Museum of Flight — The first stage of this ambitious museum will open in the fall of 1982 when the restoration of The Red Barn is completed. This building was the first Boeing factory and will be the centerpiece of the museum complex at the southwest end of Boeing Field. It owns a fleet of historic aircraft, some of which are on the site now. The museum has the distinction of having more members than any other such museum in the Pacific Northwest. Information: Pacific Museum of Flight Foundation, 2325 Financial Center, Seattle, 98161 (622-3972.)

Check with the Seattle/King County Convention and Visitors Bureau for information and specific times for airshows and events (447-7273).

Alki Point

It was here the first settlers landed in Seattle during the 1850s, and local historians delight in telling everyone about it although it wasn't particularly exciting. They arrived, built a town, and that was that. Today, Alki Point and the miles of beach, the lighthouse, and a cluster of elderly but charming beach houses make up one of the more pleasant places to walk and sunbathe in Seattle. It is a prime boat-watching area with the ferry traffic, sailboats, yachts, and freighters that round the point on their way somewhere else. Many residents surf fish there for sole while others simply walk along the 2-mile long promenade with the north wind frequently chilling them while the gulls wheel and shriek overhead. For information on the Alki Point Light Station, see Lighthouses in this chapter.

Aquarium

Seattle's Aquarium north of Waterfront Park at Pier 59 offers a unique and unusual look at Puget Sound marine life—both animal and vegetable. No collection of fish in big bowls, or performing seals and killer whales, the Aquarium's innovative displays recreate shore and underwater habitats. A huge viewing dome takes you into an underwater world filled with sea life from the Sound—sharks, several species of salmon, perch, rockfish, flounder, cod, and odd creatures—octopi, sculpins, starfish, barnacles, and varieties of shellfish. An actual fish ladder leads down to Puget Sound where the salmon fingerlings are released seasonally. After a normal life cycle, each fall, salmon make their way from the ocean, through the Sound and up the ladder to the Aquarium—the only aquarium in the world to be connected directly to life in the ocean. In the meantime, visitors may look up through a glass-bottom portion of the fish ladder to watch fingerlings (young salmon) swimming overhead. Whether viewed from below the surface or on top, playful seals and sea otters entertain constantly. The Aquarium is not limited to water creatures but also houses ducks, wrens, sea stars, and crabs in a salt marsh. Nearby a beach and pond are home to shore birds. Water anemones, sand dollars, and urchins are only a few of the saltwater creatures visible. A tide rises and falls at 3-hour intervals to expose barnacles, mussels, and similar shellfish at tide lines. Seattle's Aquarium embodies the newest ideas to permit the staff to engage in research and education while exhibits entertain. Open daily 10 a.m. to 5 p.m. winter, 10 a.m. to 9 p.m. summer. Adults $3.25; $1.25 for ages 13-17 and 62 or older; 75 cents for children 6-12; children under 5 free with an adult. Annual family pass costs $25 and entitles holder to bring in two guests on each visit and to receive newsletter. Ten free days are scheduled during the winter. The Aquarium also sponsors 4-hour cruises in Puget Sound aboard the research vessel, *Snow Goose*. Adults, $15, teenagers, senior citizens and handicapped $12, children under 12, $12. Reservations and payments 48 hours in advance (625-5030).

Arboretum

This is undoubtedly one of the most beautiful places in Seattle, and as beautiful places should be, the Arboretum is designed for people to enjoy it. The 200-acre nature preserve is located in Washington Park on Lake Washington Boulevard near the University of Washington, which oversees its welfare. One of the visual crescendos is the Japanese Garden. Visit the garden during the spring or fall, but it is a visual delight any time of year. Virtually all types of Pacific Northwest ornamental plants are displayed throughout the Arboretum along with many imported from other countries. Although the freeway leading to the Evergreen Point Floating Bridge rips through the north edge of the park, and bits and pieces of an abandoned freeway project hang over some sections of the marshes like remnants of a lost civilization, the Arboretum remains essentially a naturalist's treasure trove. The Waterfront Trail connects to the Foster Island Nature Trail (see separate listing); the other popular trails are Azalea Way and Loderi Valley, where masses (and massive) of rhododendrons are planted. It is

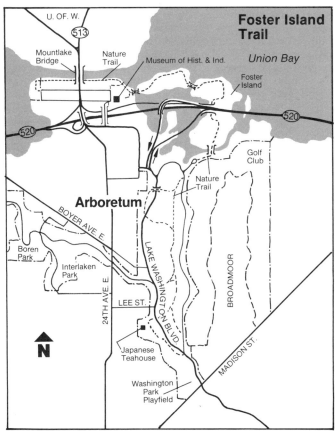

open from 8 a.m. to sunset the year around; no admission charge. Japanese Garden is open 10 a.m. to 7:30 p.m. in the summer, 10 a.m. to sunset in spring and autumn, and weekends from 10 a.m. to 4 p.m. ($1 entry fee). For information on guided tours and occasional plant sales, call 543-8800 or 325-4510.

Automobile Trips

The best source, obviously, is the AAA Automobile Club of Washington at 330 6th N. (292-5353), but you must be a member to receive the benefits of stacks of maps, brochures, discounts on publications, and other material. Perhaps the best way to see Seattle is to follow the scenic route signs along routes laid out by the Seattle Engineering Department, which we have used in our Scenic Drives in this chapter. For other ideas, check separate listings, such as Viewpoints.

Bird Watching

You don't have to be a member of the Seattle Audubon Society (Joshua Green Building, 622-6695) to be a bird watcher, and Seattle has several prime areas for you. Among the best are Green Lake, Schmitz Park, Foster Island Nature Trail, Discovery Park, and throughout the Arboretum. With so much water and so many marshes, you'll obviously see a lot of ducks, geese, and other aquatic birds. But there are an abundance of robins, sparrows, and other dry-land birds.

Blake Island and Tillicum Village

If you like salmon, boat rides, islands, and Indian culture, this could well be the main event in Seattle sightseeing. The 473-acre island lies between Vashon and Bainbridge islands and is owned entirely by the State Parks Department for use as a marine park. Tillicum Village, a concession, is the only building on the island and is one of the best eateries on Puget Sound. The longhouse-style building will seat up to 1,000, and as you enter, you will see your salmon being cooked in the traditional Indian fashion. It is filleted and held over the wood fire by cedar sticks until it is peach and golden brown, after being basted in lemon butter. The menu consists of tossed salad, relishes, salmon, baked potato in foil, green beans almondine, hot bread, wild blackberry tart, and soft drinks. During the meal Indian dancers perform their traditional North Pacific Coast interpretative dances on a large stage decorated with totemic art. There is also an Indian craft shop, and carvers frequently work on totems and smaller items at the longhouse. The tour, including roundtrip boat ride from Pier 56, costs $18.50 for adults, $7 for children under 12, $13.50 for senior citizens. Group rates are available (329-5700). Tours operate daily from June through Labor Day; weekends only the remainder of the year.

Boat Watching

Since Seattle claims the highest boat ownership per capita of any city in the nation, it only follows that watching boats steam, roar, sail, and chug by is one of the most pleasant pastimes. Obviously you can watch them from any spot along the waterfront or lakes, but here's a selection of what we consider the prime spots:

Hiram M. Chittenden Locks–Commonly known as the Ballard Locks (see separate listing).

Waterfront Park—See separate listing under Special Parks.

Fisherman's Terminal—Just off 15th W. on Salmon Bay, this is where a majority of the deep-sea fishing crafts tie up. You'll see gillnetters, seiners, trollers, tenders, and other types of commercial boats moored here. Frequently the fishermen will have their nets and other gear stretched out on the dock for repairs, which delights photographers. The Terminal Administration Building has a seafood restaurant, (The Wharf), a coffee shop, and shops specializing in commercial fishing gear.

Shilshole Bay—This is the major pleasure boat moorage on the saltwater side of Seattle, and you'll see everything from dinghies to seagoing yachts. It also is a restaurant center with Quinn's, Ray's Boathouse, Stuart's, and Golden Tides in the area. Adjoining the marina is Golden Gardens Park with beach viewing on one level and a viewpoint high up on the bluff.

Opening Day Boat Parade—Each year on the first Saturday in May the yachting season in Seattle more or less officially opens with a parade of boats from Portage Bay, where they form up, through the Montlake Cut under the bridge into Lake Washington. The parade, sponsored by the Seattle Yacht Club, usually begins about noon and lasts two hours as the sailboats, punts, cruisers, canoes, steam-powered boats, row-boats, racing shells, and whatever join the parade. The best places, obviously, are along the exact route but you'll have to arrive early with your blanket or chair, picnic lunch, and binoculars. If you can't make it early enough for a water-side seat, you might try one of the dead-end streets on the northeast side of Capitol Hill, especially those leading off E. Shelby, Boyer, and Fuhrman E. Others are found on Vista Point, East Roanoke, and Delmar Drive East. The best spots of all are along the Waterside Trail, that parallels the cut between Portage Bay and Lake Washington, and the Foster Island Nature Trail (see separate listings).; but get there early to find a spot.

Ferries

Washington State Ferries are a necessity for commuters and commercial interests in Washington and a seafaring feel for sightseers. Next to owning your own boat, the ferries are the best way to see Puget Sound and the group of islands that make up one of the most charming archipelagos in the North American continent. Ferries will take you to Bainbridge and Vashon Islands in Lower Puget Sound, and to the San Juan Islands between Anacortes and Canada's Vancouver Island. They form mobile bridges on the Sound, and you'll share them with semis, buses, delivery trucks, cars, bicycles, and walkers. Each has an observation deck and miles of glass for viewing inside out of the weather. They have restaurants and some even serve beer, which is a startling development considering Washington's reputation for blue laws that once encouraged secret drinking. They provide the most direct route to Bremerton and the shipyards, where the USS *Missouri* is berthed; to the great hiking, fishing, and sightseeing in the Olympic National Park; to the historic towns of Port Gamble and Port Townsend; to the resorts on Hood Canal; and to the saltwater fishing at Neah Bay and along the Strait of Juan de Fuca. Five-hour excursion fares are offered foot passengers from the Pier 52 terminal at the foot of Marion Street: one to Bremerton; another to Winslow on Bainbridge Island. Cost is $1.20 roundtrip for adults and 60 cents for children. Frequently when Seattleites run out of lunch ideas, they take the 2-hour roundtrip from Seattle to Bremerton, eat a picnic or restaurant lunch aboard the ferry, and watch the scenery slide past. Fares vary; for example, a walk-on one-way fare from Seattle to Winslow is $1.35, car and driver are $4.50, extra riders same as walk-on, and bicycles and riders are $1.90. Senior citizens ride at half price. Fares are complex with automobiles because they're on an escalating scale depending on length of trip and number of passengers, so we won't get into that here. For ferry information on all routes, call the Washington State Ferries' information number: 464-6400. It is manned 24 hours a day.

Note: Since the Hood Canal Floating Bridge sank in a storm in the winter of 1979, ferry service has been instituted to get travelers to the Olympic Peninsula. Check with the ferry information department for directions on the most convenient way to get there from wherever you are starting from.

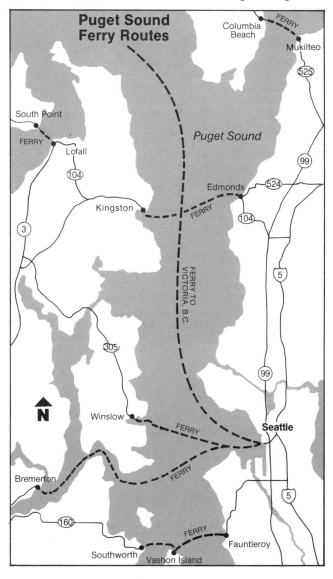

**Puget Sound
Ferry Routes**

The ferries operate on seven main routes:

Seattle-Bremerton—Pier 52. at the foot of Marion Street. To Bremerton leaving every hour on the hour from 6 a.m. until 9 p.m., less frequently thereafter until approximately 1:30 a.m. Crossing time approximately 60 minutes.

Seattle-Winslow—Pier 52. To Winslow on Bainbridge Island leaving approximately every 45 minutes except during early morning hours. Crossing time 30 minutes. Agate Passage Bridge connects Bainbridge Island and the Kitsap Peninsula mainland and is toll-free.

Fauntleroy-Vashon Island—Fauntleroy ferry dock in West Seattle at the foot of Fauntleroy Avenue near Lincoln Park. To Vashon Island only leaving approximately every 35 minutes between 5:30 a.m. and 3 a.m. Crossing time 15 minutes.

Vashon-Southworth—Vashon Island to Southworth running on roughly the same schedule as those listed above. Crossing time 10 minutes. (Note: Some ferries make the three-point run between Fauntleroy-Vashon Island-Southworth, depending on the season and time of day. Check with ferry information).

Edmonds-Kingston—Edmonds ferry terminal approximately 20 miles north of downtown Seattle via either Aurora N. or Interstate 5. Runs between Edmonds and Kingston, Kitsap Peninsula, the most direct route to the northern part of the Olympic Peninsula. Crossing time 30 minutes. Leaving approximately every 1:10 hours from 6 a.m. to 1:30 p.m. (See bridge note above).

Mukilteo-Columbia Beach—Mukilteo to Whidbey Island route. Leaving every 25 minutes between 6 a.m. and 3 a.m. Crossing time 15 minutes. Whidbey Island is the largest island in Puget Sound and one of the largest within the U.S. A trip from Seattle across the Sound by ferry to the island, then up its length to the high, dramatic bridge at Deception Pass State Park, then back south again via Interstate 5 makes an excellent day trip.

Anacortes-San Juan Islands-Sidney, British Columbia—This is considered by everyone who takes the trip as one of the prime boat trips in the country. It is a premium, all-day trip from one nation to another through the gorgeous, remote San Juan Islands. The ferry leaves early in the morning (usually about 7:45 a.m.) from the Anacortes ferry terminal and winds its way through the San Juans, stopping at Lopez, Shaw, Orcas, and San Juan Islands, passes several others, and lands at Sidney,

British Columbia (on Vancouver Island) at approximately noon. No reservations are taken on this or other ferry routes, so it is best to be early.

Port Townsend-Keystone—Port Townsend to Whidbey Island leaving approximately every hour and a half between 11:15 and 5:15. Crossing time 35 minutes. Daily during the summer. Fri. through Mon. only from Oct. 15 to April.

Other Ferry Systems connect with some of the more remote routes: the Tahlequah-Tacoma route connects Vashon Island to the South Puget Sound mainland; the Black Ball Transport, Inc., ferry runs between Port Angeles and Victoria, B.C. Before planning a trip around these lines, be sure and check with Washington State Ferries (464-6400).

Fish Watching

This may be stretching sightseeing a bit, but there are many, many people who continue to marvel at the homing instinct of salmon. And who can stand on the rim of a pool in a fish hatchery watching the thousands of fingerlings swirling around without becoming almost hypnotized by the constant motion? Ed Munro Seahurst Park, 13th S.W. and S.W. 144th just off Ambaum Road, is a relatively new King County park that has fish ladders, research facilities, and a holding pond for fish. Other good spots are: Hiram M. Chittenden Locks, Seward Park for rainbow trout, Seattle Aquarium, and the State Fish Hatchery, 125 W. Sunset Way, Issaquah.

Foster Island Nature Walk

This is an excellent place to send or take out-of-town visitors, children, or the spry elderly and is perhaps the best place in Seattle to watch boats, feed ducks, and hike all at the same time. The 1½ mile roundtrip begins at the lower end of the Museum of History and Industry parking lot (stop in at the Museum and see two major attractions in the same afternoon). The trail begins at the water's edge and immediately swoops upward over one of the numerous arching bridges built high enough to allow canoeists to pass beneath. The trail is on top of the squishy marsh and sort of floats. The wide, smooth trail leads almost to the water's edge with some side trips on deadend spurs with benches for fishing, sitting, or what-have-you. Bikes and joggers are strongly discouraged, to avoid pedestrian collisions. The trial follows one of the busiest boat lanes in Seattle because Lake Washington-based vessels must go past it and through the narrow channel called Montlake Cut in order to enter Lake Union and the Hiram M. Chittenden Locks en route to the Sound. Plaques telling of the interrelationship between water, weeds, birds, fish, and aquatic animals line the trail, which ends on the mainland in the Arboretum property. For the serious boat-watcher, an alternate trail leads up a bank overlooking the Montlake Cut, where platforms for boat viewing were thoughtfully built. Each week-end the year around and all during the summer, the boats parade through the Cut, and when a tall-masted one goes through, the Montlake Bridge raises, to the delight of watchers and the irritation of automobile drivers. This portion of the trail leads directly beneath the bridge on a narrow, but protected, walkway and ends at W. Montlake Pl. on Lake Union.

Hiram M. Chittenden Locks (Ballard Locks)

"So what," said the jaded traveler. "The boats come in, they drop down as the water goes out, the gates open and they go away." If you want to look at it that way, that's all there is to the spectacle most locals call the Ballard Locks. Yet it is a spectacle that people keep going back to see year after year for no better reason that it is (1) free and (2) fun. All pleasure boats headed for salt water from Lakes Union and Washington must pass through the locks, as must the commercial boats ranging from tugs towing log booms to the ships that berth on the lakes. If nothing else, you can marvel at the patience of the loud-voiced but tolerant locks employees who must shepherd the weekend sailors into the locks and keep them from sinking each other. Nearly 2,000,000 visitors stroll through the 7 acre botanical gardens surrounding the locks each year, and from 80,000 to 100,000 vessels go through the twin locks each year. During one peak year (1962 during the Seattle World's Fair) the count included 47,748 pleasure craft, 9,645 fishing boats, 10,597 tugs, 8,460 barges, 350 ships, 1,868 government vessels, 918 passenger, and 649 foreign vessels.

Construction of the canal and locks began in 1911, first by lowering Lake Washington from 29.8 feet above sea level to 21 feet above. Salmon Bay was elevated to the same level (21 feet). Lake Union remained at the same level, where the locks maintain the levels today. When vessels go through the locks, they are raised or lowered, depending on their direction, from 6 to 26 feet, which represents the tidal fluctuation.

The locks also permit salmon to migrate both through them and past them by way of a fish ladder, so they can continue their ancient route through Lake Union and Lake Washington to the rivers that feed them. Visitors may watch the migration from outdoor overhead walkways above the ladder or through an underground fish-ladder viewing window and stand almost nose to nose with salmon, steelhead, and other fish. The heaviest runs of tourists and fish occur during the months of June and July when sockeye salmon start their migration. Chinook run in August and September, coho in October and November.

Visitors are welcome every day of the week between 7 a.m. and 9 p.m. while the locks operate. A visitor center near the

LOCKS AND BEAGLES
~ Christopher Paul Bollen ~

Traditionally a popular sightseeing excursion, the spectacle of the boat locks in operation is both fun and free. (Beagles not part of the show).

Reflections of the uniquely easy houseboat lifestyle ripple in the shoreline waters of Lake Union.

main entrance shows how locks operate and tells of other Army Corps of Engineers projects. Hours: daily 11 a.m.-8 p.m. June 15-Sept. 15; 11 a.m. 5 p.m. Thurs.-Mon. Sept 15-June 15, (783-7059).

The locks are reached from downtown Seattle via either Aurora N. to the Fremont exit, then west on N.W. Leary Way to Market Street, and west on it to N.W. 54th; or north on 15th W. to N.W. Leary Way.

Houseboats

Seattle has one of the largest houseboat populations east of the Orient. There was a time when all houseboats on Lake Union and Portage Bay were modest—little more than shacks on floats with sewage dumped directly into the water. Some houseboats are still modest, but no longer are they free spirits; they are hooked to sewage lines. The largest colleciton of house-boats, and the widest variety in style and price, is found on the east shore of Lake Union. You can cruise slowly by car along Fairview N. along the lake shore to look at them. Over on

Portage Bay just off Lake Washington is the high-rent district of houseboats with A-frames, chalets, two- and three-story residences, which makes the bay a favorite neighborhood for young professionals. You can drive along Fuhrman E. from the University Bridge for a closer look. The best view of all, of course, is to rent or borrow a boat and cruise slowly past, peering into the people's windows. The line between window-peeking and sightseeing is a fine one, but you'll be told when you've crossed it.

Lighthouses

"Lonely as a lighthouse keeper" may apply in some parts of the world—even some parts of Puget Sound—but not in Seattle. The two here are quite metropolitan in setting; indeed, the Alki Point Light Station is right in the middle of a neighborhood and heavily used public beach. In spite of this, there is still that aura of loneliness to any lighthouse, the feeling of an outpost on the tip of some remote, dangerous shore.

The Alki Point Light Station is at 3201 Alki and was established in November, 1881. A Coast Guardsman is always on duty to answer questions from 1-4 p.m. Sat., Sun., and holidays.

West Point Light Station is at the far western tip of Discovery Park via a mile walk down a steep bluff road and past the sewage treatment facility (no noticeable odors) and out onto the point that is cluttered with driftwood, rocks, and sand. Hours are the same as Alki Point.

Scenic Drives

Whether you are a native or visitor to Seattle, one of the best ways to become thoroughly acquainted with the geography of the city is by following scenic drive routes laid out by the city engineering department. Each of the four drives are marked by small "Scenic Drive" signs attached to street signs and are relatively easy to follow.

The drives range from 30 to 40 miles in length, and each can be covered in about 3 hours' driving time, allowing for stops at particularly interesting spots, such as parks and viewpoints.

Viewpoints

Some say the best views are from West Seattle where you can look one direction to see the Olympics and the other direction to see Seattle's skyline stretched out like a painting in a doctor's waiting room. Others prefer Queen Anne Hill with views of the city stretched out below dimpled by Lake Union. Whatever your preference, Seattle has a viewpoint for it, and it is little wonder that view property has climbed as high as waterfront property in some areas.

The Park Department has wisely bought up some prime viewpoints, decorated them with artworks, walls, sidewalks,

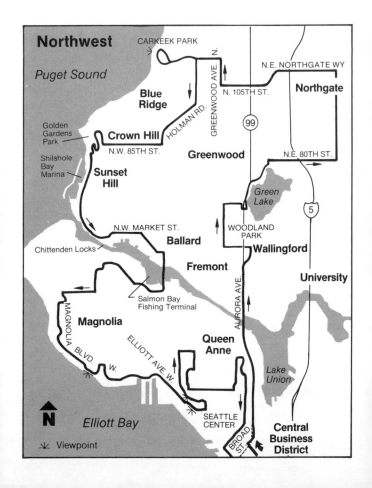

and other amenities so that visitors and residents without view property can still see the sights.

In addition to those listed below, others are available on public property if you want to do a bit of exploring. Look for deadend streets on Queen Anne Hill or overlooking Lake Washington (one of the best is on a deadend street in Washington Park). You may have the feeling you're walking on private property, but if you're in a street, it belongs to you.

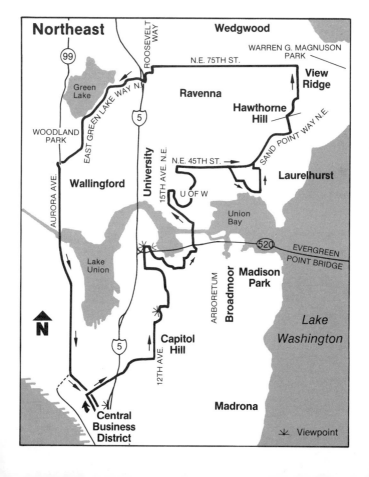

Others are part of the package in city parks, such as Lincoln Park, the Foster Island Nature Walk, Golden Gardens, and Discovery Park.

Capitol Hill

Bagley Viewpoint—10th E. & E. Roanoke. Looks out over Lake Union to Queen Anne Hill.

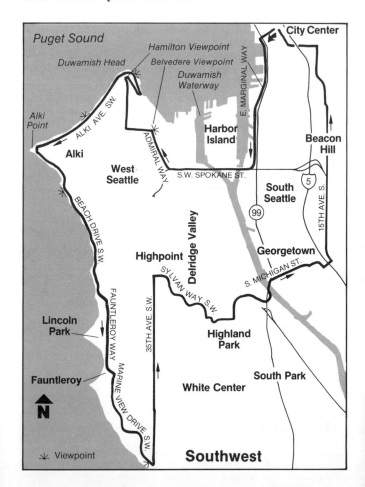

Capitol Hill Viewpoint—15th E. & E. Olin Pl. View to the east over Evergreen Point Bridge, Lake Washington, and on a clear day to the Cascades.

Louisa Boren Lookout—15th E. & E. Garfield. View to the east over Evergreen Point Bridge, Lake Washington, and on a clear day to the Cascades.

Four Columns—Pike & Boren at I-5. View to the west over the downtown area and to the Olympics.

Queen Anne Hill

Kerry Viewpoint—W. Highland Dr. & 2nd W. A great view over Seattle Center, the Space Needle, downtown Seattle and, on a clear day, Mt. Rainier.

Marshall Viewpoint—7th W. & W. Highland Dr. This one is only a few blocks west of Kerry Viewpoint, across the street from Parsons Gardens. It looks across to Magnolia and Puget Sound.

West Seattle

Belvedere Viewpoint—S.W. Admiral Way & S.W. Olga. This is perhaps the most popular viewpoint in Seattle due to its total panorama of the city skyline plus the industrial activity on Harbor Island. During beautiful weather it sometimes is difficult to find a parking place.

Hamilton Viewpoint—North end of California S.W. at S.W. Donald. This, too, is popular, but not quite as accessible as Belvedere. It shows more of Puget Sound plus the skyline.

Schmitz Viewpoint—Beach Drive S.W. & S.W. Alaska. This one is on the water level, a public oasis among the privately owned stretches of inaccessible beach.

Guided Tours

Chinatown Tour—Green tea and Japanese cookies welcome you at the start of this tour of Seattle's International District. Gather at the Center for Asian Arts for a brief slide presentation describing the settlement of Chinatown, then to Nippon Kan Hall—the social and cultural center for Japanese from 1910-1941. Next is Kobe Park overlooking Puget Sound and then to Chinatown's historic sites. Tickets for the 1½-hour tour

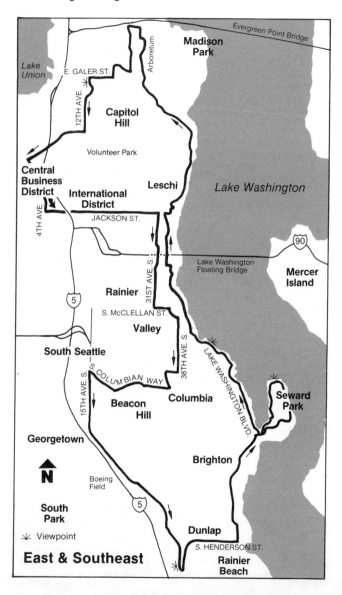

Evergreen Point Bridge

Lake Union

Madison Park

E. GALER ST.

Arboretum

12TH AVE.

Capitol Hill

Volunteer Park

Lake Washington

Central Business District

Leschi

International District

4TH AVE.

JACKSON ST.

Lake Washington Floating Bridge

90

Mercer Island

31ST AVE. S.

Rainier

5

S. McCLELLAN ST.

Valley

38TH AVE. S.

LAKE WASHINGTON BLVD.

South Seattle

S. COLUMBIAN WAY

Columbia

Seward Park

15TH AVE. S.

Beacon Hill

Georgetown

N

Brighton

Boeing Field

5

South Park

Dunlap

⚲ Viewpoint

S. HENDERSON ST.

East & Southeast

Rainier Beach

are $2 per person; tour with lunch, $6.50 for adults, $5.75 children; dinner $11 adult, $9.75 children. Call for reservations; tours usually run daily during summer, by request in winter. Large groups may arrange for separate tours, 622 S. Washington (624-6342).

Daybreak Star Indian Cultural Center—This center for Northwest Indians to meet, work, and display their artwork and crafts is located within Discovery Park near the North gate on West Government Way. Visitors are welcome Mon. to Fri. 9 a.m. to 5 p.m.; Sat & Sun. a security guard will take you on a tour of the paintings and carvings displayed on the walls. On the second Saturday of each month an Art Mart is held, and visitors can see the artists at work as well as purchase their works. See Dinner Theater listing for details on food service.

Discovery Park—Ranger-naturalists lead free guided nature walks each Sunday (625-4636). See listing in Special Parks.

Bus Tours—Several bus and boat tours are offered by Gray Line, American Sightseeing International, American discovery tours, and others. Prices range upward from $8 and can include the waterfront and Lake Washington, salmon dinners and several other longer day tours.

Kiana Lodge—Located at the tip of the Olumpic Peninsula, this lodge is for groups of 25 to 3,000 only but is well worth the time of gathering all your friends, neighbors, and family for an outing. The original lodge was built over 50 years ago on the site of an old Indian village, and additions now house a collection of Northwest Coast and Alaskan Indian artifacts. A natural forest setting features paths through azalea, rhododendron, fuschia, and begonia gardens. Steamed clams and clam nectar are served on the beach while you watch the preparation of salmon barbecued over green alder coals. Groups under 50 accepted during summer months only. Transportation can be by personal car or boat or chartered through the Kiana Lodge (683-2370). Dinner without transportation would be approximately $10 per person plus tax and any tips.

Kingdome Tours—A multi-purpose stadium located south of Pioneer Square—includes a sports museum. The 45-minute guided tours are held daily at 11 a.m., 1 and 3 p.m. Call for exact information, as tours are cancelled when events are going on. Otherwise you might be mistaken for a running back and tackled by a Seahawk. Cost $2 for adults, $1 children under 12 and senior citizens (628-3331).

Harbor Tours—Three boats, the *Barbary Coast, Harbor Tourist,* and *Goodtime* make one-hour tours along Seattle's waterfront. Tour begins at Pier 56 and cruises north to Pier 90 below Magnolia Bluff, then back south to the Harbor Island shipyards for a close-up of vessels under construction or being repaired. Half of the boats' seats are on open decks and the other half are in an enclosed area, so it is wise to take warm clothing. Season: May 1 to late September. Cost $3 adults, $2.50 senior citizens, $1.50 children 5-11, under 5 free. Every Saturday morning Japanese-narrated tours depart at 9:45. Daily trips from 11 a.m. to 4:30 p.m. (623-1445).

Jazz Tours—Each summer and autumn the Seattle Jazz Society charters the ancient, appealing passenger boat, *Virginia V,* for a combination jazz concert and Puget Sound tour. The jazz isn't avant-garde, and purposely so because the society wants to appeal to a wide cross-section of music lovers. Because the jazz tours are so popular, it is best to obtain tickets well in advance. Write the Seattle Jazz Society, Box 24284, Terminal Annex, Seattle, 98124, or call 325-7054.

Skagit Tours—One of the few tours operated by a municipal agency, and one of the most popular tours in Western Washington. The Skagit Tours are on the Skagit River at Seattle City Light's hydroelectric project in the heart of the North Cascades. The main tour is a four-hour trip through the project, including a ride on the incline lift from one level to the next, a boat trip on Ross Lake, tours through the powerhouses, and an all-you-can-eat-family-style meal. The tour starts at Diablo, 137 miles northeast of Seattle on the North Cascades Highway. Cost: $12 for adults, $8 for senior citizens over 60 and children under 17, and free for children 4 and under. However, a no-charge ticket must be requested for them. A warning: prices were expected to increase again at about press time. Naturally.

In addition, City Light offers four mini-tours in the same area: Diablo Lake-Ross Powerhouse boat trip, adults $4, senior citizens and children 4-12 years old $3, children 3 and under free. Gorge Powerhouse-Ladder Creek Falls, free; Trail of the Cedars, free; Incline lift ride, a self-guided free tour, and a museum and slide show in the town of Newhalem. Contact the Seattle City Light Skagit Tour Desk, 1015 3rd, Seattle, 98104, or call 625-3030. Tours operate from June 16 into September with reservations starting in April.

Underground Tour—One of Seattle's most popular tours, Bill Speidel's Underground Tour starts in the turn-of-the-century tavern, Doc Maynard's, 610 1st, in the Pioneer Square area. The tour begins with a short, humorous, and often accurate version of Seattle's colorful past, including biographical sketches of old Doc Maynard himself, Henry Yesler and other drunks and bandits from the 1850s. Then the tour goes through Pioneer Square for more colorful and lively Seattle history, then drops down to the underground. The underground portion is through passageways, over sidewalks and past Pompeii-like storefronts covered over when the areas was leveled out to build a decent waterfront. The tour ends at Speidel's Underground Museum about two hours, 6 flights of stairs, and 5 blocks later. Wear casual clothes and walking shoes; bring a camera, be sure it has a flash attachment. Cost of the tour is $2 for adults, senior citizens and children 6-12 $1.25, under 6 free. Reservatons required; call the ticket office, 682-4646. For 24-hour information on tour, call 682-1511.

Princess Marguerite

For most of this century Seattle has been connected with British Columbia's capital, Victoria, by luxurious cruise ships, and by the *T.E.V. Princess Marguerite*. The day trip to Victoria, something of a Little London, has been one of the must-make trips for visitors and residents alike (and you'd be surprised how many lifelong residents keep putting off the trip until "next summer"). It shouldn't be postponed. The trip is a mini-cruise that takes a half day each way and threads through the San Juan Islands to Victoria on Vancouver Island.

In early 1975 it appeared the *Marguerite* was going to join the *Queen Mary* and other liners in oblivion because her owner, Canadian Pacific Steamships, had been losing money each year in spite of increased passenger loads and increased fares. But the British Columbia government bought her as a "loss leader," gave her a renovation and put her back in business. The upper car deck was converted to a carpeted lounge with big windows, a gift shop, electric game tables, a nursery, children's play area, and special facilities for the handicapped. The main dining room was refurbished and enlarged, and the cafeteria and ballroom were reopened. Singalong music is heard in the Crown and Anchor bar, and guitarists and dance combos play elsewhere on the ship.

The *Marguerite* leaves Pier 69 each morning from May through early October at 8 a.m. and arrives in Victoria at 12:15

p.m. She leaves for Seattle at 5:30 p.m., arriving back at Pier 69 at 9:45 p.m. A round-trip ticket, good for five days, costs $25; children 5-11 $15, under 5 free. Senior citizens and paraplegics, $20 round-trip, $12 one-way. One-way fare for an automobile is $22, $6 for motorcycles, and $2 for bicycles (which are becoming a popular way to tour Victoria from the *Marguerite*). Dayrooms range from $15 to $23. No reservations required for walk-on passengers. Credit cards and personal checks not accepted at the counter. Call 682-8200 for information or reservations.

Northwest Trek

This park-zoo is one of the most humane zoos in existence because the animals are free to roam freely on the 600 acres, but man is not. Within the preserve are American bison (buffalo to most of us), black-tail and white-tail deer, moose, coyote, elk, woodland caribou, mountain goats, beaver, black bears, timber wolves, wolverine, mink, and bighorn mountain sheep. The bird population includes ducks, geese, and trumpeter swans.

Visitors ride on tram buses powered by propane with naturalist-guides giving lectures along the 50-minute, five-mile route. The preserve also has short hiking trails, special exhibit areas, a concession, and picnic areas.

It is located on State 161, 6 miles north of Eatonville, and helps round out a weekend outing to Mt. Rainier. It is open daily from 10 a.m. until one hour before sundown April through October, and Wed.-Sun. Nov.-Mar.

Admission is $4 adults; $2 children 4-16; $2.50 senior citizens showing Medicare card; free for children under 4. Special group rates are available on request (206) 832-6116.

Industrial Tours

These businesses offer tours to both individuals and organized groups. Arrangements can be made in the case of conventions to tour other firms, but such arrangements should be made through the Seattle/King County Convention and Visitors Bureau.

Bethlehem Steel Co. —4045 Delridge Way S.W. (938-6800). Hard hats and safety glasses are issued for a visit to this steel manufacturing company. You'll see open-hearth furnaces and molten steel being poured into forms. Call 2 weeks in advance for the hour-long tour offered Mon.-Fri. at 9 a.m., 10 a.m., 1 p.m. and 2 p.m. Minimum age is 15 years. Everyone should wear low heels, no open toes, and slacks are recommended strongly.

The Boeing Co. —Everett (342-4801). Tour begins with a half-hour movie or slide show of the company's products. Buses then take you to the Product Development plant and a viewing platform in the world's largest building to see the assembly of a 747. Tour lasts 1½ hours, Mon.-Fri. at 9 a.m. and 1 p.m. Call well in advance for a reservation and directions. Children 12 and over only.

Chateau Ste. Michelle —Woodinville (485-9721). A new showplace for Ste. Michelle Vineyards. The grapes are grown some 190 miles away in the Prosser-Grandview area of eastern Washington. A reproduction of a 17th century French chateau has been built to house the 150,000 sq. ft. winery and wine shop. The 87-acre grounds include trout ponds, a greenhouse, creek with footbridge, and picnic areas among the trees. Open for free guided tours and tasting daily, 10 a.m.-4:30 p.m., except certain holidays. Take the Woodinville exit (23) off I-405 and follow State 522 into the town of Woodinville. Turn onto State 202 and in 2 miles you are there.

Coca Cola Bottling Co. —1150 124th N.E., Bellevue (455-2000). Tours given during school year Mon. and Fri. 10 a.m. and 1 p.m. by reservation only. Slide show of the machinery used. Tours see the sterilizing and filling of bottles. A sample of Coke, of course. Maximum group size is 30; third grade and above. Call a week in advance.

Goodwill Training and Rehabilitation Center—Corner of Rainier & Dearborn (329-1000). A people-oriented tour where you'll see and talk to the multitude of employees at various training stations. They learn, among other skills, sorting, sewing, electrical repair, and furniture refinishing. After the 30-minute tour, you'll see the Goodwill museum of antiques and collectibles thrown away by the unsuspecting and gathered by the staff. Hours: 8 a.m.-4 p.m. Advance reservations required.

KING Broadcasting Co. (Channel 5)—320 Aurora N. (343-3000). Tickets are available for the live broadcast of the "Seattle Today" program which begins at 9 a.m. weekdays or "Seattle Tonight" program at 7 p.m. Advance notice of 1 to 2 weeks for tickets; 18 is minimum age. Call the promotion department after January, 1981 regarding tours.

KIRO Broadcasting (Channel 7)—3rd & Broad (624-7077, Ext. 338). Tours are given on Wed. and Thurs. afternoons at 1, 2, 3, and 4 p.m. Two weeks' notice preferred for families (7 is the minimum age); 3 weeks' notice for large groups.

KOMO Radio and TV (Channel 4)—4th & Denny Way (223-4062). Afternoon tours of radio and TV production work during fall and winter months. Prefer a weeks' notice; fifth grade and older only.

Lighthouse for the Blind—2501 S. Plum (322-4200). Chair caning, weaving, assembly of mops, brooms, and airplane parts are among the wide variety of products made by skilled blind and handicapped persons. Visitors always welcome by calling a day or two in advance; Mon.-Fri. 8:00 a.m. to 4:30 p.m.

NOAA Ships—Southeast end of Lake Union. The National Oceanic and Atmospheric Administration's white ships are open for tours when in port. Each ship has different research specialties, so you may want to see more than one. Weekdays during working hours. Information: 442-7657.

Pacific Northwest Bell—1101 4th (345-6349). School classes or groups may visit the communications center for a 45-minute tour of the operators' positions and office switching machines.

Preservative Paint Co.—5410 Airport Way S. (763-0300). Learn about paint manufacture from the raw materials to packaging. No minimum age for this 45-minute to 1½-hour tour, but children 12 and older seem to enjoy it more. Dress casually, as it can be dusty and the chance of accidentally brushing against wet paint is there. Available the year around, Mon.-Fri., between 9 a.m. and 2 p.m. by reservation; contact Rob Hogg.

Rainier Brewing Co.—3100 Airport Way S. (622-2600). See beer hop to the bottle or can in this modern brewery. Families or small groups may drop in for a 30-40 minute tour between 1 and 6 p.m. Mon.-Fri. Groups larger than 12 should call for reservations; children must be of walking age. Samples given to those of legal drinking age.

Seattle Times—Fairview N. & John (464-2111). See the complete operation of a large daily newspaper—composing room, news room, mail room, wire services, and printing. Minimum age is 10. They usually accept reservatons for group tours only, but call and if there is room on a scheduled tour, they will sometimes take a family along.

Art in Public Places

There are people in Seattle who make a hobby of fountain watching, and they can tell you the exact location of every public fountain in the city. Not the common drinking fountain, we hasten to explain, but those fountains that transcend the ordinary into the realm of art.

Rare is the person at the Seattle Center who can walk past the International Fountain without stopping to watch the 217 nozzles spraying pure water upward in intricate designs while music is played on the elaborate sound system.

Seattle's art in public places is not limited to fountains (although there does seem to be an abundance of them, perhaps because there is an equal abundance of water). There are vast murals, monolithic sculpture, statues, intricate metalwork, and a scattering of abstract artworks that might even impress an Easter Islander.

So take the time to explore, using this list as a guide. You don't have to be quiet while viewing them, as you would in a museum, nor should you feel compelled to say something profound about them. In fact, you don't have to even like them to enjoy tracking them down and wondering why the city government bothered commissioning them.

Not surprisingly, the largest collection is in the Seattle Center, which is dominated by the International Fountain, the Horiuchi mural, and the grand arches over the Pacific Science Center pool.

Seattle Center

Mercer Street Parking Garage—Monolithic sculptured concrete panels on corner walls—Charles W. Smith.

Playhouse, Grand Courtyard—"Fountain of the Northwest," an illuminated bronze sculpture—James FitzGerald. Also, a river rock sculpture, "Barbet," by James Washington.

Northwest Square, which faces the Playhouse Courtyard— "Sea Shell Fountain," 12 tridacna shells and freeform cement—Philippine Artisans.

North Mall—Julius C. Lang Memorial Fountain, in a lighted pool—Francoise Stahly.

Veterans' Building—"Doughboy Bringing Home Victory," a cast bronze statue on a granite base—Alonzo Victor Lewis.

Central Plaza—"International Fountain," which represents a giant sunflower and has 217 nozzles—Kazuyuki, Matsushita and Hideki Shimizu.

Flag Plaza Pavilion, Grand Stairway—"Flame #2," sculptured bronze on a marble base—Egan Weiner. Stairway fountains—Lawrence Halprin and Bob Price.

Coliseum, North Court—Two Chinese concrete lions—carved under supervision of the Taiwan Handicraft Promotion Center. "Evolution of Man," "Flight of Gulls," and "Seaweed," cast bronze sculptures in 40-foot by 120 foot basin—Everett Du Pen.

Amphitheater—Free-standing glass mosaic mural in 16 shades on 54 concrete slabs — Paul Horiuchi.

Pacific Science Center, Northwest Garden—"Gamma," a sculptured concrete fountain—Jack C. Fletcher. Northeast Pool — "Great Gull," a bronze sculpture — G. Alan Wright.

The Lagoon—"Water Sparkler," a fountain with 145 garden sprinklers set in the illuminated lagoon run on a tape sequence — Jacques Overhoff. "Variety Club Fountain" — copper sculpture and seascape pool with life-size beachcombing children — Tom Hardy.

Downtown

Seattle Ferry Terminal, Alaskan Way at Marion—Joshua Green Fountain — George Tsutakawa.

Pioneer Square Park—Pergola, built ca. 1909, restored — Julian F. Everett. Totem Pole, replica of one brought from Tongass, Alaska, in 1899, burned in 1938, replaced in 1940 — Tlingit Indian carvers. Chief Seattle drinking fountain sculpture (bronze) — James A. Wehn.

Norton Building, 801 2nd—"Totem," welded copper sculpture — Harold Balazs. "Restless Bird," cast stone sculpture — Philip McCracken.

Rainier National Bank, 1110 2nd — Walnut and colored glass screen — James FitzGerald.

Prefontaine Place, Yesler & 3rd—Fountain, dedicated 1926—Carl F. Gould.

Seattle City Light, 1000 block of 3rd — 1959 glass mosaic mural "Water into Electricity" — Jean Cory Beall.

King County Administration Bldg, 500 4th — "Merchant Seamen" murals, formerly hung in Marine Hospital — Kenneth Callahan.

Seattle Municipal Bldg., 600 4th — Two bronzed walnut screens, ca. 1959 — Everett Du Pen. Pylon fountain, bronze, and cast mosaic-stone, 1959 — Glen Alps.

Public Safety Bldg., 600 block of 4th — Memorial to Gold Star Mothers (Carrara marble) 1951 — Dudley Pratt.

Seattle Public Library, 1000 block of 4th — Screen (etched brass, bronze, fused glass) 1960 — James FitzGerald. Granite sculpture "Kinship of all Life," Creation Series #6, 1968 — James W. Washington, Jr. Casein and rice paper collage "Thrust Fault"—Paul Horiuchi. Treated sheet steel screen "Activity of Growth," 1960 — Glen Alps. Bronze sculpture "Pursuit," 1960 — Ray F. Jensen. Cedar sculpture "Alice," 1967 — James Wegner. Copper alloy "Fountain of Wisdom," 1960 — George Tsutakawa.

Seattle-First National Bank, 1001 4th — Bronze sculpture "Vertebrae", 1968 — Henry Moore. Two small fountains — George Tsutakawa. Paving mural, "Sea Marks" — Guy Anderson. Two granite, carved in relief benches — James W. Washington, Jr. Bronze sculpture "Penelope" — Emile-Antoine Bourdelle. Hanging sculpture, stainless steel wires — Harry Bertoia.

Financial Center, Pacific National Bank of Washington, 1215 4th—Sculpture "The Divers"—Roy Stenger.

Washington Bldg., 1325 4th—Abstract sculpture—James FitzGerald.

Fidelity Lane, 1622 4th—"Rosetree" (bronze) — Tom Hardy.

IBM Bldg., 1200 5th—Fountain, bronze, 1964—James FitzGerald.

Logan Bldg., 5th at Union—Hammered bronze "Morning Flight," 1959—Archie M. Graber.

Rainier National Bank, 1402 5th—Aluminum and walnut sculpture—Charles W. Smith.

Rainier National Bank, 510 Olive Way—Red cedar sculpture "Progress," ca. 1956—Dudley Carter.

McGraw Place, Westlake at Stewart — Statue of Gov. John Harte McGraw, bronze — Richard Brooks.

Naramore Fountain, 1100 block of 6th — Bronze, 1967 — George Tsutakawa.

Plymouth Chapel, 1200 block of 6th — Stained glass created by California studio to specifications of architect John Morse.

Westlake Square Park, 6th at Stewart — Fountain, ca. 1965 — Jean Johanson.

Federal Building, 2nd & Madison — Stone Sculpture "Landscape of Time" — Isamu Noguchi.

Central Seattle

Jefferson Terrace, 800 Jefferson — Abstract aluminum sculpture, "Tall Shape" — Glen Alps. Thomas Jefferson Memorial Fountain, bronze, 1969 — James FitzGerald.

Seattle University, Library, 12th & E. Columbia — Two paintings — Paul Horiuchi.

Madrona School, 1121 33rd — Three carved cedar abstract sculptures for children, 1961 — Henry Rollins.

Volunteer Park, Seattle Art Museum terrace — Black granite sculpture, "Black Sun," 1969 — Isamu Noguchi. Chinese tomb figures. Rams, camels from approach to tomb of 15th Century Ming prince; tigers, warrior and civil officer from tomb of Manchu noblemen, 17th or 18th Century. "Fifteen planes," stainless steel sculpture — David Smith. East of Seattle Art Museum — Cedar sculpture — "Rivalry of the Winds" — Dudley Carter. North — Statue of William H. Seward, bronze — Richard Brooks. Wading pool environs — Children's play sculpture, 1962 — Charles W. Smith.

Washington Park (Arboretum) Tea Garden — Stone lanterns — Japanese.

Museum of History and Industry, 2161 E. Hamlin — Cast-iron sculpture, "Man in Space" — Armando O. Orozco.

Magnolia Branch Library, 2801 34th W. — Abstract sculpture — Glen Alps.

Kerry Park, West Highland Dr. — Kinetic, volumetric space-frame, steel — Doris N. Chase.

Tilikum ("friend") Square, 5th & Denny Way — Statue of Chief Seattle, bronze, 1912 — James A. Wehn.

Denny Park, 9th N. & Denny Way — Bust of Dr. Mark Matthews, 1941 — Alonzo Victor Lewis.

Myrtle Edwards Park, north of Pier 71 — Stone sculpture "Adjacent, Against, Upon" — Michael Heizer.

Belgrade Park, 3rd & Bell — Concrete sculpture "Gyro Jack" — Lloyd Hamrol.

North Seattle

University of Washington, 15th N.E. overpass — Bronze sculpture, "Girl with a Flat Hat" — Phillip Levine. E. 41st entrance — Statue of George Washington, bronze, ca. 1909 — Lorado Taft. Suzallo Quadrangle — "Broken Obelisk," Cor-Ten steel sculpture — Barnett Newman, Rainier Vista — Drumheller Fountain, 1961 — Lawrence Halprin.

Pacific National Bank, 4501 15th N.E. — Steel sculpture — Charles W. Smith.

Safeco Plaza, Brooklyn Ave. N.E. & N.E. 45th — Bronze fountain, 1973 — George Tsutakawa.

U.S. Post Office, N.E. 43rd & University Way N.E. — Two murals — Jacob Elshin.

Woodland Park Totem pole — Chief William Shelton, Tulalip Indian Reservation. South entrance — Spanish War Memorial, bronze — Allan G. Newman. Bird-bath, brick with carved bird insets — Richard Beyer.

Ballard Branch Library, 5711 24th N.W. — Copper alloy fountain, "Of Sea and Life," 1963 — Howard Duell. Wall-sculpture, laminated wood, 1963 — Archie M. Graber.

Shilshole Bay Marina — Bronze statue of Leif Ericson — August Werner.

Northgate Shopping Center, 5th N.E. & N.E. Northgate Way — Giant-plant fountains, Totem Pole Pool, bronze, 1963 — George Tsutakawa.

Northwest Hospital, 1551 N. 120th — Totem Pole — Don Keys.

Lake City Branch Library, 12501 28th N.E. — Bronze semicircular gates, 1965 — George Tsutakawa.

South Seattle

Lake Washington Floating Bridge, east tunnel entrance — Pacific Rim Motifs, concrete tablets — James FitzGerald.

Mt. Baker Park, Lake Washington Blvd. S. — Granite reproduction of ancient Japanese lantern, 1923.

Seward Park, Lake Washington Blvd. S. — Torii, Gateway of Welcome, presented by local Japanese in 1939.

Belvedere Place, Admiral Way at Olga — Totem, replica of Haida pole — Flieschman and Morgan.

Southwest Branch Library, 9010 35th S.W. — Wall sculpture, "Mother Reading with Child" — Charles W. Smith.

Burien Library, 14700 6th S.W. — A.N. Thompson Memorial Fountain, 1972 — George Tsutakawa.

Sea-Tac International Airport — Acrylic painting, "Spectrum Delta II" — Francis Celantano. "Kalpa," 4 paintings, acrylic — Christopher English. Sculpture in glass and neon, "Infinity Column" — John Geise. Acrylic painting, Untitled — Thomas Holder. Sculpture, ebony, vermillionwood and ivory, "Tent Frame," — Paul R. Jenkins. Central Plaza Sculpture, enameled aluminum — Robert Maki. Oil painting, "Garden Zipper" — Alden Mason. Wood sculpture, "Night Flight I" — Louise Nevelson. Serigraph on mirror-coated plexiglas, "Star Quarters," — Robert Rauschenberg. Untitled, room with computer-controlled sound and light, light display — James Seawright/ Peter Phillips. Acrylic painting "York Factory A" — Frank Stella. Acrylic sculpture, untitled — John Wharton.

Water Operations Center, 2700 Airport Way S. — Stainless steel fountain, 1975 — Ted Jonsson.

Hilton Inn, near Sea-Tac Airport — Painting "Space Owl" — Jane G. Johnston, Coffers — Irene McGowan. Painting — Paul Horiuchi. Sculpture — James Wegner. Raccoon mural — Patricia K. Nicholson. Frieze — Archie M. Graber. Metal wall sculpture — Gordon Anderson. Mural — Guy Anderson.

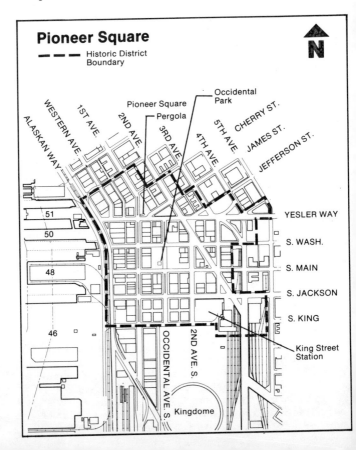

WALKING TOURS

Seeing Things & Places In Depth

SEATTLE is full of enclaves with a special historical, trade, or shopping interest for visitors and residents. These spot locations can really only be appreciated on foot. Zipping by in a car does not allow you to savor the flavor of the atmosphere, the people, and the infinitesimal multiginae that contribute to the uniqueness of each area. While there are many isolated areas with their own charm, these are the ones we like:

Pioneer Square

Pioneer Square is one of those pleasant anachronisms in 20th century America when our enlightened society appears intent upon demolishing everything that might be considered old-fashioned. Somehow the wrecking-ball renters overlooked Pioneer square, and it remains an oasis of elegant brick amid aluminum, glass, and concrete—not to mention asphalt parking lots.

It is Seattle's birthplace. It was the area chosen in 1852 when the original settlers abandoned Alki Point because of the hard, windy winters and poor moorage for visiting sailing vessels. The small harbor of Elliott Bay offered better protection, and the local Indians, led by a compassionate chief named Sealth, were generous with both land and information.

After they settled in, the settlers offered free land to a sawmill man named Henry Yesler to set up his rig on the waterfront, and he went to work leveling the forests on surrounding hills. He built a skid for the logs down what is now Yesler Street, and it became known as Skid Road, a term that was absorbed into America as Skid Row. (And don't you dare say it in Seattle. Saying Skid Row here is as bad or worse form than calling San Francisco 'Frisco).

When the whole town burned in 1889 because a glue pot spilled in the basement of a cabinet shop, the rebuilding began before the ashes of the frame buildings cooled. But this time they were a little smarter. They used bricks. Then, with the rebuilding expanded to include construction of a bigger and better waterfront, the city began raising the streets in the downtown area by regrading hills, both to build the port and to eliminate the lumps that made downtown traffic nightmarish.

Some of the streets were raised as much as 18 feet, which turned the first floor of the brick buildings into basements. At first the sidewalks remained at the original level with stairs up to the street for crossings, but gradually the sidewalks were paved over, sometimes with thick glass skylights, and dimly lit, dank arcades resulted. But the first floors were soon abandoned as basements. This phenomenon can be seen today in the *Underground Tours* operated by Bill Speidel, along with irreverent (sometimes irrevelant) tour-guide spiels (see Tours).

As the city spread out over the hills to Lake Washington and north and south like a locust invasion, the Skid Road section became what we associate with Skid Roads—cheap hotels, wino havens, and something of a city within a city, a Bowery, a place where nice people did not go.

The rehabilitation of Skid Road was a gradual thing, and the name was changed by its supporters to Pioneer Square. There were some close calls with the wrecking balls, but in 1970 it was declared a historic district by the city, and the city, state, and federal funds began arriving.

Although it is spreading in all directions, the area is generally defined as being bordered on the north by Cherry, the south by Jackson, the east by 3rd, and the west by Alaskan Way. The core of the district is along the brick street of Occidental Way S. which has been turned into a mall and park.

It has some 16 art galleries, about the same number of restaurants and cafes, three or four bookstores, 20 or 30 specialty shops, and several taverns.

Begin the walk at 1st and Yesler and walk beneath the pergola in *Pioneer Square Park*, once a major street car stop and a place to meet friends. The pergola originally was one of the "new" Seattle's most ornate pieces of ironwork but fell into a sad state of disrepair along with the rest of the district. But a grant from United Parcel restored it to its former elegance.

Also in the park is a tall totem pole carved by Tlingit Indians of Southeast Alaska. It is a replica of one collected by a group of businessmen on a jaunt to Tongass Island, Alaska, in 1899 (actually, they stole it). The Tlingits agreed to carve a new one after the original was damaged by fire, then charged an exhorbitant fee as revenge for the way the first was taken.

Across 1st from the park is the *Bahama's Restaurant, Discotheque & Deli.* Across Yesler is the *Merchants Cafe,* and directly east of the park is the *Pioneer Building,* one of the finest of the brick buildings of the era. In its basement is the *Brasserie Pittsbourg,* a French restaurant that is highly rated. It supposedly is the oldest cafe in Seattle that has been continuously operating since before the turn of the century.

Antique stores and taverns abound, and some have the most intriguing and worthless but necessary junk you're likely to see outside a trivia museum.

The visitor center of the *Klondike Gold Rush National Historical Park* (pause for breath after reciting that) is open at 117 S. Main. It is the first element of a park that eventually will run all the way to Dawson City, Yukon. It features old movies about the Klondike and dispenses information on Chilkoot Pass.

At the corner of 1st and Main stand the *Grand Central Building,* one of the prime restoration projects in the district. It formerly was a hotel, but the owners invested private capital to expose the old, gorgeous brick and refurbish it to accent its rich architecture. Inside it are a used bookstore, numerous galleries

Restored to its turn of the century elegance, the cast-iron pergola of Pioneer Square provides tired travelers with a shady respite.

and craft shops, specialty shops, and restaurants. Some Pioneer Square visitors see this building and explore no farther.

The rear door of the Grand Central opens onto *Occidental Park*, a curious mixture of cobbled park and ugly architecture. A shelter of sorts was built on one corner that looks as though the architect got confused and stopped in mid-design. The angular parasol (I think that is what it is supposed to be) is the most out-of-character piece of architecture in the district, and resembles a cross between a service-station sign on a freeway ramp and the skeleton of a billboard.

A block east on S. Main is the bricked-in oasis called *Waterfall Garden Park*, a gift from United Parcel Service.

Stay on Occidental and follow the brick street down to an area of quality galleries, decorator shops, and the *Seattle-First National Bank* with its museum atmosphere.

Other points of interest include:

The Iron Horse — 311 3d S., a restaurant-tavern where railroad photos and artifacts are displayed and slides of old steam engines are projected on the wall. Sit at the bar so your drinks will be delivered on a train set running up and down the bar.

From Pioneer Square you can walk to the Kingdome or the International District, wander up 1st for a walk on the wild side, or swing down and take in the waterfront. Or you can cut up a block past the parking lot at Yesler and James that looks like a sinking ship, and return to the downtown area via 2nd — if you're walking only. Second is one-way going south away from town.

Waterfront

While other port cities around the country knew that their waterfronts had charm with a tangy air scented by salt water, cresote, and fish, Seattle not only ignored its waterfront; it built an early American freeway, called the Alaskan Way Viaduct, like a wall of China around it. The wall still stands, its traffic noise making conversation well nigh impossible at times and as a concrete screen to keep office workers from gazing out across the Sound when they should be typing or posting bills.

Fortunately, somebody got wise and stubborn and began changing the waterfront from a blighted area to one with exotic shops, stand-up fish-and-chips bars, and even a city park.

Begin your exploration at Pier 70 at the foot of Broad Street because your chances of finding a parking spot are better there.

Plan on buying something—maybe lunch for starters—while ambling around the two-story converted warehouse. The cavernous building houses more than 40 shops. On the lower level you'll find *Juan's, Barney Bagel & Suzy Creamcheese, The Smuggler Restaurant,* the *Pier 70 Tavern and Chowder House* (virtually hanging over the water mixed in with a peanut butter shop), and shops with toys, leather goods, antiques, imported gifts, candles, and wines.

The upper level has parking and more shops, including a record store, the *Northwest Senior Craftsmen* outlet, (where you can buy a print of By Fish's famous retirement gift, "Free At Last"), *The Top of the Pier* restaurant, and a boutique or two.

Now take a walk south past working piers, past Pier 69 where the *Princess Marguerite* docks each evening between runs to Victoria, to Pier 59. There you'll see a plaque on the concrete guard rail marking the spot where the steamship *Portland* landed on July 17, 1897, with nearly two tons of gold from the Klondike. Its arrival kicked off the stampede to the Klondike through Seattle, and almost overnight lifted Seattle out of a depression that had begun four years earlier. Also on Pier 59 is the OmniRama Theater, a restaurant, and a book and gift shop.

Right next door is Seattle's *Aquarium* and newest major park, named of course, the *Waterfront Park*. It isn't a traditional park (and neither is the *Gas Works Park* on Lake Union, but that's still another story). It has no grassy lawns but it does have a large angular bronze fountain and a pavilion with a design borrowed from Stonehenge, and lots of space for sitting, walking, and looking.

Next door, for those who didn't bring their brown bag or picnic lunch are the *Sourdough Bakery and Restaurant* on Pier 57, called *Miner's Landing*. They serve a wide variety of seafood and will put it in containers for picnics. The eatery shares the pier with one of the largest import houses on the waterfront, *Pirate's Plunder*.

Now we're getting busy. The next stop is Pier 56, *Trident Imports* (elephant bells, South Pacific furniture, clothing, and a lot of things you won't need but will want), and *The Elliott Bay Fish and Oyster Co.* restaurant with inside and outside dining and an outdoor fish bar with food to go.

Next is the *Seattle Harbor Tours* office and dock, then, on Pier 55, an honest-to-goodness waterfront store for fishermen: *Fisheries Supply Co.* with miles of rope and line, charts, compasses, nets, spark plugs, and you name it. Beside it, on Pier 54, is *Ivar's Acres of Clams*, one of the city's most popular restaurants and the place that got the Ivar Haglund eating empire off and running.

Pier 53 is the home port for Seattle's two great fireboats, the *Alki* and *Duwamish,* the latter with the largest pumping capacity (22,000 gallons a minute) in the world. On summer Saturdays and Sundays the fireboats pull out into the bay and spray their hoses like floating peacocks and whenever a special event is being held in the area. You'll need a camera to prove to friends back home how beautiful water spraying off a boat is.

Pier 52 is the *Washington State Ferries* dock for those bound "overseas" to the islands or the Kitsap Peninsula. Feel free to ride the escalator up to the top deck, or save it after completing the waterfront tour and get up to 1st Avenue on the skybridge that leads from Pier 52 over the streets and beneath the viaduct. If you've walked off all those snacks you've picked up along the way, stop in at *Bruccio's* for a refill or a cool drink.

Pier 51 is fronted by *Ye Olde Curiosity Shop*, which the staid and cautious *National Geographic* once called "Seattle's most fantastic store, perhaps..." The most popular and grotesque exhibit is called Sylvester, a 6-foot tall, 137-pound mummy found in the Gila Bend Desert in 1895. Poor Sylvester... The shop also has numerous Indian, Aleut, and Eskimo artwork, elephant and walrus ivory, and to keep Sylvester company, a collection of shrunken heads from Ecuador, and other exotic, weird things.

Pier 48 is the *Alaska Ferry* dock, and the Alaska Travel office operated by the state is also on the pier. The ferries are in on Fridays. The Port of Seattle's Alaska Square Park at Pier 48 features a colorful Tlingit totem pole carved in Haines by Indian artisans. The same Alaska Indian Arts craftsmen carved the 7 big panels on the face of the terminal building at Pier 48.

The most interesting part of the waterfront ends here. The piers keep going south a mile or so but guests aren't welcome, except at the Coast Guard Station and Museum on Pier 36. So you'd as well turn around and forget about seeing the rest of the waterfront unless you go on a Harbor Tour.

From the waterfront you can either retrace your steps, or continue on to a 1st Avenue tour headed north to your point of origin, or down to Pioneer Square, only three or four blocks away.

First Avenue

While many Seattleites try to ignore it, and the Chamber of Commerce avoids it in brochures, and the historical restoration crowd wants to take it over, 1st is one of the city's unique resources. It is funky, rough, gaudy, a little dirty, and pretends to be nothing other than what it is: What you see is what you get, one might say.

A Salvation army store is at the corner of 1st and Pine (after you pass the Midtown porno movie house). This is one of the many "army" stores of one kind or another along the street, and it has castoff clothing, furniture, books, etc., that may or may not have any value. But browse to your heart's content.

Of historical interest is the Alaska Trade Building (1915), which at one time was the printing plant for the largest daily labor newspaper in the country, the *Seattle Union Record*. At that time the U.S. Attorney General called this state the "Soviet of Washington," which delighted the Wobblies at whom the insult was intended.

When you reach 1st and Pike, you're getting into the curious mixture of stores that run from so called Army-Navy Surplus Stores to dirty movies to bingo parlors, now that the latter is legal again.

In 1405 you find the Eclipse Hat Shop, one of the few remaining stores in Seattle, and probably anywhere, that cleans and blocks hats.

In the next block (1224) you'll find one of the oldest pet stores in Seattle, Town & Country's Barnier Pet Store, with puppies lolling around in the window tearing at your heart strings.

The 1300 block is a busy one. There's OK Loans (1311), reportedly the oldest hock shop in the city and one of several along the street. Occasionally you can get a good buy on musical instruments, cameras, TV sets, silver, weapons, and that sort of thing, but don't expect to find something the owner underpriced; they wouldn't be in the business if they didn't know the value of items hocked.

Also on the block (1303), is Seattle Tattoo Emporium, one of the last left in Seattle and a harking back to the World War II and Korean War days when the street was a main thoroughfare for sailors and Marines.

Scattered along most blocks are so-called "penny arcades" where a single penny won't buy you a single thing. Most have become dirty-movie palaces.

The 1000 block offers passport photo shops, a few pawn shops, a surplus store or two, and even a gallery has intruded.

At 1st and Madison is Warshal's, a long-time sporting goods and camera store that has a well-earned reputation for integrity. If an item they stock turns out to be no good, they'll tell you so and tell you not to buy it. Or if you do buy something that is unsatisfactory before they have a chance to test it, they want it back to return to the manufacturer.

From Marion Street (the 900 block) on south, the street gets a bit classier, the buffer zone between the funk and the flash with the Pioneer Square restoration area beginning a block away.

Across Madison is the Federal Building, where security is so tight you can hardly find your way around, but the bookstore on the main level is a dandy.

You must remember, however, that you can expect to be approached by at least three panhandlers along the way, some of whom are genuinely down and out, but most who simply want another jug before the night ends. The street can get rough on occasion, and most of the taverns are the type that make you want to find a corner so nobody can get behind you. Unless you have more than the normal amount of curiosity, the daylight hours are best for touring 1st Avenue. Otherwise, you're on your own.

Pike Place Market

Pike Place is a two-plus-block street that curves north from the western end of Pike. The Market is largely built on stilts out over the edge of a bluff that looks across Elliott Bay. From this vantage shelf a number of the Market's restaurants offer eye-boggling views from windows facing west.

Starting originally in 1907 as a place where vegetable and fruit growers gathered to sell their produce to city dwellers, the Market has grown into a small city all its own. As the number of farmers decreased or an industry took over their lush Kent valley farm lands for factories and parking lots, artists and craftsmen moved into empty stalls along with restaurants, antique shops, and a startling variety of small specialty businesses. Today, more than 100 shops, individuals, produce sellers —even a modern bank—operate at the west end of Pike and in the main arcade facing Pike Place from both sides. Warren-like lower levels with steps and ramps at odd junctions invite strollers and visitors to browse, wonder, and sometimes buy.

The Market's fresh fruit and vegetable sellers and the variety of restaurants draw thousands of visitors daily. Seattleites regularly shop for home-grown produce in stalls. When there's time, the shopper walks the length of the main arcade checking quality and prices for lettuce, cabbage, cukes, and seasonal fruits. On the way back he or she picks up those items mentally noted on the first pass. Competition remains keen. At the end of the day a merchant-farmer (or one of his hard-working offspring) may drop in a few radishes with heads of lettuce or quote a special price for more than one item. It's a friendly place that teems with a cross-section of humanity.

Change is endemic to the Market. Shops open and close irregularly. At the north end of the main arcade and outside to the west when the sun shines, craftsmen and artists set up a sales counter or table for the day. The count varies from day to day with more craftsmen showing their wares during the summer and in the weeks before Christmas. The Market includes antiques, plants, meat, fish, gifts, grocers and delis, bakery, restaurants, and spice shops.

Corner Market at Pike Place and 1st has been restored and rehabilitated. Merchants in this market include: beauty salon, caterer, crumpet place, flower shop, herb shop, oriental market, bookstore, meat markets, and restaurants.

Sur La Table (84 Pine) offers unusually fine cooking ware. Starbuck's Coffees, Teas, and Spices (1912 Pike Pl.) rates a visit just to sniff the enchanting odors, an advertising come-on unbeatable by anything in print.

Take time on your Pike Place walking tour to sample the atmosphere and you'll find yourself returning again and again. Many Seattleites consider the Market their most favorite place.

Seattle Center

Although the center wasn't built until 1962, it is difficult to remember Seattle without it or to imagine what the city would be like if it didn't have it. The recreational, cultural, and entertainment center of Seattle, it is the most exciting "people" place in the Northwest. It was the site of the Century 21 World's Fair, one of the few World's Fairs in history to pay its own way.

The city went all out to make it beautiful, and the 74 acres offer a combination of imaginative architecture, lush green grass and trees, and public art. Fountains gurgle and splash wherever one turns. It was designed to be used rather than stared at. Office workers go there for picnic lunches or walks, and it is one of the highest priority items on every visitor's agenda.

Fun Forest for the children is reason enough for going. They can clench their fists and eyes and get scared on the Zipper, the Matterhorn, the Wild Mouse, bumper cars, and numerous other rides. For the less strong of heart and stomach, there are concession games of baseball, dart and ring tossing, miniature golf, the Moon Walk, and others.

The Space Needle is close by. The revolving restaurant and viewing deck occupy the top of a tall, rather elegant tripod that has become a symbol of Seattle. The ride to the observation platform costs $2 for adults whether you plan to eat in the restaurant or not; children ride for $1. Statistics: Height is 605 feet above ground level, and the restaurant is at the 500-foot level. The steel structure weighs 3,000 tons, and the foundation sinks 30 feet into the ground, anchored by 5,800 tons of concrete. The restaurant's outer ring of tables makes a 360-degree revolution every hour and seats 275. Elevators travel upward at the rate of 800 feet per minute, taking 43 seconds to the top.

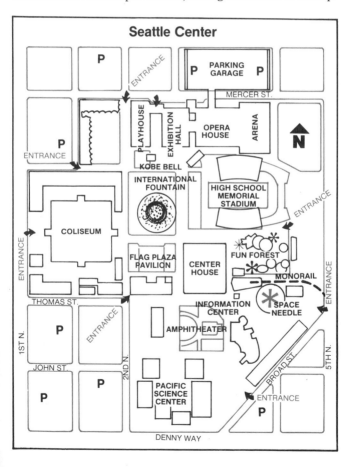

The Pacific Science Center with its broad, shallow pools and soaring futuristic arches, occupies the southern end of the center and has been very successful in translating science into everyday—and fun—terms. Five buildings make up the complex. Highlights: Eames Theater, where films are shown and meetings held; the Kwakiutl House, a replica of a Northwest Indian ceremonial house; the mathematics area where you can operate calculators, play games, and study the matter of probability and other heavy subjects; full-scale models of manned and unmanned spacecraft permit climbing into them to see how the astronauts live; the Star shows, an 8,000 sq. ft. overhead domed screen that shows the mysterious galaxies and makes you feel, indeed, small.

In addition to all this, the center hosts frequent traveling exhibits of photos, artwork, and artifacts. A scientific game area allows visitors to push buttons that make weird things happen inside machines.

The Balcony Book and Gift Shop stocks everything from nature and science books to puzzles, shells, toys, and Indian and Eskimo crafts.

Admission: adults $2.50, 17 & under $1, preschoolers free. Senior citizens pay $1.50. Hours: 10 a.m. to 5 p.m. daily. Information: 625-9333.

Laserium is a cosmic-laser-light concert also in the Science Center Bldg. Laserium I, the original, shows Wed.-Sun.; Laserium II, a new edition, shows Tues., Thurs., Sat. Show times are 2, 4, 8 and 9:30 p.m.; additional late shows on Fri. and Sat., at 11 p.m. Admission to the Science Center not included except for matinees at 2 and 4 p.m. Buy your ticket separately at the entrance. $4 per person, call for special group rates (382-2885).

Center House is another major building, originally called the Food Circus Building. Inside this gigantic, old fortress that formerly was an armory, the Center House Court indoor park features restaurants in an atmosphere, where you can take your food to eat at tables and engage in people watching. Above, boutiques ring the surrounding overhead area, and the Fountain level downstairs features a variety of shops and boutiques. The Seattle Center Administrative offices, including the invaluable lost-and-found office at the Information Office, occupy the second floor of the building.

Coliseum —Where many rock concerts and trade shows are held. The ice shows also appear in the Coliseum.

Opera House — Home of the Seattle Symphony and most musical events, such as the Seattle Opera, traveling symphonies, and ballets. It has great acoustics, is air-conditioned, and seats 3,100.

Playhouse — Used by the Seattle Repertory Theater and other theater groups, seats 890, and has a beautifully landscaped courtyard. Frequent photo and art exhibits are hung in the lobby.

Arena — Used more frequently for conventions than spectator sports. It is connected to the Display Hall for convenience during large exhibitions and conventions. The Arena seats up to 6,000.

Mural Amphitheater — A large outdoor stage area with the giant mosaic mural, "The Seattle Scene," by Paul Horiuchi as a backdrop. The stage is surrounded by a pool and has a sloping grass amphitheater. Free concerts are held here — rock, pop, jazz, and classical. It is a centerpiece for the Bumbershoot Festival held each summer.

Other Seattle Center highlights include:

International Fountain — Electronically operated and lighted, the fountain plays a constantly changing pattern of water accompanied by music.

Flag Plaza Pavilion — This was a popular spot during the World's Fair and now is used for exhibits such as flower shows, festivals, and special events.

For information on galleries, children's theaters, and the monorail, see appropriate listing elsewhere in the book. Information: Call 625-4234.

Monorail

When the Alweg Monorail was built during the 1962 World's Fair, there was talk about its being extended from downtown Seattle to Seattle-Tacoma International Airport. For reasons known only to politicians, the extension never came and probably never will, even though it is popular, quiet, and fast. Today it runs back and forth along a 1.2-mile track from the Seattle Center to Westlake Mall, between 4th and 5th at Pine. It makes the trip in 90 seconds, and offers shoppers or visitors the alternative of parking near the Center and riding it to and from downtown. Hours: Mon. to Thurs. 10 a.m. to midnight; Fri. and Sat. 10 a.m. to 12:30 a.m.; Sun. until 10 p.m. Cost: 35 cents, senior citizens 10 cents, each way.

GINGERBREAD

Touring the original residential regions of Seattle reveals a treasure of historic homes. Trimmed with gingerbread icing intricacy, the eclectic elegance of these homes provides walking fans with a wealth of individual tours.

ENTERTAINMENT

Doing, Seeing, Participating

CULTURAL activities are booming in Seattle despite the city's addiction to outdoor pursuits on weekends. Several equity acting groups hold forth on the boards. Music groups abound, and the Seattle Symphony and Opera are rated excellent. Of all the entertainment categories, after-dark goings-on attract fewer habitues. The middle ground offers less than the pinnacle of fine music and theater productions and the mire of an excess of porno movie houses and what used to be called "penny arcades," although inflation long ago killed the penny. While the selection within categories can be ragged in spots, and weak in professional dance, practically every taste in entertainment can be satiated in Seattle.

Tickets for most events are sold at Fidelity Lane, 1622 4th (624-4971), The Bon Marche at the downtown, Northgate, and Southcenter stores, Seattle Ticket Service, 710 Cherry (382-0888), and U-District Ticket Center, 4530 University Way N.E. (632-7272).

Theaters

On Stage

A Contemporary Theater (ACT) — 100 W. Roy St. (Box Office, 285-5110; Business Office, 285-3220). A resident professional (equity) theater specializing in contemporary plays. Also conducts A Children's Theater and programs for senior citizens.

Bathhouse Theater — 7312 W. Greenlake Drive N. (524-9110). Both children's and adult's productions sponsored by the Parks and Recreation Department.

Driftwood Players of Edmonds — 950 Main, Edmonds, Mailing address: P.O. Box 385, Edmonds, 98020 (774-9600). Community sponsored and operated theater that also sponsors student productions.

The Empty Space Association —919 E. Pike (325-8787; Box Office, 325-4443). Experimental plays and varied repertory. Free summer plays in Volunteer Park.

Glenn Hughes Playhouse — 4045 University Way N.E. (Business Office, 543-5140; Box Office, 543-5636). University of Washington School of Drama theater.

Intiman Theater —Shares Second Stage Theater with Musicomedy, 8th between Pike & Pine (447-4651 or 624-4541). Highly rated small theater that presents classic dramas in an intimate atmosphere.

La Pensee Players —201 N. 70th (783-2428). A serious community theater that produces experimental and original scripts, sometimes involving dance, puppetry, story theater, and improvisation.

Mountaineer Players —P.O. Box 122, Seattle, 98111 (623-2314). Produces an annual play in the outdoor forest theater near Bremerton. Sponsored by the Seattle Mountaineers, an outdoor club.

Musicomedy Northwest —Seattle's only nonprofit community musical-comedy theater presents three large-cast, traditional, full-orchestra musical comedies, such as "South Pacific" and "My Fair Lady." Tickets are $14 for top seats. The cast and orchestra, as many as 150 total, perform as volunteers. Shows at the Second Stage, 8th between Pike & Pine. For information call 325-3633.

Penthouse Theater —University of Washington Campus (Box Office, 543-5635; business, 543-5140). An arena theater operated by the University.

Pioneer Square Theater —107 Occidental (622-2016). Produces a wide variety of new plays.

Poncho Children's Theater —700 50th N. (in Woodland Park) (633-4567). Children's theater in conjunction with Woodland Park Zoo performed by junior high students.

Puppet Power —500 N. Aurora (329-5534). Presents puppet plays for children and adults throughout the area.

Seattle Repertory Theater —Seattle Center Playhouse, 225 Mercer (Box Office, 447-4764; Business Office, 447-4730). Professional, equity theater with six plays a season (October-April) running eight performances each.

Showboat Theater — University of Washington Campus (Box Office, 543-5636; Business Office, 543-5140). A proscenium theater operated by the university.

Skid Road Theater — 102 Cherry (622-0251). Legitimate, experimental theater, with lunchtime (brownbag) performances. Frequent performance in Pioneer Square's Occidental Park.

Dinner Theaters

Cirque Dinner Theater — 131 Taylor N. (622-5540). This was the first built in Seattle and specializes in light, fast-paced comedies. Dark on Mon. $18 per person week nights; Sun. brunch, Fri. and Sat. nights, $20. Reservations required.

Music Hall — 7th & Olive. Caberet Theater with an off-again, on-again history. Call for information (583-0818).

Daybreak Indian Dinner Theater — Discovery Park. (285-4425). Salmon served Makah style, Indian fashion show, guitarist, hoop show, Tlingit Cape Fox Dancers. Fridays by appointment only. Call for dates and prices. 1980-81 prices, $17.50 per person in groups of 5 or more, $15 senior citizens and children under 12.

Classic Theaters

Many of Seattle's grand old theaters have fallen victim to the wrecker's ball, and actual tears were shed by theater lovers when the Orpheum and Palomar gave way to a hotel and parking lot, respectively. But there are a few grand old ladies of the theater era remaining, in part, one suspects, because Seattle had so many to begin with. The master theater designer, B. Marcus Priteca, was from Seattle, and he was kept busy in his hometown building his peculiar combination of elegant and gaudy structures.

Not all theaters built in the grand manner still perform grand functions, as we soon shall see. But at least they stand, monuments of a more flamboyant time and as a reminder that theaters do not have to be horrendous boxes with seats in them. This tendency to erect theaters with a built-in terminal ugliness has led us to recommend the Yellow Pages and theater ads for movie houses. There isn't much else we could say about them other than list them.

But here's a list of some of Seattle's more interesting theaters, both stage and screen.

Coliseum —5th & Pike. A Priteca designed building that was one of the first giant movie houses in the country. Built in 1915, it was for years the largest theater in the West.

Embassy —1409 3rd. This is one of two or three downtown theaters that have been running almost continuously since before World War I; 1911 in the Embassy's case. It now is a porno house with one nice built-in feature for the shy—it has a rear box office for those who want to sneak in without being seen.

Fifth Avenue Theater —1308 5th. This gaudy, elaborate and beloved old cavern of a theater is a great example of the lost art of building theaters. Fortunately it was taken over by a group of investors who restored it and turned it into a Broadway-Style Theater with long-run stage shows.

Music Box —5th near Pike. While this one can't compete with the Fifth Avenue or Paramount, it has a certain informal charm that helps make movie-going a complete experience.

Paramount —901 Pine. Also designed by Priteca, the Paramount opened in 1927 and is still recognized as one of the most acoustically perfect theaters in the West. It now is devoted almost entirely to rock concerts. It is almost as grand as the Fifth Avenue, and its long, winding passageways to restrooms and sub-lobbies can make you wonder if you're going to make it. It also has a fabulous Wurlitzer pipe organ restored to mint condition.

Movie Theaters of Special Interest

Most theaters, obviously, devote their energies to first and second-run films. Several movie theaters in Seattle specialize in cult films, classics, pornography, and ancient films you aren't likely to see on television. Some of them are:

Harvard Exit —807 E. Roy (323-8986). The Exit specializes in quality films that the first-run houses either do not keep around long or don't want to be bothered with. (Examples are "The Emigrants" and "The New Land," both of which ran at the Harvard Exit for months.) The theater also picks up films on the fifth and sixth time around that have become either cult films or minor classics. The management's taste in excellent films is impeccable. So is their hot spiced tea, and coffee served to patrons before the films start.

The Movie House —N.E. 50th & University Way N.E. (523-3935). This funky, small theater has had a knack of picking up ancient films and starting them on their way to the classic category. Examples include the Sherlock Holmes films (one of which the management bought the distribution rights), the Lone Ranger series, "King of Hearts," and the forgotten comedy classic, "Ruggles of Red Gap." It is the only movie theater that accepts reservations. It also has a small coffee shop.

OminiRama Theater — Pier 59 on the waterfront (622-1869 or 622-5440). Tilt your seat back to a 45-degree angle and view the picture projected up and around you in a 52-foot dome. This is a commercial theater but is similar to three others in the country that are connected to science museums (San Diego, Detroit, and St. Paul). The hour-long show is normally $2.75 for adults, but with a combined ticket to the Seattle Aquarium next door the fee is reduced to $1.50. Call for group rates.

Pike Place Cinema — Post Alley in the Economy Market Bldg. (622-2552).

Toyo Cinema — 5608 Rainier S. (722-9368). A Japanese movie house showing films both with and without English subtitles. It is a theater that existed for some time as an ethnic house that later was discovered by film buffs.

University Cinema — 5510 University Way N.E. (524-1010). A small University District house that plays many old greats, such as Chaplin classics, W.C. Fields, Buster Keaton, etc.

Music

Seattle has such a variety of musical events, ranging from classical to rock, that there is literally something for every taste nearly every week. So well established and mature is Seattle's cultural atmosphere that critics from the East Coast and California are amazed (and envious).

It is impossible to produce an accurate list of events in the musical category because schedules change, new names are added while others are dropped, and often not even the organizations themselves are certain of concert dates very far in advance. At any rate, here's a list of the major musical organizations, and be sure and watch the newspaper entertainment sections for up-to-date listings.

For University of Washington performances, obtain a copy of *Spectrum,* a listing published quarterly by Continuing Education, 543-2590. Copies are mailed on request, free.

A word of warning: Many small groups are listed here under the name and address of the current president. Since organizations hold elections nearly every year (just after this book is published, it seems), some of these addresses and telephone numbers may be out of date.

Major Groups

Seattle Opera Association — 305 Harrison (447-4753). Founded in 1964, the opera has quickly made an indelible mark on the international opera scene under the innovative and imaginative management of general director Glynn Ross. It quickly rose to the top ranks of United States opera and in 1975 went international with the first American performance of the complete Wagnerian "Ring." The opera kicked off what it calls the Northwest Festival, an annual summer production of "The Ring" in German and English, which attracts an international following. In addition, the opera offers five productions each year from September through May, English language performances, tours, children's matinees. Performances are always in the Seattle Opera House in the Seattle Center.

Seattle Symphony Orchestra — 305 Harrison (447-4700). Founded in 1903, the symphony presents 12 subscription concerts each year, October through April, on Monday and Tuesday evenings and Sunday afternoon concerts, all in the Opera House. The symphony tries for a balance between the "museum" pieces and modern music, with an occasional premier performance. Rainier Miedel is the musical director and conductor.

The Philadelphia String Quartet — 5821 Vassar Ave. N.E. (523-1554). A few years ago Seattle "stole" the famed quartet from Philadelphia, which became quartet-in-residence at the University. The group gives some 20 concerts each year under auspices of the School of Music.

Seattle Youth Symphony — 400 Boren N. (623-2001). One of Seattle's favorite musical groups, the Youth Symphony continues to startle and amaze music lovers with the professional quality of the orchestra and soloists. The young symphonists present three major concerts each year, which are usually sold out before the season begins, but blocks of tickets are available for the blind and low-income seniors and youth groups. Vilem Sokol, a UW music professor, is the conductor and musical director.

Other Musical Groups

Allspice —3034 118th S.E., Bellevue (543-8668). Specialty ethnic music from nearly every part of the world.

Cascade Youth Symphony —2000 68th W. Lynnwood (774-6899). For talented music students.

Collegium Musicum —UW School of Music (543-1200). Faculty and student concerts and recitals.

Contemporary Group —UW School of Music (543-1200). Faculty performing group, including members of the Philadelphia String Quartet.

Gilbert and Sullivan Society —4233 Baker N.W. (782-5466). The group presents an annual major production at the Seattle Center Playhouse, children's theater, lecture recitals, and maintains a G&S library.

Highline Civic Symphony —2515 S.W. 169th Pl. (243-5387). A 60-member orchestra composed of local talent that gives concerts occasionally.

Ladies Musical Club —1137 Hárvard E. (324-5796). For outstanding women in music who perform in concerts. Sponsors artists in Seattle Concert Series, "brown bag" concerts.

Musicians Association of Seattle, Local 76 —2650 3rd (623-0025). Professional musicians' union co-sponsors 12 concerts with Seattle Art Museum on Sunday afternoons in fall and spring. Free.

Norwegian Male Chorus —Norway Center, 300 3rd W. (284-1152). Established 1889, the performing group is the oldest and largest a cappella male chorus in Seattle.

Sea-Chordsmen —(Seattle Chapter of the Society for the Preservation and Encouragement of Barbershop Quartet Singing in America, Inc.) or SCSPEBQSAI! 3726 147th S.E., Bellevue (746-5052). Annual show, frequent sing-outs for schools, banquets and benefits.

Seattle Classic Guitar Society —2519 Montavista Pl. W. (283-1710). Sponsors recitals, workshops, lectures, and master classes.

Seattle Community Symphony Orchestra —939 N. 105th (783-6998). Sponsored by the city parks department, the group usually gives four free concerts a year.

Seattle Jazz Society —P.O. Box 24284, Terminal Annex, Seattle, 98124. Promotes live jazz performances, sponsors jazz cruises (see Tours) and other events.

Seattle Master Singers —3200 37th W. (783-4097). Choral performances by a chamber choir of 25.

Seattle Philharmonic Orchestra — P.O. Box 177, Seattle, 98111. (324-8982). Three to five concerts a season by amateur musicians with small admission fee.

Seattle Symphony Chorale — 305 Harrison (447-4700). Choral group allied with symphony that performs four to six times annually.

University of Washington Groups

The UW sponsors a number of musical groups composed of students and faculty which give performances throughout the year. In each case, the school of music or the Office of Lectures and Concerts should be contacted for program information. Some of the groups are: Chorale, Concert Band, Madrigal Singers, Opera, Percussion Ensemble, Sinfonietta, Symphony Orchestra and the Soni Ventorum Wind Quartet.

Dance

Alvfotter — 7350½ Mary N.W. (783-7508). Specializes in Swedish dances from about 300 years ago.

American Contemporary Dance Company — 2320 1st , P.O. Box 1164, 98111 (623-2232). Performances and demonstrations; children's classes. Skinner Releasing Technique taught.

Baba Karim Middle Eastern Dance Troupe — 6003 38th N.E. (522-3909). Folk and tribal dances of Middle East and North Africa. Two large shows a year; participants in festivals and community events.

Bailadores de Bronce — 5260 16th N.E. (525-0094). Folk dances of Mexico performed in full costume.

Bill Evans Dance Company — 704 19th E. (322-3733). Modern dance company performs in Seattle Playhouse, Opera House, and UW's Meany Hall.

Cabata'an Folk Dancers — c/o Filipino Youth Activities, 810 18th. (323-6545). Filipino folk dances performed at selected charities and festivals.

Cape Fox Dancers — 8023 12th N.W. (285-4425). Tlingit Indian dance group from Southeast Alaska. Performs Northwest Coast Indian dances with traditional songs.

Community Square Dancers — N.W. 85th & 3rd N.W. (783-8112). Traditional square dancing and calls performed at "G" Note Tavern.

Cornish Dance Theater — 710 E. Roy (323-1400). Cornish

School's dance company gives performances and supplies dancers for productions in the area.

Madrona Dance Center — 800 Lake Washington Blvd. (625-4303). Performances, residencies, and master classes in dance; low-fee classes for all ages. Sponsored by the Seattle Park Department and Dance Advisory Council.

Skandia Folkdance Society — P.O. Box 5378, University Station, 98105 (784-7477). Preserves traditional Scandinavian dances, classes, dance mixers.

Square and Folk Dance Federation of Washington, Inc. — 18749 23rd N.E. (342-8758). Promotes square and round dancing in Washington. Publishes *Footnotes Magazine*.

Beautiful by day, Seattle is brilliant by night as the setting for an exciting variety of entertainments.

After Dark

View bars

The views with booze are one of the pleasures of Seattle's nightlife, especially those which have a piano player who strokes the keys instead of assaulting them. New ones open; old ones close, but these are places to start.

One of the many views of the black-at-night waters of Puget Sound, and gliding ferry lights, the harbor scene, and the twinkling of Bainbridge Island in the far distance is from the piano-bar lounge of the *Edgewater Inn,* down near the north end of the docks along the waterfront. It's dark, so it's just you and the Sound.

The best sky-high view of the Sound at night—but a better place to watch a sunset—is the cocktail lounge of the *Mirabeau Restaurant* on top of the big-black-box Sea-First Building downtown.

If you're looking for a no-city view of the Sound, the artistic Olympic Mountains, and setting sun (an unbeatable combination), there is a whole strip of places along Shilshole Bay in Ballard.

At the mouth of the Hiram Chittenden Locks—a sight in themselves—is *Ray's Boathouse,* a pleasantly hip place with a nice bar.

The more razzle-dazzle lounge experience of a cocktail sunset, or by the light of the moon, is available inside the riveted steel hull of *Stuart's.*

Overlooking the huge yacht parking lot of Shilshole Marina, and then to the mountains and water, is a large lounge at Quinn's Fishmarket and Bar.

Right by the locks, and with no magnificent view to boost it, is the smaller lounge at *Hiram's at the Locks.*

There are some great urban landscapes too. Across Mercer Street from Seattle Center is a neat little complex called the Hansen Baking Company, which contains one of THE saloons of Seattle. But, first the view. An old church, refurbished into a restaurant somewhat sacrilegiously called *Sundays* is part of the complex. There is a second-floor lounge—and a very hip neon-and-stainless disco bar in the basement. From this second floor lounge, and extremely comfortable bar, look out over the lit arches of the Pacific Science Center, the Space Needle, and into a backdrop of downtown lights.

Before we leave the Hansen Baking Company—which really was one—we have to mention *Jake O'Shaughnessy's* ... THE saloon we just mentioned. Jake's almost has a personality of its own. It's hard to put your finger on just what makes it click. But it does. It feels and looks like a great big, somewhat-refined turn-of-the-century, somewhat-sophisitcated-Irish saloon. An Irish tenor bartender who holds forth at will and whim, the most complete bar in town, with a great bottle display to browse and pick-and-choose. No view.

You can catch a downtown view from the lounge high atop the *Hilton Hotel* downtown. The view is not this bar's best feature—although it is a great lookout tower. Famous for pick-ups, dancing, and usually high quality bands.

A favorite downtown view spot is the *Cloud Room* of the not very tall Camlin Hotel. The bar is elegant and relaxed, very tasteful, and it sits in a pocket of large buildings along one wall. On the other wall is a large open-air patio, which looks out on the quiet hulk of Capitol Hill. It is not breathtaking, but if feels the most like Seattle.

From atop a hill one may look out over in-city Lake Union at the University of Washington. A warm view of a very quiet city can be had from the small piano bar (great) lounge of the ritzy *Canlis Restaurant* at the south end of the Aurora Avenue Bridge. Unless you're planning to drop a bundle on the best charcoal-broiled steaks in town, wait 'til later in the evening to visit the lounge, which quiets down and becomes very intimate.

Three of the best night-time views of the city are nonalcoholic. Across the street from the *Embers* along the Harbor Drive in West Seattle, the city stands in profile, reflecting across the salt water. Close enough to be big, far enough away to see the whole thing. Fabulous!

The most breathtaking way to see the city on a mild night is to take a round-trip ferry ride on either the Winslow or Bainbridge run. It can be unforgettable, but remember that salt air is chilly, and really bundle up so you can stay outside on the deck.

The third is just plain driving on Interstate 5 between downtown and the University district.

Pioneer Square

There's been a regular entertainment boom down in historically restored Pioneer Square. Every month it seems another small tavern or restaurant is booking an act. The fare ranges from sometimes big-name jazz, to blue-grass pickers, country rock and rollers, spicy Afro-Latin jazz, and even records.

A luxurious tavern (beer and wine only) called *Parnell's* (313 Occidental S.) has booked some fine moderate jazz acts. When it's not live, it's jazz records and good ones. Uniquely comfortable, with Tiffany lamps, low padded seating, and good contemporary art on the walls.

Some big-name performers, and some who should or will be, perform jazz, rock, and blues at *Hibble & Hyde's* (608 1st).

Billed as "Seattle's Only Second Class Tavern," *The Central Tavern* (207 1st) is indeed humble, but rock, country rock, and crazy goof-off rock can be hand for both the feet and ears. Wed.-Sat.

Pioneer Square's seen good times and bad times for a long time, but it's always been the saloon capital of the state. It has some fine bars to this day, which are still serving from ornately carved back bars.

The *Merchant's Cafe*, (109 Yesler) which bills itself as the oldest restaurant in Seattle, has preserved the bar and comfortable feel of the old days. A quiet place for talking.

A louder place for talking, and the more wire-up, hip, young crowd is the *J&M Cafe* (201 1st S.) A high-ceilinged big old saloon, which preserves two vast and lovely old bars; it's usually bustling.

A half-and-half contemporary and pioneer-days world meets in the stylish *Old Timers Cafe* (620 1st) on Pergola Square. Again a grand old bar, but everything else is redone to accompany the rich, hip piped-in music.

A vast saloon down by the Kingdome called *F.X. McRory's* is brought to you by the folks from Jake O'Shaughnessy's over by Seattle Center. Same style but a triple shot.

Elsewhere in Town

The *Planter's Bar* of the Washington Plaza, which doesn't have much going for it in the way of decor, often books some of the best MOR solo performers that play this town.

Down in the Denny Regrade area, just north of downtown, is a comfortable bar in the Sixth Avenue Motor Hotel (2000 6th), called the *Tally-Ho Sixth Avenue*. The entertainment varies, but it is again MOR as a rule.

Another strictly MOR room—this time just a ways west of Seattle Center—is *Ivar's Captain's Table*, (333 Elliott W.), an attractive lounge with a slightly more mature musical format.

In the University District, at the University Tower Hotel (4507 Brooklyn N.E.) is another branch of the *Tally-Ho* lounge, which tends to book the same acts, although on occasion something a little hotter and hipper gets a month-long gig.

Overlooking Seattle's huge commercial fishing fleet at Fisherman's Terminal in Ballard is *The Wharf*, which also books solid MOR acts for the more mature audience.

Also to be kept in mind is the wide variety of entertainment available east of Lake Washington and on the Airport Strip down by Sea-Tac Airport.

Dancing

If you're looking for a polka in an authentic setting and are willing to drink only wine and beer, there's a little place off the beaten track in Ballard called the *International Schooner* where polka is a weekend experience. It feels like the Continent, and is a hell of a lot of fun.

There really is only one place for the foxtrot et al in town, and that is the show room of the *Edgewater Inn* along the waterfront. The management conscientiously books acts which, no matter what else they do, will play music for people who like to dance in traditional one-two-three-FOUR styles.

Just down Alaskan Way from the Edgewater in Pier 70, where the *Pier 70 Restaurant and Chowder House* dishes out the consistently hottest and best live, get-down dance music in town. Groups as big as 10 members and electronic amplification take to the stage and pull out all the disco sound stops. Plus—a beautiful view of the sound.

Not disco, not square, the *Top of the Hilton* downtown is also a main dance hall—and our lengendary "meat market" for pickups.

A huge and lively, always jampacked disco scene happens nightly at *The Golden Tides* down on the Shilshole Bay strip in Ballard.

Another elegant, small disco, with hip neon accessories and stainless steel dance floor is *Sunday's* in the Hansen Baking Company Complex by Seattle Center. It's the full act at Sundays.

Other mainstream acts can be seen-heard at *The America's Cup*, 1900 N. Northlake Way; the *Brick Oven*, 409 Roy; *Norselander*, 300 3rd W.; *Quinn's Fishmarket and Bar*, Shilshole Bay Marina, and *Slightly French*, 12531 Aurora N.

One of the most famous middle-of-the-road places recently

reverted to its original name and is coming back strong at *the* ballroom dancing place, ***Parker's Restaurant and Lounge***, 17001 Aurora N. For a period of several years it was known as the Aquarius Tavern, but nostalgia, and good business sense, brought back the original name.

Comedy Bars

A relatively new form of entertainment in Seattle are the bars and night clubs featuring comedians, both professionals and those from the audience who want to enter show business. Here is a list of places that feature "open mike" entertainment:

Bahamas Underground—1st & Yesler Way. Show starts at 5:30 p.m.

The Owl Cafe—5140 Ballard N.W. Mon., 9 p.m.

Mother Morgan's—211 S. 1st, Kent.

Skippers Tavern—2307 Eastlake E. Wed. Sign-up at 8 p.m.

Komedy Store—In Gasperetti's Roma Cafe, 4th & Main. Wed.-Sat. Best comics on Fri. and Sat. nights.

Old Timers Club—620 1st. Thurs. Sign-up at 7 p.m. Show starts at 8.

G-Note Tavern—85th & 3rd N.W. Sun. evenings at 8.

Slightly French—12531 Aurora N., (367-2908) features Wayne Cody's zany Komedy Store, with films, stand-up comics, and whatever else crosses the management's mind.

Other Places of Note

There are a couple of neat bars up on Capital Hill. Perhaps the premier elegant bar of the city is in ***Henry's Off Broadway***. Tasteful elegance, yet casual, it is a jam-packed, lively experience. Mirrors, comfort, and an occasional flash from the in-bar oyster bar.

Also on Capitol Hill is ***B.J. Monkeyshines and Lion O'Reilly's:*** old bar, brass, and mock old-saloon feel is what distinguishes the place.

There is a tiny, elegant bar in ***Labuznik Restaurant*** on 1st. After 9:30 p.m. it is *très intime,* perfect for whispering sweet nothings.

By Dawn's Early Light

Back in the old days when Seattle (and the entire state of Washington) was ruled by the so-called Blue Laws, hanging out at night was a lot more fun than it is now. The police payoff system, rancid though it was, meant little to the average citizen other than it permitted people to stay out all night drinking illegally in places where policemen hung around to keep the peace — and, of course, to protect their investments in the payoff system. But things have loosened up on drinking, and late-night sin isn't so much fun.

There are a few places (all legitimate and law-abiding, of course) that stay open all night. Since the authors of this guide-book don't include roaming the streets in the wee small hours as part of the research (it isn't nearly as much fun if you're happily married), we can't vouch for the atmosphere or clientele in most of these places. The first two listings, however, should be pretty tame places:

Cafe de Park — Park Hilton Hotel, 6th & Seneca
Thirteen Coins — 125 Boren N., & 18000 Pacific Highway S.
Beth's Cafe — 7311 Aurora N.
Steve's Broiler — 1937 4th.
The Doghouse — 2230 7th.
Nifty's — 1102 S.W. Spokane.
Randy's — 10016 E. Marginal Way
Cricket — 2947 Eastlake E.
Hattie's Hat — 5231 Ballard N.W.

If you have a thirst late at night that the pop machine down the hall can't satisfy, two Washington State Liquor Control Board stores are open after dark. The store at 602 2nd stays open until 10 p.m. Fri. & Sat., and the 6th & Lenora store is open until 11:30 Mon.-Sat.

Electronics

Television Stations

Six television stations serve the Seattle area.
KCTS-TV Channel 9, the educational station
KING-TV Channel 5, the NBC affiliate
KIRO-TV Channel 7, the CBS affiliate
KOMO-TV Channel 4, the ABC affiliate
KSTW-TV Channel 11, independent
KCPQ-TV Channel 13, independent

Radio Stations

Country & Western
KMPS-AM, 1300
KWWA-FM, 106.9
KERI-FM, 104.1
KWYZ-AM, 1230
KMO-AM, 1360
KGAA-AM, 1460

Middle of the Road
KPLZ-FM, 101.5
KIRO-AM, 710
KIXI-AM, 910
KOMO-AM, 1000
KASY-AM, 1220
KTNT-AM, 1400
KRKO-AM, 1380
KRPM-AM, 1450
KLAY-AM, 1480
KRBO-AM, 1490

Easy Listening
KQIN-AM, 800
KMPS-FM, 94.1
KEZX-FM, 98.9
KIXI-FM, 95.7
KSEA-FM, 100.7
KBIQ-FM, 105.3
KBRD-FM, 103.9

Jazz
KZAM-AM, 1540

Esoteric
KRAB-FM, 107.7

Classical
KUOW-FM, 94.9
KING-FM, 98.1
KXA-AM, 770
KPLU-FM, 88.5

Rock
KZAM-FM, 92.5
KJR-AM, 950
KISM-FM, 92.9
KISW-FM, 99.9
KZOK-FM, 102.5
KZOK-AM, 1590
KING-AM, 1090
KZAM-FM, 92.5
KNBQ-FM, 97.3
KRPM-FM, 106.1
KYYX-FM, 96.5
KYAC-AM, 1250

Religious
KBLE-AM, 1050
KGDN-AM, 630
KFWY-AM, 1560

All Talk
KVI-AM, 570
KAYO-AM, 1150

These stations will announce snow and ice information and if schools are closed for the day or operating on an emergency schedule: KIRO, KING, KOMO, KJR, KMPS, KAYO, KYAC, KQIN, KIXI, KVI.

SPORTS AND RECREATION

Fun & Games for Every Season

MANY PEOPLE in Seattle are so recreation minded that they know little and care less of what goes on inside the city limits; the city is a condition they tolerate five days each week, a place to live and work between outings. With the possible exception of outdoor ice skating in the winter (it's too mild here), there probably is no sport played anywhere else in the nation that isn't available in Seattle.

But that is only the beginning. Outside the city — within sight on a clear day — are the Olympic and Cascade Mountains where one can rock climb, hike, car camp, canoe, kayak, swim, ride horses or simply pause and look. Also within sight of the city, and even right in the city, one can walk on beaches, dig clams, fish for salmon, ling cod, sole. Other diversions include sailing, water skiing, swimming, cruising, scuba diving...the list is very long.

Because Seattle is surrounded (almost) by water — fresh to the east, salt to the west — and the mountains are less than an hour's drive away and more than 12 million acres of them are in public ownership, it is easy to understand why many residents treat the city simply as a launch pad for fun.

Interestingly, with all this self-propelled sports activity, Seattle has become a success story in spectator sports and each professional team — Seahawks, Sonics, Sounders, Mariners and others — receive enthusiastic support in terms of seats sold.

Archery

This isn't one of the major sports in Seattle, in part one suspects because it isn't particularly strenuous. But there is one public range, at Carkeek Park at the west foot of N.W. 110th St. The park has six practice ranges but you'll have to bring your own targets. Another range is in Redmond at Marymoor Park, 6046 W. Lake Sammamish Parkway, N.E.

Badminton

This is by no means a major sport in the area, but Community Centers occasionally organize leagues if there is sufficient demand. Call the local Community Center for details.

Baseball

For years Seattle had the Rainiers baseball team as part of the Pacific Coast League, the Triple A variety of baseball, and games were played in Sicks Stadium on Rainier Ave. S. Then, with the wisdom that brings smog to cities, Seattle decided to become a "major league" city. They got into the American League with the Seattle Pilots. For one year. Then the franchise was sold and Seattle sports fans screamed "Foul!" In one of those legal maneuvers only attorneys can understand, Seattle interests took the American League to court. But, instead of taking them to court to get the League out of town and behind bars, or at least several million dollars poorer, Seattle took them to court to bring them *back* to town! And they won. Seattle got an expansion franchise out of the case and a promise from the ethical baseball league that the city would have a team. And now we do. The Mariners.

The team began playing in April, 1977, after selecting 30 players from existing AL teams. Ticket prices are $7.50, $6.50, $5.50, $4.50, and $1.50 general admission in the Kingdome. Information: P.O. Box 4100, Seattle, 98104 (628-3300).

We also have the college teams at the University of Washington, Seattle University, and Seattle Pacific College, plus uncounted dozens of Community Center league teams, Little League teams, Babe Ruth teams, and what have you. During the season, select a Community Center at random if you're a baseball buff, and you'll find someone playing baseball. Sandlot baseball, unfortunately, has disappeared with real grass.

Dozens of slow-pitch leagues are formed around the city by the Park Department. For information, call the Community Center nearest your home, or the headquarters: 625-4671.

Basketball

For several seasons Seattle has had an excellent NBA team called the SuperSonics (abbreviated to Sonics). The mediocre record of wins and losses suddenly changed in 1978 after Coach Lenny Wilkens took over. They won the NBA championship in 1979. The Sonics play in the Kingdome. Ticket information, (628-8448). Their headquarters are at 221 W. Harrison on the edge of the Seattle Center.

Among the college teams, the Seattle University Chieftains have usually attracted the most national attention, thanks to stars such as Elgin Baylor and, more recently, Frank Oleynick. Call the Athletic Department, 626-5305, for game and ticket information.

The University of Washington's Husky basketball team has never generated the enthusiasm and boxoffice response of the football team, but the basketball teams are usually exciting to watch. Information: Athletic Events ticket office, 543-2200.

Seattle Pacific College fields another popular team, the Falcons. Athletics office: 281-2085.

For the participant rather than spectator, the Park Department each fall organizes fast-break, slow-break and half-court leagues, as well as an occasional open night for people to organize their own games, called open shooting. Call the local Community Center or headquarters, 625-4671.

Bicycling

Getting acquainted with Seattle's outstanding views, waterfront and boating activities, and people on a bicycle offers more action than walking and more intimate experiences than driving. As you pedal along a beach walk or pump up and down hills to take in old neighborhoods with interspersed viewpoints, you can absorb each new experience before a new one interrupts. Walking can be too slow—and too much work. But, on a bicycle a continuing succession of encounters with people and environment unfold with a minimum of physical exertion.

All of Seattle and suburbs are laced with planned bicycle tours. Many are marked with the familiar two-wheel symbol of the bike trail. Every type of trip can be experienced from easy, level rides around Green Lake to the up-and-down challenging

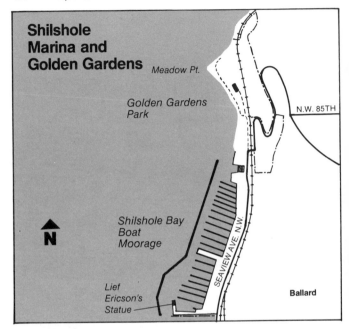

rides on Queen Anne and Mercer Island. Rental bikes are available mainly at Green Lake and in some of the shops (see list below). Many Seattleites own their own lightweight touring bikes as a result of their interest in long-range touring.

Bicycle Trips

Following are only a few of the most popular bicycle trips or tours around Seattle and neighboring islands and suburbs.

Bicycle Sundays — During summer months a 6-mile stretch along Lake Washington is closed to auto traffic from 10 a.m.-5 p.m. every third Sunday. Check with the Seattle Parks Dept. or Police before you go freewheeling.

West Seattle Beach Ride — Begin at the west side of the Spokane Street Bridge over the Duwamish Waterway on Harbor Avenue S.W. near S.W. California Place. You'll be looking at an ever changing view of Elliott Bay, the Olympics in the background, and across the water to Seattle's downtown skyline, so pick a clear day. Your ride will be level on the water side of Harbor and Alki Avenues around Duwamish Head, along Alki Beach and Park, past Alki Point Lighthouse, on to Schmitz Viewpoint Park, and beyond to Lincoln Park and the landing for ferries to and from Vashon Island. Generally easy. About 12 miles and 2 hours round-trip. Turn around at any point for a shorter trip. Picnic areas, restrooms, food shops, and takeout foods available along the route.

Green Lake Ride — Probably the most popular bicycling path in Seattle, a round-trip of Green Lake is 3 miles and is mainly flat. You're likely to encounter many walkers and joggers but no motor traffic. Traffic moves counterclockwise around the lake. Green Lake Park East and West includes fishing, swimming both in the lake and a pool, playfields, and picnic areas. The Green Lake Ride offers a destination from the University of Washington along the Ravenna Park bicycle path. Generally easy. Three miles and about 30 minutes. Bike rentals are available near the lake. Restaurants and shops are nearby.

Queen Anne Hill Ride — Cycling around Queen Anne Hill affords a look at one of Seattle's oldest residential areas with viewpoints interspersed for a look in all directions.

Shilshole Bay-Salmon Bay Rides — These two rides are located along both sides of the Salmon Bay waterway from Fisherman's Terminal to Shilshole Bay and Golden Gardens Park on the north side of the waterway and along Commodore Way to Discovery Park on the south side of the waterway.

Magnolia View Ride — High above Puget Sound, Magnolia Bluff offers views of the Olympics, shipping in Elliott Bay, West Seattle, Mt. Rainier, and Seattle's downtown skyline.

Lake Washington Ride — A succession of waterfront park areas along Seattle's eastern edge afford low, level riding on paths and streets from the University of Washington's Arboretum to a circle tour of Seward Park.

Burke-Gilman Trail — This 12.5-mile premium bicycle and hiking trail in the Seattle area represents a concept that is being watched closely by other cities. The city and county took over an abandoned stretch of railroad bed that ran from Gas Works Park on Lake Union to Kenmore, taking a swing through the edge of the UW campus and along the west shore of Lake Washington. After the city and county acquired it, the roadbed was cleared of rails and ties,graded smooth, surfaced, and given to bikers. From the city start at Gas Works Park on Lake Union and follow the marked bikeway around Lake Union, through the University of Washington campus to University Village shopping center. At this point the trail intersects with the bikeway to Green Lake or you may make a loop trip through the University District along 15th N.E. and back to Gas Works Park. Continuing on the Burke-Gilman Trail at University Village, you will pass Warren G. Magnuson Park, Matthews Beach Park, a rest area at N.E. 130th, and go around the northern tip of Lake Washington to Kenmore Logboom Park. Auto parking, restrooms, and picnic tables are available at all parks on the trail.

Waterfront Park Bike Path — See Myrtle Edwards and Elliott Bay Parks chapter.

Other rides include Capitol Hill, Laurelhurst, Lake Union, and Seattle City Center within the city limits. Nearby are interesting trips around Mercer Island, Bainbridge Island, Whidbey Island, Newport-Lake Sammamish, and Vashon Island. Or, experienced cyclists can circle Lake Washington in about 50 miles of varied riding.

Bicycle Clubs and Information

Various clubs offer touring, racing, and information sharing about bicycles. Cascade Bicycle Club sponsors a 24-hour hotline (522-BIKE). Leave your name and telephone number on the recording, and someone will return your call and answer any question on biking. Bicycle Paper (P.O. Box 842, Seattle, 98111) is published monthly from April to Sept. and is available at most bike shops. Two other clubs are:

Mountaineers, Bicycle Section, 6039 Beach Dr. S.W., Seattle, 98136.

Washington State Bicycle Association, Box 16533, Seattle, 98115 (523-0701). List of racing organizations may be obtained from this association.

Washington State Highway Department locates 61 different routes for bicyclists and publishes maps. Write Bicycle, Engineering Services Div., Highway Administration Bldg., Olympia, WA 98504.

The City of Seattle's Engineering Department publishes a Bicycle Guidemap, free.

Bicycle Races

Races at King County Marymoor Park in Redmond on Mon. and Fri. nights at 6:30. Training rides at 4 p.m. Mon.

Entry fee, sponsored by Marymoor Park Velodrome, all riders welcome. Track is banked at 25 degrees and is open to the public every day.

Bicycle Rentals

Alki Bikes, 2722 Alki S.W. (938-3322). Near Alki Ave. bike
   path.
The Bicycle Centers, 5026 University Way N.E. (523-7008).
   Near but not on Burke-Gilman Trail or University bike
   path from Green Lake. Also 4529 Sand Point Way N.E.
   (523-8300). Near Burke-Gilman Trail.
Gregg's Greenlake Bicycle Center, 7007 Woodlawn N.E. (523-
   1822). Close to Green Lake path and near Burke-Gilman
   Trail.
Northlake Schwinn Cycle, 17171 Bothell Way N.E. (365-5919).
   Near Burke-Gilman Trail in Forest Park Shopping Center.

Boating

Boat Racing

Each summer Seafair sponsors an unlimited hydroplane race on Lake Washington, usually in early August. It is one of the most popular events in the city in spite of the loud groaning by residents of whatever neighborhood on the lake the city and Seafair decide to take over for the weekend. Seafair also sponsors smaller-class hydroplane races, usually on Green Lake, earlier in the summer.

One of the most beautiful types of boat racing are the shell races held in the Lake Washington Ship Canal occasionally throughout the year with the University of Washington crew competing against other college crews.

One of the most spectacular motorboat races is held each summer in the 11-mile-long Sammamish Slough, actually a sluggish river emptying Lake Sammamish into Lake Washington. The race is usually held in April and usually is divided into two parts: a boat race and a water-ski race. When the slough isn't being used for races, it is a popular trip for canoeists and kayakers, especially beginners or those testing a new craft.

Sailboat Racing — Sailing detractors say watching sailboat races is as exciting as watching grass grow or watching paint dry. Don't you believe it. The Seattle Yacht Club, 1807 E. Hamlin (325-1000), and the Corinthian Yacht Club, with clubhouses on Shilshole Bay and Leschi Park on Lake Washington (322-7877) are the major clubs. Both sponsor numerous races throughout the year. Check the newspapers or call the clubs.

Boat Ramps and Moorages — Public

Puget Sound — Don Armeni, Harbor S.W. off S.W. Maryland; Eddie Vine, N. end of Seaview N.W.; Seacrest Marina, Harbor S.W. & S. Washington (day).

Salmon Bay and Lake Washington Ship Canal — 14th N.W. & Shilshole N.W.; N. 36th, Corliss N. & Northlake Way.

Lake Washington — Atlantic City, S. Henderson & Seward Park S.; Lakewood Moorage, Lake Washington Blvd. S & S. Genesee; N. & S. Leschi Moorages, Lakeside S. off E. Alder; Sayres Memorial Park, Lake Washington Blvd. S. & 46th S.; S. Ferdinand & Lake Washington Blvd. S.; S. Day & Lakeside S.

Duwamish Waterway — 1st S. & S. River.

Boat Rental Prices

Whether you want to sail, fish, scuba-dive, water ski, sightsee, or simply go for a boat ride, there's a place somewhere in the Seattle area to rent a boat of your choice. You can rent yachts for

THE STARS OF THE FLEET

Sailboat racing remains a favorite Seattle sport and spectacle.

extended Puget Sound cruises, with or without skippers and crews; you can rent a kicker-boat with motor and fishing gear to go after salmon (and dogfish, of course) off Whidbey Island and Point No Point; you can join a sailing club and take instructions; you can rent a paddleboat at Green Lake; you can canoe through the Arboretum. The choice is yours.

Before giving you a sampling of some two dozen places to rent boats, we can talk briefly about price.

Sailboats — The smaller models, for day use only (up to 16 feet), average about $10 an hour. The 25- to 30-foot models run from $75 a day and up with better prices for a weekly rental. When you get into this class and larger, some charter firms require you to use their own skipper at an additional cost.

Canoes — These range from about $2 an hour at the University of Washington Canoe House on up.

Paddleboats — At Green Lake these rent for $4 an hour and up.

Rowboats — At Green Lake, $2.75 an hour.

Kicker boats — For the uninitiated, these are simply outboard boats with a 20-horsepower motor used in Puget Sound for salmon or bottom fishing. These cost roughly $15 a day without motor. Motor rentals begin at around $5.50 an hour. Most rental places also have fishing gear available at about $5 a day, some slightly higher. Rental places open around 4 a.m. for the early risers who want to get their salmon before going to work.

Water ski boats — For obvious reasons, it is hard to find a variety of boathouses that will rent these high-powered craft because they are accident prone and expensive to repair. Those few places that do rent them charge roughly $25 an hour or $75 to $100 a day depending on the size of boat and motor.

Boat Rental Locations

The Boathouse — 9812 17th S.W. (763-0688). Rents canoes.

Goodtime Charters — Pier 56 (623-1445). Charter for large groups, 3-hour minimum. Price ranges from $500 to $875 depending on size of group. Can take from 100 to 300 aboard cruise boat.

Green Lake — Rentals on east end of lake (527-0171). Rowboats and paddleboats.

Kelly's Landing — 1401 N.E. Boat St. (623-3470). Rents Hobie 16, canoes, and small sailboats. Open 7 days a week in summer.

Laebugten Wharf, Inc. — 16111 76th Pl. W., Edmonds (743-2211). Kicker boats and fishing equipment for salmon fishermen. Charter service available.

Ledger Marine Charters — 101 Nickerson (283-6160). Charter boats, power and sail, from 26-footers and up with one-week minimum. Can provide skippered charters for single-day group trips.

Lloyds Boat House — 1660 Harbor S.W. (932-1050). Kicker boats rented by half or all day, motors, and bait.

Northwest Marine Charters — 2400 Westlake N. (283-3040). Charters both sail and power boats from 26-footers up. Special arrangements can be made for skippered one-day outings.

Ray's Boathouse — 6049 Seaview N.W. (783-9779). Rents kicker boats, motors, and fishing gear; rowboats.

Sailboats Unlimited — 2046 Westlake N. (283-4664). Charters and rentals.

University of Washington Waterfront Activities Center — (543-2217). Somewhat difficult to find. Turn right into parking lot off Montlake Bridge, north end, and follow waterfront to end of lot at new building. Canoes for rent by hour or day.

Windworks Sailing School & Charters — 7001 Seaview N.W. (784-9386). Cruising sailboats from 26 to 40 feet for trips through Puget Sound, San Juans and Canadian Gulf Islands. Skippered charters available.

Sailing Lessons

Pick a beautiful summer day in Seattle and you'll see hundreds, if not a thousand or more sailboats flitting across Lake Washington and Puget Sound. It is nearly as popular as power boating and certainly a lot quieter. There are a number of sailing courses available through private clubs or organizations such as the University of Washington Alumni Association. Public courses are easier to enroll in and only these are listed. For information on others, contact the Coast Guard Auxiliary, Power Squadron, a community college, or a private yacht club.

American Red Cross — In cooperation with the city parks, the Red Cross offers classes open to anyone 13 years or older who can pass the Red Cross swimming test. The course includes 24 hours of instruction, 12 in the classroom and the rest on water. To register, call the Park Department, 100 Dexter N., 98101 (625-4671); or the Red Cross, Box 24286, Seattle, 98124 (323-2345).

Wind Yachts, Inc., 6300 Seaview N.W., 98107 (784-0110), offers year-around instruction focused on sailing larger boats during the 16-hour courses.

Bowling

There are some three dozen bowling centers (they aren't called alleys any more) in Seattle, more in outlying areas, many of which have restaurants and nurseries. Most also have billiard tables (there are few pool halls left in Seattle). Check the Yellow Pages for a complete list of nearby lanes.

These organizations will assist you with league sign-up and tournament information: Greater Seattle Men's Bowling Assn., 1512 N.E. 117th (365-2973), and Greater Seattle Women's Bowling Assn., 2366 Eastlake W. (325-8530).

Boxing

Although Seattle has produced a few contenders in the middle and heavyweight categories (Eddie Cotton, Boone Kirkman, and Pete Rademacher), there is little emphasis on boxing here now. Gyms are scarce and most lean toward the health spa or Oriental martial arts clients.

Bridge

There are at least three bridge clubs in Seattle and occasional competition at the Seattle Center. For information and instruction, Seattle Bridge Center, 1515 Dexter N., (282-6414).

Chess

The Main Library of the Seattle Library system, 5th & Madison, offers free chess games Wednesdays from 1-6 p.m. For information on other clubs, call the library, 625-2665, since others meet on an infrequent basis in branch libraries.

Curling

The Granite Curling Club, 1440 N. 128th (362-2446 or 362-9927) offers free instruction. Season runs from October through April. Initiation fee; $25, dues $12 per month, $2 per game. Call for schedules of competition.

Fishing

It has been often said that to understand the Northwest mystique, you first must go winter steelheading when the temperature is below freezing and you have to keep dipping the rod into the water to clear the ice off it, and you stand there shivering and never catch a fish. Or you must catch some sea-run cutthroat, or a salmon headed for the spawning beds, or dig a clam, or go out in Puget Sound in a kicker-boat before dawn and sit in a fogbank, lost and wondering if a freighter is going to run you down. If the Northwest has a mystique, fishing and all that goes with it are part of it.

Fisheries biologists say there are some 150 species of fish in Puget Sound and about 36 in Lake Washington (including the saltwater fish that migrate in). Thus, most anglers go after the more spectacular fish — the salmon, steelhead and sea-run cutthroat trout — and there isn't so much competition for the bottom fish that are equally good on the dinner table.

These lesser known marine fish include cod, hake, flounder, sole, perch, and surf smelt. The freshwater fish include rainbow trout, largemouth bass, sunfish, mountain whitefish, and crayfish.

Also of major importance to sports fishermen are the marine shellfish (there are few right in Seattle, however, so don't get your hopes up), which include several types of clam, goeducks, Dungeness crabs, shrimp, octopus, and squids.

Your best bet is to check in at a sporting goods store for information on seasons, license fees, and tips on where to fish for which species. In many cases you'll have to drive a few miles away from Seattle, especially for clam digging and obviously for stream fishing. However, there are numerous piers maintained by the Seattle Parks and Recreation Dept. where no license is needed.

Public Fishing

Puget Sound — Waterfront Park at the end of Pier 57 is a public fishing pier and a popular place for father-and-son teams of bottom fishermen. Also on the waterfront, the public seawall just north of Pier 70 is popular. Others include: Alki Avenue breakwater and the pier at the south end of Golden Gardens Park.

Green Lake — Fishing anywhere on the lake or at three piers: N.E. corner near the ball field (juveniles only); N.W.

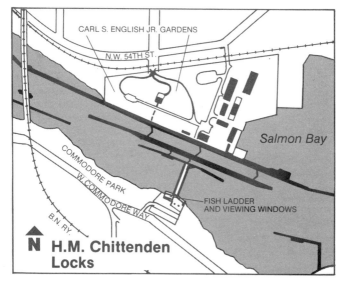

CARL S. ENGLISH JR. GARDENS

N.W. 54TH ST.

COMMODORE PARK

W. COMMODORE WAY

B.N. RY.

Salmon Bay

FISH LADDER
AND VIEWING WINDOWS

**N   H.M. Chittenden
Locks**

corner near "Duck Island;" and S.W. corner by the Aqua
Theater.

Lake Washington — Madison Park at the foot of E. Madison;
just south of Madrona Beach near the foot of E. Jefferson; Mt.
Baker Park, S. McClellan & 35th S.; Seward Park, Lake
Washington Blvd. & S. Juneau; N. Leschi Moorage, Lakeside S.
and Alder E.

Ship Canal — South side of Hiram Chittenden (Ballard)
Locks.

Charters

Puget Sound — Bait, tackle, and usually coffee are provided
on these local salmon charter boats. Will also fish for bottom
fish on request. Viking Charters (634-2939), U.S. Inc., 7342
15th N.W. (789-6702), Mager, 3605 50th S.W. (935-9274). Ben-
dixon Charters, Shilshole Marina (283-3963), Bob Meehan
(778-7580), Bud Darling (774-1349).

Ocean Charters — Charter boats in the Pacific off the coastal
towns of Westport, Ilwaco, Sekiu, and Neah Bay in particular,
have become a major industry. There are many in Seattle who
do not consider their year complete without at least one trip out
into the ocean for salmon, just as there are many tourists who

come here with that one thing in mind. In most cases, it is possible to arrange for a charter-boat trip from Seattle via toll-free numbers to the coastal towns. More and more charter firms are stressing other fish now instead of only salmon, so check with the firm to see what they suggest you go after.

In addition to the day trips, there are tuna and albacore charter boats from the coastal towns. Check chambers of commerce, sporting goods stores, and the *Fishing and Hunting News* for details. The charter season for salmon runs from around May 1 through September.

Football

University of Washington

Not long ago tickets to the University of Washington Huskies games were a scalper's delight. Since the Seahawks arrived, tickets are easier to get. Ticket information: 543-2200.

Professional

Seattle Seahawks — After a lot of guessing by the populace and jockeying for position by potential owners, Seattle gained a professional football team that plays in the National Football League. The Seahawks' principal owners are the Nordstrom family, and the team is coached by Jack Patera, who in a short time was able to make a bunch of unproven young players and some aging castoffs from other teams into an exciting, go-for-broke team. All home games are played in the Kingdome with both radio and TV coverage by KIRO. Tickets are steep, beginning somewhere around $12. Office, 5305 Lake Washington Blvd., Kirkland (827-9777); ticket sales, (827-9766).

Golf

There are more than a dozen private golf courses in the Seattle area and some two dozen public courses. It is best to call the public courses in advance for reservations. Most, obviously, are out of town.

Nine holes cost $4 to $5 weekdays; $4.25 to $5.75 weekends: 18 holes, $4.50 to $5.75 weekdays; $5 to $6.25 weekends. Annual golf cards are $440. Public courses below are 18-hole except those designated 9H.

Ballinger Park, 7008 230th S.W., Mountlake Terrace (776-7775), 9H

Bellevue Municipal, 5450 140th N.E., Bellevue (885-6009)

Sports and Recreation   77

Brookside, 19115 N.E. 155th, Woodinville (788-1038), 9H
Carnation, Carnation (333-4151)
Cascade, Cedar Falls Rd., North Bend (888-0227), 9H
Colony Park, 5621 Kent-Des Moines Rd., Kent (852-8844), 9H
Earlington, 1115 S.W. Interurban S. (242-4221)
Foster, 13500 Interurban S. (242-4221)
Greenlake, 5701 W. Green Lake Way N. (623-8084), par 3
Interbay, 2501 15th W. (625-2820), 9H, par 3
Jackson Park Municipal, 1000 N.E. 135th (363-4747)
Jefferson Park Municipal, 4101 Beacon S. (762-4513)
Lake Wilderness, 25400 Witte Rd. S.E., Maple Valley (432-9405)
Maplewood, 13020 Maple Valley Highway, Renton (255-3194)
Mt. Si, Snoqualmie (888-1541)
Si View, North Bend (888-1817)
Snohomish, 7806 147th S.E., Snohomish (568-2676)
Snoqualmie Falls, Fall City (392-1276, toll-free)
Tall Chief, Fall City (222-5911)
Tyee Valley, 2401 S. 192nd (878-3540)
Wayne, 16721 96th N.E. Bothell (485-6237)
West Seattle, 4470 35th S.W. (932-9792)

Practice Golf Ranges

Harris-Conley, 1440 156th N.E., Bellevue (747-2585)
Interbay, 2501 15th W. (283-3170)
Jefferson Park, 4101 Beacon S. (763-8989)
Puetz Evergreen, 11762 Aurora N. (362-2272)
Renton, 2000 Lake Washington Blvd. N., Renton (255-1817)
Valley, 5813 Kent-Des Moines Rd., Ken (852-6700)

Gymnastics

This isn't one of the sports biggies in Seattle, but instruction and competition are sometimes offered by the Park Department (625-4671), Seattle Pacific University (281-2000), and the University of Washington's Continuing Arts Education (543-2300). Also, the YMCA (447-4547) and the YWCA (447-4888). For privately owned schools, check the Yellow Pages.

Handball, Squash, Paddleball

Some private clubs (Washington Athletic Club and the newer franchise clubs, for example) offer these sports. Otherwise, your best bet is the YMCA, listed elsewhere in this section.

Hang Gliding

This sport, which is about as dangerous as executing a swan dive from a jet, is popular among the daring, but there are few places it is practiced near Seattle. The best spot, according to enthusiasts, is near Morton, where each weekend in good weather hand-gliders from all over the Northwest gather to hang out. The Pacific Northwest Hang Glide Association has been formed. Information: Recreational Equipment (323-8333). Also, Ultralite Sports, 14800 Westminster Way N. (363-6364) gives lessons.

Hiking

This is one of the most popular sports in Seattle and the whole Northwest with at least 250,000 (at last count) participating in it. The government owns some 12 million acres of the state, much of which is available to hikers and climbers. If you have no experience in hiking, or backpacking as it often is called, your best bet is to join a club or take a course in the highly specialized and potentially dangerous sport. With hypothermia a major problem even in summer, you should know what you're doing before you strike out across the forest floors, glaciers, and peaks.

The Mountaineers is the oldest organization, 719 Pike (623-2314). The club offers courses and trips in the whole range of outdoor experience (except hunting, a real no-no); short hikes, expedition hikes, rock climbing, mountaineering, bicycle trips, canoeing and kayaking, skiing, and snowshoeing in the winter.

The Washington Alpine Club, Box 352, Seattle, 98111, sponsors ski instruction and occasional caravans for camping trips to other parts of the state, as well as the climbs for which it was named.

The Sierra Club has a Seattle chapter, which also goes on frequent outings, usually in connection with an area it is attempting to save. Information: 4534½ University Way, Seattle, 98105 (623-9314).

Several firms in Seattle specialize in wilderness trips and mountain climbing for the inexperienced.

Rainier Mountaineering, Inc. has the National Park Service concession for leading climbs on the king of mountains. Information: Rainier Mountaineering, Paradise, WA 98397. Telephone (long distance 1-569-2227).

R.E.I. Mountain Schools offers month-long courses from April through September with instruction in all the basics of backpacking; how to choose a pack and boots as well as survive on freeze-dried food. Climbing and alpine travel courses also. Information: R.E.I. Mountain Schools, P.O. Box C88126, Seattle, 98188 or call Recreational Equipment Inc. (562-4894).

Equipment rentals — Packs, boots, climbing gear but not sleeping bags are available at the major outdoor-recreation stores in Seattle. Recreational Equipment, Inc., 1525 11th (323-8333) has the best selection and prices.

Courses are offered by the Parks Department, most community colleges, and at Recreational Equipment on Thursday evenings. If you want to find out in advance how you'll enjoy rock climbing before investing in a course, try yourself out on the 25-foot tall Schurman Rock in Camp Long, 5200 35th S.W. Make reservation first: 935-0370.

Guidebooks — All hikers, whether novice or expedition-class, feel naked in the Northwest unless they have the excellent series of guidebooks published by The Mountaineers on various sections of the mountains around the state, and the classic hiking-climbing text, *Freedom of the Hills.* The guidebooks include *Trips and Trails, 101 Hikes, 102 Hikes,* and for the lowland hiker, *Footloose Around Puget Sound* — plus others.

Guidebooks frequently accomplish two things: they point out the most spectacular, and they bring hordes to those attractions. To avoid crowds (and to satiate your hunger for gorgeous maps), contact the various forest rangers in the state and the national parks. They will supply maps with marvelously detailed trails, streams, and major features shown.

Signpost is a magazine published by Signpost Publications, 16812 36th W., Lynnwood, 98036 (747-3947). An informative, sometimes outspoken, bimonthly for hikers, kayakers, climbers, and backpackers with 10 newsletters a year for subscribers. A separate firm with the same name also publishes guidebooks and how-to-do-it books on outdoor subjects.

The National Park Service and National Forest Service have combined forces to furnish information on questions such as up-to-date trail information, cutting of Christmas trees and firewood, and environmental concerns. They also supply maps (50¢ each) and answer questions at Forest Service-Park Service Joint Recreation Information, Rm. 110, Federal Bldg., 915 2nd, Seattle, 98174 (442-0170). Dial 442-7669 for a recording about trail, road, and campground conditions, snow levels, and other pertinent information.

Hockey

Professional hockey is one professional sport that didn't fare too well in Seattle, and the Totems gave up and left town about 4 years ago. A new team has been formed, the Breakers, and are part of the Western Canada Hockey League. For information: 624-9121.

Horse Racing

Few states are more schizophrenic about gambling than Washington. While travel agencies, air, and bus lines make a bundle off gamblers intent on breaking the banks at Reno and Vegas, Washington has seemed content letting its money flee south to the tables. On the other hand, Longacres race track has been an establishment in the Seattle area so long that we tend to forget that people actually do go there to gamble on which horse will run faster than other horses.

The track is between Southcenter and Renton, near Sea-Tac, on Interstate 405. Post time is 4:15 p.m. weekdays, 1:15 p.m. on holidays and weekends. Admission to the track on race days is $2.50 for the grandstand, $4.50 for the clubhouse dining area. Cocktail lounges are scattered throughout the track for convenience. Children under 10 are not permitted at the track except during Saturday morning workouts. The track is closed Mondays and Tuesdays.

The racing season runs from mid-May to late September.

Occasionally during the racing season the track offers free Saturday morning workouts where guests have an opportunity to talk to trainers, vets, and jockeys about horses, betting, and whatever else track touts talk about. (Try saying that rapidly!)

The Special Events Department can make arrangements for groups from 20 to 300; call the track at 226-3131 during the racing season, 624-2455 during the off-season for information.

Horseback Riding

There are no riding stables or trails in the city limits but several on the outskirts of town, where horses may be rented.

The best public riding area for those who own horses is Bridle Trails State Park in Kirkland. Riding stables in the area include:

Aqua Barn Ranch, 15277 S.E. Renton-Maple Valley Highway, Renton (255-4618). Open year-around; trails on 500 acres. Instruction.

Gold Creek Stables, 16528 148th N.E., Woodinville (483-2787).

Lake Serene Pony Farm, 3915 Serene Way, Lynnwood (743-2112). Trail riding for children ages 3-14.

Kelly's Riding & Boarding Ranch, 7212 Renton-Issaquah Rd. S.E. (392-6979).

Red Barn Ranch, 17601 S.E. Lake Moneysmith Rd., Auburn (854-3690). Seattle Park Dept. facility open to groups only. (See listing in Parks section).

Horse Shoe Pitching

Pits are available at Lincoln Park, Woodland Park, Rainier Playfield (Rainier & Oregon), and Broadway Playfield (11 & E. Pine). Bring your own shoes.

Jogging

A nice thing about jogging in Seattle is that people do it everywhere, and you could jog through the Federal Building without attracting much attention (maybe a little, though). But the most popular spots are around Green Lake, where joggers do their thing by the hundreds; the Arboretum; Volunteer, Lincoln, and Seward Parks; and all Community Centers. Near park headquarters at Discovery Park there is a half-mile fitness "parcours" with 15 types of exercises to complete along with jogging. Some joggers prefer adding a bit of sightseeing to their route and jog down Alaskan Way along the waterfront or through any neignborhood they please. They can even run on the city golf courses, which is unusual in cities.

For long-distance runners, the Runners' Hotline (522-7787 daytime; 324-6537 night) will tell you about competition events.

Kingdome

They're calling it Kingdome. The King County Multipurpose Stadium was approved in 1968 by voters, but the site selection rhubarb that followed delayed construction several years. When a site was selected, on the edge of Pioneer Square at King Street and Occidental, a new element was introduced to Seattle's skyline.

Now the sterling statistics: it covers 9.1 acres and is 250 feet high and 660 feet in diameter. It will seat 64,772 for football games which includes 15,057 chair seats with arm rests, 39,233 on sidelines, and 25,489 in the end zone. For baseball games, it will seat 59,623 with 13,082 chair seats with arm rests, 16,649 between first and third base, and 41,799 between the foul lines. (For a tour see listing in Guided Tours, Sightseeing section.)

For personality shows it will seat approximately 80,000.

It has 17 restrooms for men, 15 for women; 87 water fountains, 2 freight-passenger elevators, and 51 concessions. It has a sports museum and space for 2,700 cars on the site. Shuttle buses run north and south from the stadium.

The professional football, baseball, basketball, and soccer teams play in the Kingdome.

Lawn Bowling

Jefferson Park Lawn Bowling Club — 4103 Beacon (762-9728). Queen City Law Bowling Club — 6018 Whitman N. (782-1515) or Seattle Parks Dept. Instruction and games at Woodland Park N. 63rd & Whitman N., and Jefferson Park Golf Course, S. Dakota & Beacon.

Model Airplane Flying

This noisy and fascinating sport is permitted at the Interbay Playfield, 17th W. & W. Barrett; Carkeek Park; and Genesee Playfield, 43rd S. & Genesee. Marymoor Park in Redmond has a model airport opening at dawn in the spring and summer months; shows and races are held there.

Model Boat Racing

These tiny hydro races are held at infrequent intervals on the west shore of Green Lake. Check with the Park Department for information and clubs (625-4671).

Oriental Martial Arts

Judo, karate, kung-fu, and the other forms of the violent art are offered both commercially and by public programs throughout Seattle. Its popularity is due in part to the late actor, Bruce Lee, who was from Seattle and was buried here after his untimely death. Instruction for both men and women are offered by most community colleges, the YMCA and YWCA, and at Community Centers.

Ping Pong

National Table Tennis League, 707 5th N. (282-7700) is headquarters for the International Table Tennis League, which organizes title matches throughout the world. Seattle Sockeyes Professional Ping Pong Team, same address and telephone as NTTL. Washington State Table Tennis Assoc. welcomes all players at Connolly Center, Seattle University, Mon.-Wed.-Fri. evenings.

Polo

The Seattle Polo Club isn't in Seattle, of course. It is at N.E. 116th & 150th N.E., Redmond. Free matches are held throughout the summer on the outdoor field and during the winter in the Central Park Stables at Bridle Trails State Park. Information: 885-1504.

Rugby

This sport hasn't caught on strongly in Seattle yet, but its day surely will come. It is played on an intramural basis by some schools, particularly private schools, and the Seattle Rugby Club (285-4279) organizes occasional games.

Seafair

This community festival used to be a parade, the hydroplane races, and pirates running about making a lot of noise. It has grown up a bit to include these things plus an almost year-round schedule of activities. Among them are tug-of-war contests, the milk carton boat race on Green Lake, a wacky soccer game between the Seafair Pirates and the Sounders, the Bon Odori festival in the International District, bicycle competitions, soap box derbies, golf tournaments, kite flying events, art shows, and on and on. Even a chess tournament. If you don't like parades, don't like your meals disturbed in restaurants by clowns dressed as pirates, don't like the noise and crowds con-

nected with the unlimited hydroplane races, this clearly is not
your type of event. But there are thousands, if not millions, who
consider Seafair the highlight of the year, and it has become as
much a part of Seattle life as rain and skiing and bicycle
Sundays. Information: your local papers or Seafair, Inc. 901
Occidental S. (623-7100).

Skating

Roller skating has become competition for skateboarding
and is permitted around Green Lake and in The Seattle Center.

Prices in rinks average around $1.50 plus skate rental.

Burien Ice Chalet, 15444 1st S. (243-4242)

Crossroads Skate Palace, 16232 N.E. 8th, Bellevue (746-9150
for recording; 746-9590 for more info)

Highland Ice Arena, 18005 Aurora N. (546-2431)

Roll-A-Way Skating Rink (Roller), 6210 200th S.W., Lynnwood
(778-4446)

Skate King (Roller), 2301 140th N.E., Bellevue (641-2046); 225
S. 140th Burien (244-7000); 12526 N.E. 144th, Kirkland
(821-8711).

Sno-King Ice Arena, 19803 68th W., Lynnwood (775-7511)

Southgate Roller Rink, 9646 17th S.W. (762-4030)

**The sheltered waters of the Puget Sound make long, inter-island
courses a relaxing sport for larger sailboats.**

Skiing

Moisture-laden storms from the Pacific turn Seattle's skies rainy and cover mountain slopes with enough snow to hide rocks, tree stumps, and slope irregularities. To take advantage of so much snow, numerous ski resorts offer a variety of lifts, slopes, and social amenities at or near the high passes in the Cascades. Except for Crystal Mountain most areas operate almost exclusively on a day basis with few or no overnight accommodations.

For years Paradise on Mt. Rainier offered great snow accessible only with portable rope tows. Now, even those are gone. Snow conditions vary widely from the sometimes wet and heavy "Snoqualmie Premix" to fluffy, dry powder at the top of "Internationale" at Alpental. Two other resorts offer consistently dry snow, but they are far from Seattle — Mission Ridge 13 miles outside of Wenatchee and Mt. Baker 60 miles east of Bellingham.

Despite the sometimes heavy snow and/or light rain, skiing attracts thousands of devotees to the slopes every winter weekend. Busloads of students in private and PTA-sponsored ski-school classes continue to expand the numbers crowding the slopes on Saturdays and Sundays. The crush of skiers on those two days has prompted operators to light slopes for night skiing. But, some of the best skiing on uncrowded slopes with no lift lines is available to week-day skiers. Most of the areas operate 7 days a week during the season. Many offer night skiing from 3 to 7 nights a week. All areas offer lessons by professional instructors operating from established ski schools. All areas operate ski shops for repairs and equipment rentals. A day lodge at each location serves lunches, beverages, and snacks. A ski patrol renders assistance in case of injuries.

Following is a list of ski areas arranged by location. Prices noted are for the 1980-81 season.

Snoqualmie Pass

Two ski areas operate at or near the summit of Snoqualmie Pass where Interstate 90 crosses the Cascade Mountains. The pass is 46 miles east of Seattle with four lanes the whole way. Unless chains are required or one or more lanes are blocked by traffic or avalanches, you can easily drive to the summit in about an hour.

Alpental — Newest and most challenging with the highest and steepest slopes of any resort at Snoqualmie Pass. Slopes suitable for intermediate and beginners also. Open Tues.-Sun. for day and night skiing. Equipped with 4 chairs, one T-bar, and 2 rope tows. Restaurant with beer stube. Condominiums nearby. Lift rates: weekends & holidays — $13 all lifts; midweek $9.50 — (1-434-6112).

Snoqualmie Summit/Ski Acres — Two popular areas now combined into a single ownership with shuttle bus service between the areas. One lift ticket is good for both areas, which operate daily for both day and night skiing. Some overnight accommodations at the Summit and condominiums at Ski Acres. Baby sitting. Lift rates: weekends & holidays, $11; midweek — $9. (1-434-6161).

Other Areas

Crystal Mountain — A destination resort plus day skiing, Crystal is 76 miles S.E. of Seattle via Highway 410. Operates daily for day and night skiing. Outstanding facilities with 6 chairs, T-bar, and 9 rope tows. A bar and restaurant occupy a warming hut at the top of the high chair. Cafeteria in day lodge. Overnight facilities operate their own restaurants, bars, swimming pool, dormitories, and apartment suites. Condominiums. Child care. Lift rates: $13 every day.

Sno-Country Stevens Pass — 70 miles northeast of Seattle on U.S. Highway 2. Operates Wed.-Sun. for day and night skiing. Four chairs weekdays, 7 Sat. and Sun.; children under 6 free. No overnight accommodations. Restaurant, cafeteria, beer stube. Child care on weekends. Lift rates: weekends & holidays — $14; midweek — $12.50. (1-937-2500).

White Pass — 105 miles southeast of Seattle on U.S. Highway 12. Operates daily. Three chairs, one poma, free rope for children under 12. Day lodge with cafeteria, lounge. Condominiums across highway with pool, restaurant, and general store. Lift rates: weekends & holidays — $12; midweek — $9 (1-509-453-8731).

Ski Touring

Newest winter sport to attract thousands of weekenders tired of waiting in long lift lines is cross-country ski touring. Sometimes called Nordic or alpine skiing, touring offers solitude, quiet, and outdoor activity without the cost of lift tickets.

Ski touring also opens up new areas for viewing and, for many, leads to overnight wilderness camping. Since cross-country ski touring gets you away from crowds, you should be prepared with proper equipment and training. Following is a listing of services keyed to training for cross-country ski touring and outings:

Family Adventures, Inc. — Box 312, Leavenworth, 98226 (1-509-548-7330) offers workshops for ski touring. Group outings into Enchantment Lakes.

Recreational Equipment, Inc. — 11 & E. Pine (323-8333). Instruction and rental equipment.

Snow Reports

Weather and snow conditions at favorite areas assume major status, and four services provide daily or twice-daily reports via telephone. Most of the local radio stations also broadcast snow condition reports on a daily schedule that varies with each station. For telephone reports in season:

Avalanche Report — Snoqualmie Pass area (442-SNOW). Mt. Baker area, a long distance call from Seattle (599-2714).

Cascade Ski Report (634-0200)

Northwest Ski Report (634-0071)

Crystal Mountain Report (634-3771)

Highway Dept. Report of road conditions (464-6010)

Numbers are often busy, try again if you get a busy signal.

Skin Diving

Skin diving around the Seattle area began as the city did — at Alki Beach. Some of the best diving in the Seattle area may still be found there and at nearby Seattle park access areas. Entry can be made all along the 3-mile water-side strip starting at the 1600 block on Harbor Ave. S.W. around to 64th S.W. and Alki S.W. Smaller access sites are along Beach Dr. S.W., off Golden Gardens Park north of the Shilshole area and on the beach areas of Discovery Park. Scheduled underwater tours with sea life identification by park personnel are offered at Discovery Park. Call Seattle Park Department (625-4671) for more information.

Skin divers are represented by a state-wide council and a number of clubs with interests in underwater photography, bottle recovery, scientific study, sightseeing, and exploration.

Covered seating at the University of Washington Stadium is only a short walk from the boat dock for boat bound sports fans.

For specific information on interesting diving locations see *141 Dives in the Protected Waters of Washington and British Columbia* by Betty Pratt-Johnson (available at dive shops). To join or inquire about club membership, contact any dive shop.

Soccer

This exciting sport has boomed almost as much in the Seattle area as tennis, and has become as popular for Little League organizers as baseball. During the winter it is difficult to find a playfield anywhere in Seattle, Mercer Island, and Bellevue that doesn't have youngsters in uniforms racing back and forth with parents shouting from the sidelines. So, when professional soccer was brought to town, it had a built-in audience, and nearly every game of the pro team, the Sounders, is well attended or sold out.

The Sounders play from May to September in the Kingdome. For ticket information call Seattle Sounders Soccer Club (628-3551).

Stargazing

University of Washington observatory near the north campus entrance is open to the public summer evenings. On clear nights look through a 6-inch telescope or a spectroscope that shows the spectrum of bright stars. A slide show on cloudy evenings. And it's free.

Swimming

Beaches

The Park Department has six public swimming beaches at parks along Lake Washington: Madrona, Madison, Mt. Baker, Matthews, Pritchard, and Seward Parks, and two separate beaches on Green Lake. For the extremely hardy, there are public beaches where you can swim if you feel you must in Puget Sound: Alki, Golden Gardens, Carkeek, and Lincoln Parks.

King County, Division of Parks — Sixteen pools are scattered throughout King County. Call Recreation Services, Division of Parks, for location of outlying pools and other information (344-3982). Fees for adults and children during public swims are: 1 hour 50¢; 2 hours $1; Adult-only swims are $1. Also sponsor lessons and swim teams. Listed below are a few of the indoor pools near Seattle:

Bellevue, 601 143rd N.E. (747-4245)
Evergreen, 606 S.W. 116th (246-1610)
Federal Way, Kenneth C. Jones Pool, 30421 16th S. (839-1000)
Foster, 4414 S. 144th (242-2287)
Lindberg, 16740 128th S.E., Renton (226-9230)
Mercer Island, 8815 S.E. 40th (232-7370)
Mount Rainier, 22722 19th S., Des Moines (824-1728)
Northshore, 9815 N.E. 188th, Bothell (486-9177)
Redmond, 17535 N.E. 104th (885-3600)
Shoreline, 19030 1st N.E. (363-4845)

Seattle City Parks and Recreation Department — Pools under the directorship of the Park Department are all indoor except one and are open year around for lessons and public swims. Fees for public swims are $1 for adults, 50¢ for 18 years old and under. Call the individual pool for scheduled swim times.

Ballard, 1471 N.W. 67th (783-7176)
Colman (50 meter, Olympic size), an outdoor pool connected
    with Lincoln Park, open June through Labor Day only,
    Fauntleroy & Cloverdale (938-2027)
Evans, 7201 E. Green Lake Dr., N. (625-4258)
Helene Madison, 13401 Meridian N. (362-5344)
Meadowbrook, N.E. 107th & 30th N.E. (365-9933)
Medgar Evers, 500 23rd (324-2560)
Queen Anne, 1st W. and W. Howe (625-2282)
Rainier Beach, Rainier S. & S. Henderson (723-5919)
Sealth, 2801 S.W. Thistle (935-6006)

YMCA Pools — Fees for non-members are $5 for adults or family; none is Olympic size.

Downtown, 909 4th (447-4547)
West Seattle, 4550 Fauntleroy S.W. (935-2270)
East Madison, 1700 23rd (322-6969)

YWCA Pool — Located downtown at 5th & Seneca (447-4868). Fees for non-member use: adults $2.50; under 12, 50¢; and teens 12-17, $1.50.

Tennis

Almost overnight tennis became THE game in Seattle, and the city was hard-put to keep up with the demand for more public courts. After spending a small fortune on backpacking gear, canoes, kayaks, and other relatively expensive sports, the surge of tennis with its very low investment resulted as much from economics as from Billie Jean King and Seattle's Tom Gorman.

Indoor Facilities — There are many private facilities or clubs in Seattle and the vicinity requiring membership dues paid yearly or by the month. Seattle Tennis Center, a Seattle Parks and Recreation facility, is the first publicly owned indoor center in the area. As well as the 10 indoor courts there are 4 adjacent outdoor courts. Reservations may be made up to a week in advance; and court fees are $6 for singles and $8 for doubles for an hour and fifteen minutes of play. Open 7 days from 7 a.m. to 10:30 p.m. Empire Way S. and S. Walker St. (324-2980).

Reservation System — The Seattle Parks and Recreation Department (P & R) has established a reservation system for 9 outdoor tennis courts scattered around the city. These may be reserved daily between 10 a.m. and 10:30 p.m. and must be made in person up to a week in advance at the Seattle Department of Parks and Recreation's Public Information/Scheduling Office at 5201 Green Lake Way N. from 9 a.m. to 10 p.m. 7 days a week. The rate for 75¢/hour; $2/hour for Tournament use; with lights $1.30 extra. Courts that may be reserved are : *Bitter Lake,* N. 130th & Greenwood; *Meadowbrook,* N.E. 107th & 30 N.E.; *Broadway,* E. Pine & 11th; *Mt. Baker,* S. McCllelan & 35th S.; *Lincoln Park,* Fauntleroy S.W. & S.W. Webster; *Ballard Pool,* 15th N.W. & N.W. 67th; *Lower Woodland* (2 courts), Stoneway N. & Green Lake Way N. A note of caution: Your fee will not be refunded if it rains.

At last count, nearly 550 courts at 175 different locations in and around Seattle reflect the game's popularity, so the reservation system definitely should be considered before challenging a friend, getting dressed, and finding you've no place to go.

Court Locations — Following is a list of the courts in and near Seattle that were complete as this book was being written. More are being built.

Key: The first number is the total courts at that location. (O) — outdoor; (L) — lighted courts; (R) — rebound board.

Richmond Beach High School, 196th & 22nd N.W. — 1 (O)
Hillwood Park School, 3rd N.W. & N.W. 195th — 2 (O)
Shoreline High School, 18560 1st N.E. — 4 (O)
Bothell High School, 18125 92nd N.E. — 4 (O)

Anderson Junior High, 9815 N.E. 188th — 4 (O)

Hamlin Park, 15th N.E. & 160th — 2 (O)

Shorecrest High School, 15345 25th N.E. — 4 (O)

Bitter Lake Community Center, N. 130th & Greenwood — 4 (L)

Othello Playfield, S. Juneau & 42nd S. — 2 (O)

Seward Park, S. Juneau & Lake Washington Blvd. — 2 (O)

Van Asselt Community Center, Beacon S. & S. Myrtle — 2 (O)

Rainier High School, 8815 Seward Park Ave. S. — 6 (O)

Alki Community Center, 58th S.W. & S.W. Stevens — 2 (O-L)

Hiawatha Community Center, California Ave. S.W. & S.W. Lander — 3 (O-L)

Delridge Community Center, Delridge Way S.W. & S.W.. Alaska — 2 (O)

Georgetown Playground, Corson S. & S. Homer — 1 (O)

Lowman Beach, Beach Dr. S.W. & 48th S.W. — 1 (O)

Lincoln Park, Fauntleroy S.W. & S.W. Webster — 8 (O) 6 (L) (R)

Sealth High School, 2600 S.W. Thistle St. — 2 (O)

Highland Park, 11th S.W. & S.W. Thistle — 1 (O)

South Park Community Center, 8th & S. Thistle — 2 (O)

Hutchinson Community Center, 59th S. & S. Pilgrim — 2 (O)

Lakeridge Park & Playground, Rainier S. & S. Cornell — 2 (O)

Ingraham High School, 1819 N. 135th — 6 (O)

Victory Heights Community Center, N.E. 107th & 19th N.E. — 1 (O)

Hale High School, 10750 30th N.E. — 4 (O)

Meadowbrook Community Center, N.E. 107th & 30th N.E. — 6 (L)

Matthews Beach Park, N.E. 93rd & Sand Point Way — 2 (L)

Lake Forest Park Elementary School, 18496 Ballinger Way — 2 (O)

Lakeside School (Private), 14050 1st N.E. — 2 (O)

Wilson High School, 1330 N. 90th — 2 (O)

Green Lake, 7312 W. Green Lake Dr. N. — 2 (O)

Green Lake Community Center, 7201 E. Green Lake Dr. N. — 3 (O)

Froula Playground, 12th N.E. & N.E. 72nd — (O)

Roosevelt High School, 1410 N.E. 66th — 2 (O)

Cowen Park, University Way N.E. & N.E. Ravenna Blvd. — 3 (O) (R)

Ravenna Park, 20th N.E. & N.E. 58th — 2 (O)

Ravenna Blvd./Freeway, N.E. 65th under I-5 — 1 (O)

Woodland Park, Aurora & N. 50th — 14 (O) 10 (L)

Lincoln High School, 4400 Interlake N. — 2 (O)

Wallingford Playfield, N. 43rd & Wallingford N. — 2 (O)
University Playground, N.E. 50th & 9th N.E. — 2 (O) (R)
University of Washington — 26 (0)
Laurelhurst Community Center, 4554 N.E. 41st — 4 (O) (R)
Rogers Playground, Eastlake E. & E. Roanoke — 2 (O)
Montlake Community Center, 1618 Calhoun — 2 (O-L)
Madison Park, E. Madison & Lake Washington Blvd. — 2 (O)
Helen Bush School (Private), 405 36th E. — 1 (O)
Whitman Junior High, 9201 15th N.W. — 4 (O)
Soundview Playfield, 15th N.W. & N.W. 90th — 2 (O)
Ballard Community Center, 28th N.W. & N.W. 60th — 2 (O) (R)
Ballard Pool, 15th N.W. & N.W. 67th — 4 (O-L)
Gilman Playground, 11th N.W. & N.W. 54th — 2 (O)
Magnolia Community Center, W. Garfield & 34th W. — 4 (O) 2
    (L)
Rodgers Park, 3rd W. & W. Garfield — 2 (O)
Observatory Courts, Warren N. & Lee — 2 (O)
Kinnear Park, 7th W. & W. Olympic Pl. — 1 (O)
Volunteer Park, 15th E. & E. Prospect — 4 (O)
Miller Community Center, 20th E. & E. Republican — 2 (O-L)
Broadway Playfield, E. Pine & 11th — 3 (O-L)
Garfield Community Center, 23rd E. & E. Cherry — 3 (O-L)
Beacon Hill Playground, 14th S. & S. Holgate — 2 (O) (R)
Mt. Baker Park, S. McClellan & 35th — 2 (O-L)
Franklin High School, 3013 S. Mt. Baker Blvd. — 1 (O)
Jefferson Park, S. Nevada & 16th S.— 2 (O)
Genesee Playfield, 46th S. & S. Genesee — 2 (O-L)
Rainier Community Center, Rainier S. & S. Oregon — 2 (O-L)
Cleveland Playground, 13th S. & S. Lucille — 3 (O) (R)
Cleveland High School, 5511 15th S. — 3 (O)
Rainier Beach Community Center, Rainier S. & S. Cloverdale
    — 2 (O)
Rainier Playfield, Rainier S. & S. Alaska — 2 (O)
Brighton Playground, 42nd S. & S. Juneau — 2 (O)
Discovery Park, 36th W. & W. Government Way — 2
Leschi Park, Lakeside S. off Alder — 1 (O)
Madrona Playground, 34th E. & E. Spring — 2 (O-L)

Associations

YMCA

The YMCA of Greater Seattle offers a wide variety of
programs for men, women, and children in five categories:

Youth (camping, Youth Basketball, etc.), Family (parent-child, day care, Youth Shelter, etc.), Fitness (cardiovascular testing, aerobics, sports, etc.), International (refugee aid, tours, etc.), and Individual and Community Development (forms, urban issues, etc.).

Association headquarters are at 909 4th. A 24-hour program number is 382-3202. Branches are: Auburn Valley, 1005 12th S.E., Auburn (854-1541), Downtown, 909 4th (382-5000), East Madison, 1700 23rd (322-6969), Eastside, Bel-Red Rd. at 144th N.E., Bellevue (746-9900), Fauntleroy, 9260 California S.W. (937-1000), Highline, 17874 Des Moines Way S. (244-5880), Metrocenter, 909 4th, (382-5013), Northeast, 5003 12th N.E. (524-1400), Northwest, 1708 N.W. Market (782-8100), Shoreline, 1220 N.E. 175th (364-1700), Snoline, 7315 212th S.W., Edmonds (776-3148), and West Seattle, 4550 Fauntleroy Way S.W. (935-2270). The YMCA operates resident camps at Camp Orkila on Orcas Island and Camp Colman at Lakebay in southern Puget Sound.

YWCA

One of the widest varieties of physical-fitness and adult-education programs outside the educational system is offered by the YWCA. Classes in creative writing, art, metric conversion, speech and drama, crafts, foreign languages, bridge, health, and self improvement are among the subjects available.

Another program for downtown workers on their lunch hour is called the "Brown Bag Speakers' Series," with experts from various fields speaking for a nominal fee.

Physical-fitness programs include exercises, swimming, yoga, ballroom dancing, volleyball, judo, and karate. Several programs for children also are offered.

The YWCA operates several branches. For information on membership and programs, call the main branch, at 1118 5th (447-4871).

SHOPPING

Browsing Is Half the Fun

ONE of the nicer things about Seattle is that you can have a
lot of fun spending your money. Some of the most imaginative
shops on the West Coast are found tucked away in remote
corners of the city stocked with things you can probably live
without, but once you own them they will brighten your life a
bit. With the Scandinavian and oriental influence so strong
here, there is an emphasis on fine craftsmanship and imaginative design, and you might find things here that are available in
few other cities.

As much fun as it is compiling such a section, we have
found it an equally frustrating job because we cannot hope to
compete with the Yellow Pages, nor do we want to. Instead, we
are limiting the major listing to places we know, then giving a
bonus by listing the dozens of places where you can buy things
at cut rates in the Bargain Shopping section.

One problem about exciting little shops is their habit of
appearing, then mysteriously disappearing before word-of-
mouth has become strong enough to support them. As we've
said elsewhere, you'd best call first to be sure (1) they still exist;
(2) they're going to be open when you arrive. And, if you find a
good one, let us know.

Department Stores

Frederick & Nelson — 5th & Pine (682-5500). This store is a
   division of Marshall Field & Co., and we know of one
   emigrant from the Chicago area whose mother breathed a
   little easier for her daughter's welfare when she found that
   Marshall Field was represented in Seattle. If nothing else,

stop in for a can of Frango mints. Branch stores are located at Aurora Village, Bellevue, and Southcenter shopping centers.

The Bon — 4th & Pine (344-2121). The Bon is likely to be a little more lively inside. Another plus is the parking garage across the street on 3rd with a skybridge leading to The Bon for those occasional rainy days. The Bon also is popular with the younger set for the latest in clothing styles and hit records. Stores at Northgate and Southcenter.

Sears Roebuck Co. — 1st S. & S. Lander (344-4830). Catalog telephone shopping (682-2000). This is the largest department store in the area and supposedly the largest west of the Mississippi (it was the last we heard). If it isn't available on the floor, trot to the catalog sales department and you can get it delivered within a day or two. Inside tip; a popcorn freak we know says the popcorn that Sears sells is superb. Branch stores on Aurora N., in Renton, Ballard, and Overlake Park (Bellevue).

J.C. Penney Co. — 2nd & Pike (624-3550); catalog telephone shopping (292-9066). Everything you'll find in your hometown "Penney's" plus, since this is a very large store. Branches in Aurora Village, Ballard, Northgate, Southcenter, West Seattle, and Bellevue.

Nordstrom — 1501 5th (628-2111). One of the most stylish of the department stores with an emphasis on clothing for all ages and sexes. One of the few stores in Seattle to stock large selections of large-sized shoes. Branches in University District, Northgate, Aurora Village, Southcenter, and Bellevue.

Clothing

Women's Clothing

These stores are among Seattle's most expensive.

Bagatelle — 4110 E. Madison (329-2524)
John Doyle Bishop, Skinner Bldg. (682-4177)
I. Magnin — 6th & Pine (682-6111)
Lady Albert Ltd. — 1335 5th (622-3970), Rainier Square
Littler's — 1331 5th (223-1331), Rainier Square
The Mediterranean — 523 Union (622-2949)
Totally Michael's — 1333 5th (622-4920), Rainier Square

Men's Clothing

Albert Ltd. — 1210 4th (623-3970)
Brooks Brothers — 1401 4th (624-4400)
Klopfenstein's — 600 Pine (622-2360); Northgate (364-9300);
Southcenter (243-1433) ; Aurora Village (542-1113); Bellevue
(454-2450)
Littler's — 1331 5th (223-1331), Rainier Square
Michael's Bespoke Tailor — 407 Union (623-4785)
Yankee Peddler Shoppes — 4218 E. Madison (324-4218); 1409
N.E. 45th (633-1409)

Tall & Small Shops

High & Mighty — Southcenter (246-6061); Alderwood Mall
(771-5115), and Sea-Tac Mall (941-3626)
Pacific Big & Tall — 1313 3rd (622-2936); Aurora Village
(546-3333)
Shelly's Tall Girls Shop — 1516 5th (622-8926); Northgate
(365-1220)
Mich's Small & Short Men's Shop — 622 S. Jackson (682-7364)

Formal Wear Rentals

These firms are members of the American Formalwear
Association. They also have other branches.

Brocklind's Inc. — 901 Olive Way (682-5898)
Winter's Formal Wear — 200 Broadway E. (324-3171)
Tux Shops — 1521 6th (622-3900)

Downtown Baby Sitting Services

Browsing through stores with small children in tow can be
frustrating as well as expensive. A small person we know, long
ago, was practicing her acrobatics in a small exclusive ladies
clothing store while mother was busy with the sales clerk. The
manikins in the window display joined in with disastrous re-
sults, and the parent fled the store after paying a sizable sum for
restoration. We're certain your children are better behaved and
store insurance policies cover this sort of accident but — these
nurseries accept drop-ins while shopping.

Kindergarten — Frederick & Nelson, 5th & Pine (682-5500).
    Ages 3 to 8.

Little Red School House — The Bon Marche, 4th & Pine (344-8799). Ages 2½ to 9.

Downtown Covered Shopping

Rainier Square Pedestrian Concourse — Also known as the Rainier Tunnel. Some downtown businesses can now compete equally with the large covered shopping malls outside of town. The western terminus of the tunnel is the lobby of the Rainier Tower Bldg. on 4th Ave. (once insude, you lose the feeling of

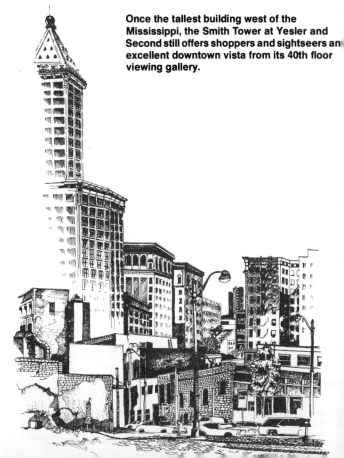

Once the tallest building west of the Mississippi, the Smith Tower at Yesler and Second still offers shoppers and sightseers an excellent downtown vista from its 40th floor viewing gallery.

being crushed if the building topples). The carpeted concourse continues to 6th Ave. with entrances to a variety of stores and restaurants. Included among the shops are Eddie Bauer, Littler, Lady Albert, B. Bailey books, Totally Michael's, Fifth Avenue Record Shop, a gourmet kitchenware store, home furnishings, Crepe de Paris restaurant, and White Henry Stuart Cafe. Exits lead directly to the Hilton Hotel, Skinner Bldg., 5th Avenue Movie Theater, Washington Athletic Club, and of course, Rainier Bank and the parking garage.

Unique Shopping Centers

In and around Seattle a sprinkling of creative and unusual enclaves of shops and unusual stores attract browsers and shoppers interested in the quaint and unusual. Some of the most interesting of these little centers that we like are described briefly below along with the two giants.

Southcenter — Interstate 5 and 405. Enormous covered mall with 7,200 parking spaces and more than 100 stores. Branches of major department stores plus numerous specialty shops.

Northgate — Interstate 5 and N.E. Northgate Way — Another large covered shopping mall on the north side similar to Southcenter.

Hansen Baking Company — No, this isn't an industrial tour, so read on. Until sometime in 1974 it was what it says it is: a large bakery on Mercer & 1st N. just north of the Seattle Center. Then, the bakery went elsewhere and the old, hulking brick building was sandblasted, spruced up, and a few fountains added to convert it into one of Seattle's newest and most compact shopping attractions. It is especially popular with foot-weary refugees from Seattle Center. The shops range from a bakery, clothing and kitchen shops, and the Game Gallery. The restaurants include the highly praised Jake O'Shaughnessey's, and Sunday's.

University District — Centered at 45th and University Way N.E. Not an enclosed shopping center but a mixture of shops — inexpensive restaurants, boutiques, arts and craft stores, bakeries, and the location of the University Bookstore — one of the largest bookstores in the nation. The "in" place for the young to buy their pants, tops, clogs, and jewelry. Avenue Arcade and Sun Loft listed below are also in this district.

Avenue Arcade — 4518 University Way N.E. An old Penney's store remodeled inot three levels of shops — jewelry, men's and women's apparel, gift shops, interior design, import shops, ice cream and spice shop, and the Walking Crepe Company (a restaurant).

Capitol Hill — This area sort of sprawls between Broadway and 15th, Olive and E. Roy, and edges its way down the hill toward town on Pine and other streets. Several of the shops are listed in our Specialty Shop section, particularly the more exclusive furniture stores such as *Keeg's* and *Del Teet's*. There are a number of bookstores — *The Book Project*, 1502 E. Olive, *A Different Drummer*, 420 Broadway E. — and several cafes and restaurants listed in the Restaurant section. As a matter of record, we twice have gone to the Boondock's restaurant on Broadway, grew disheartened at the long wait, and went across the street and down a few doors to the Jade Pagoda for a gigantic Chinese dinner.

Old Milltown — 201 5th S., Edmonds. Originally, this big old building housed the Ford Motor Company agency in Edmonds. Completely refurbished, it captures a feeling of an old-time shingle mill with its rough-hewn wood. Many shops are fitted out with antique hardware.Old Milltown contains a restaurant, health food store, wine shop, local artists' cooperative, pottery shop, leather shop, boutique, ice cream store, coffee, tea & spice shop, basket shop, antiques, and a gallery.

Old Bellevue — Main Street west of Bellevue Way. This section of Bellevue is developing into a unique collection of antique stores and unique shops — custom jerelry, pottery, picture framing, tennis, kitchen, crafts, gifts, imports, plants, bath, florists, and interior galleries.

Pier 70 — At the foot of Broad on the Sound. Originally a working dock and warehouse built in 1902. The two-story wooden warehouse's exterior has been sandblasted and the interior renovated to enclose over 40 shops and several restaurants. A few of the shops included are candy, import candle, jeans warehouse, jewelry, toy, book and art gallery. One of the restaurants, the Top of the Pier, has a good view of the Sound.

Gilman Village — Juniper & Gilman Blvd., Issaquah. This cluster of shops began as several restored old houses connected with a boardwalk and decking. Now other buildings have been tastefully added to extend the charm of this passel of shops. Included in the cluster are *The Boarding House* restaurant, shops for linens, kitchen utensils, plants, antique jewelry, fabrics, yarn, clothing, stained glass designer, and *The Country Mouse*, an outlet entirely devoted to handcrafted items of all kinds from craftspersons in the area.

Firdale Village Art Center — Three-quarters of a mile west of Aurora on 205th, Edmonds. Arts and crafts plus specialty shops including yarn, pottery, weaving, plants, clothing, books, fashion designer, interior decorating.

Specialty Shops

This category could go on forever because we're lumping several types of stores into one listing. The resident will likely already know many of these shops, and the out-of-town visitor will want to visit them; it is unlikely, however, that the out-of-towner will buy a love seat in Seattle to ship back home to New Orleans. So here's a grab-bag of more than passing interest. Specialty shops tend to be clustered in places like Pioneer Square, along the waterfront, in and around the Seattle Center, and in enclaves around the city and in the suburbs.

Uwajimaya — 6th S. & S. King (624-6248). Japanese imports from foods to records to printed matter. Southcenter and Bellevue also.

Sur La Table — 84 Pine (622-2459). Cookware for the gourmet.

La Tienda — 4138 University Way N.E. (632-1796). African, Peruvian, Polish and Mexican rugs, clothing, jewelry, etc.

Del Teet Furniture Co. — 127 Broadway E. (323-5400). Excellent contemporary furniture.

McBreen Inc. — 905 E. John (323-2336). Furniture and design services.

Keeg's — 310 Broadway E. (325-1771). Kitchenware, toys, posters, Danish furniture, mostly imports.

The Grandmother Shop — 214 1st S. (624-2601). Children's clothing, toys, and dolls.

Fifth Avenue Record Shop— Rainier Square (624-6507), Rainier Square. Excellent selection of popular, classical and rock records plus several offbeat recording labels.

Jafco — 520 Westlake N. (464-1424). Catalog showroom; discount prices on name-brand small appliances, cameras, jewelry, sporting goods, toys, etc. Several suburban locations.

Johnson-West Music Service — 500 Denny Way (682-6883). The best selection of sheet music in town.

Teresa of Hong Kong — 517 Pine (622-0455). Oriental fashions for milady including kimonos, pajamas, Happi coats, and ivory and jade carvings.

Toys Galore — 1514 5th (622-7117); Southcenter (246-7060). Ordinary and extraordinary gifts for the youngsters.

Opus 204 — 204 Broadway E. (325-1782). Imported leather, rugs, textile, and baskets from Africa.

Baby & Co. — 1936 1st (622-4077). A boutique of clothing, costume jewelry, accessories, and footwear for the adult baby.

Courtney Branch — 109 S. Main (622-2165). Fine pottery and tableware all made in the Northwest.

Tobo Oriental Imports — 504 12th S. (324-2100). Japanese variety store, crammed wtih handsome pots, dishes, gifts.

Specialty Food Stores

When your family or companions gather round the table and say, "Oh yuk, THAT again!" it's time to go down to the Pike Place Market and gather your dinner from the concentration of

Shoppers descend on the numerous specialty shops of Pike Place Market to seek out items generally not available elsewhere.

specialty food shops there. But if the market doesn't appeal to you, try some of the other shops located in and around Seattle.

The Wedge — 4760 University Village Pl. N.E. (523-2560). Good selection of imported and domestic cheeses.

Brenner Bros. Bakery & Delicatessen — 120th N.E. & N.E. Bellevue-Redmond Rd. (454-0600). Out of town and a little difficult to find but worth the trip for their superb breads and bagels.

Silversten's Bakery — 100 Mercer (283-3797). Their Scandinavian pastries are tops.

Boehm's Homemade Swiss Candies — 559 N.E. Ravenna Blvd. (523-9380) and the original chalet store, 255 N.E. Gilman Blvd., Issaquah (392-6652). Superb candies from broken chocolates to mint truffles, English toffee, and other mouth-watering tidbits.

Husky Delicatessen — 4721 California S.W. (937-2810). Tasty bulk ice cream and cones, imported foods including such exotic items as reindeer meatballs.

Brehm's Deli & Grocery — Pike Place Market (622-9172). Outstanding source for foods hard to find elsewhere, such as freshly ground creamy peanut butter, spoon cheese, sweet mustard chow-chow pickels, old-fashioned deli olives, dates, imported Greek feta cheese, and the biggest assortment of fruitcake ingredients in Seattle.

DeLaurenti (Italian & international foods) — Pike Place Market (622-0141). An old-style market with open bins for beans, dried fruit, and similar foods. Not limited to but heavily specializing in Italian style foods — breads, cheese, wines, and a host of items you won't find anywhere else plus a complete delicatessen. Also at 317 Bellevue Way N.E., Bellevue (454-7155).

So-Lo Sweet Shop — 630 S.W. 153rd (244-8525); 630 Stewart (625-1711). Have your dessert and eat it too — with up to 75 percent fewer calories.

Specialty Spice Shop — Pike Place Market (622-6340). Pungent smells guide your nose to this source for bulk spices, tea blends, coffee mixes at varying prices. Many items not found elsewhere.

Starbuck's Coffees, Teas and Spices — 1912 Pike Pl. (622-8762). Coffees are roasted in Seattle; also sell brewing and grinding devices. Other stores in University Village, Broadway District, 10214 N.E. 8th, Bellevue.

Truffles — 3701 N.E. 45th (522-3016). Wine, meats, tea, French cheeses; a step above your basic grocery store. Also gift boxes and baskets.

A & J Meats — 2401 Queen Anne N. (284-3885). Some customers come from Mercer Island to buy their weekly supply of meats. Aside from their choice selection of regular meats, Al or Jerry will make up rouladen, chicken kiev, or hors d'oeuvre trays that make you wish you had forgotten to invite the guests.

Fish Markets

There is nothing wrong with properly frozen fish, but if you want fresh seafood, here are the approximate seasons. King salmon begin arriving about May 1, silvers June 15, sockeyes about July 1, pinks in August, especially in odd-numbered years (underwater calendars?), and chums (also called dogs or falls) arrive near the end of September. Bottom fish — cod, sole and snapper — come in year-round; fresh crabs come on the market in December. Due to Indian fishing there is a limited

Offering a huge selection of fresh produce, fish and meat, amid crafts displays and street entertainers, the Pike Place Public Market retains an authentic atmosphere that appeals to Seattleites and visitors alike.

supply of fresh salmon year-round, but the above are the commercial seasons.

Port Chatham Packing Co. — 632 N.W. 46th (783-8200). Smoked salmon at its best. Also you can bring in your own catch for smoking, canning, or airmailing to the folks back home.

Pike Place Market — These three seafood markets are near each other in the main floor of the market and will pack a salmon for sending across the country; City Fish Co., Pure Food Fish, and Pike Place Fish.

Totem Smokehouse — 1012 Western (223-1710) Canned alder-smoked salmon, sturgeon, oysters, and clams. Also in Kirkland at 7307 N.E. 120th (823-6611).

Wild Salmon Fish Market — 1800 W. Emerson Pl. (283-3366). Located in Fishermen's Terminal where all the boats tie up, the salmon don't have far to go; also crab and shrimp. Market owned by a group of salmon fishermen.

Wine

Washington has never been known for its enlightened liquor laws, although it is getting better all the time. For years the laws were so protective to the state's small wine industry that those in love with the immortal grape were forced into smuggling to accumulate a decent wine cellar. But that is changed now, and with it came a splurge of wine how-to books and columns (yes, we know: ask anybody lurking around the west end of the Pike Place Markets. But we're talking about a different kind of wine experience).

We won't get into the specialized material here, in part because all experts on wine share a single trait; they disagree with each other constantly. But here's a list of some major wine shops in the Seattle area:

Cellar Wine Shop, 14411 Greenwood N; *Cork and Bottle,* 511 Broadway E.; *Esquin Wine Merchants,* 1516 1st S.; *Gourmet Shop,* 12511 Lake City Way N.E., *La Cantina;* University Village and 104 Bellevue Way S.E., Bellevue; *Mondo's World,* 4223 Rainier S.; *Pam's Wine and Gourmet Gift Shop,* Westwood Village; *Pike and Western Wine Merchants,* Pike Place Markets; *Vintage Cellars,* 1624 4th.

Nearly all of these shops will arrange a wine tasting party for you in your home, in a hotel suite, a room of a restaurant, or elsewhere. They also offer classes in the basics of the art of wine. For example, a class of six week's duration offered by the La Cantina costs $40. Most wine tasting parties, by the way, are usually given by the shops at no charge unless extensive planning is involved. Several give 10 per cent discounts on cases.

There's still another way to get into wine: join the Enological Society of the Pacific Northwest. It is open to anyone over 21. Write to the society, 200 2nd N., Seattle, 98109. The society has monthly programs, dinners featuring food and wine from different parts of Europe, and an annual festival held in August at Seattle Center.

Now. If you're really hooked on wine and think you can do better than the French or the Californians and want to make your own, here's a list of shops that carry wine-making equipment — plus the forms you have to fill out for the federal government. There's no fee for the permits but the government wants to know who is making wine and where, and it is a no-no to make more than 200 gallons a year. That is usually sufficient for the average family anyway:

Aetna Wine Supply Co., 708 Rainier S.; *Arbor Winemaking Supplies, Inc.*, 8824 Roosevelt Way N.E.; *Cellar Wine Shop*, 14411 Greenwood N.; *Liberty Malt Supply Co.*, Pike Place Markets; *The Party House*, 10408 16th S.W.

Delis, Picnics, and Brown Bags

With the growth of delis, brown-bag specialists — not to mention a broadening (no pun intended) middle class in Seattle with enough money to seek out new luxuries — the custom picnic is here. Even catered picnics aren't unusual. Of course, there are still those who believe in preparing their own picnic hamper or portable cooler, or at the most ambitious, stopping off at Dag's, Herfy's or Col. Sanders for the makings. When this book first appeared, delis were something you found in other cities. Now they're more apparent than service stations.

B & B & Ben Gula's Delicatessen — 414 Olive Way (622-4575). Picnic buffet platters include meats, cheeses, potato salad, cole slaw, pickles, and bread along with paper plates and napkins.

B & B Corned Beef House No. 1 — 103½ Pike (624-8173). Complete line of deli goods. Catering.

Barney Bagel and Suzy Creamcheese — Pier 70 (623-4270). In addition to sandwiches to go, they have fresh fruit, potato salad, and more than 50 kinds of sandwiches. They will deliver week-days, north to Ballard Bridge and south to Boeing Field during noon hour.

Chinese Kitchen — 2413 E. Union (322-6666 or 322-6040). Family style dinners or individual combinations for take-out or delivery. Delivery after 5 p.m. weekdays and 4 p.m. weekends.

City Picnics Sandwich & Delivery Co. — 412 Spring (682-8183) and 117 S. Main (682-2067). Good selection of sandwiches and salads for eating-in or take-out. Spring Street restaurant delivers on foot within a 7-block radius.

Duke's — 236 1st W. (283-4400). An assortment of sandwiches ranging from ham and jack cheese to turkey and cranberry. Cheesecake and assorted desserts. Pâté, too.

International Kitchen — 2201 N.E. 65th (524-4004). Prepares a variety of picnics to take to nearby Ravenna Park. Take along your own bottle of wine.

La Mediterranean Delicatessen — 528 Broadway (329-8818). Specialties of creole chicken with mushrooms, polynesian salad, 32 varieties of cheescake, deli meats, and cheese trays.

Leschi Mart — 103 Lakeside. (322-0700). Homemade pâté, barbecued ribs and chicken, beer and wine.

Matzoh Momma's — 509 15th E. (324-6262). One of the best delis in town. Specialties are homemade breads, bagels, chicken soup, and blintzes.

The Mouse House — 170 S. Washington (623-6885). Near the Kingdome; take a picnic to the game. Super-size sandwiches.

Pike Place Market — This is obviously the best and the most fun if you have the time to wander through picking up your food from various shops. If you're doing it on a noon hour, you'd best scout ahead of time, then break up the shopping list into several pieces to distribute among your party. Better yet, tell everyone to bring something they like and see what kind of picnic you wind up with.

Rosellini's Gourmet Kitchen — 4th & Vine (622-1970). You can bring your own basket by earlier, and they'll lay it out for you with napkins and plastic cutlery. A wide range of snacks and hors d'oeuvres, pasta, sliced meat sandwiches. Advance notice for a large group. A bit more expensive than the others.

Snug Restaurant — 1414 2nd (682-4304). Pay a deposit on the basket, checkerboard linen, and wine glasses, and picnic in grand style with a French or English meal. Delivery free with minimum from Pioneer Square to Denny Way; call before 11 a.m.

Uwajimaya — 6th S. & Sl .King (624-6248). The major Japanese supermarket in Seattle. A delightful place to visit even if you're not going on a picnic.

Washington Plaza Hotel — (624-7400). Call a day ahead for a sumptuous wine and cheese picnic boxed with amber cellophane and a bright red bow.

As for locations for the picnic itself, you have hundreds from which to choose. Seattle is sprinkled with tiny pocket parks intended for the neighborhood they serve. Check the Parks and Recreation listing, then explore on your own. Chances are you'll be able to find parks that are virtually unused. Other prime locations include the waterfront, Seattle Center, the Ship Canal, Foster Island Nature Walk, or any of the viewpoints listed separately.

Antiques

While the Pacific Northwest isn't old enough to have its own antiques — most have been imported — there are numerous shops with excellent collections and reasonable prices. The antique business is in a growth stage, and new shops are opening frequently throughout town. For the moment, they tend to cluster in the downtown area, Pioneer Square, Capitol Hill, and north on Queen Anne Hill, Fremont, University, Ballard, and the Greenwood Districts plus the Pike Place Market. Here we have just listed some of the more centrally located and unique shops.

Antiques 'N Things — 1010 4th S. (622-9117). Glass, costumes, dolls, and toys.

Antique Mall—114 Alaskan Way S. (622-5130). Has 17 shops in the same building.

Globe Antiques — 529 Pine (682-1420). European imports from the 17th century. Silver, porcelain, and Oriental rugs. Appraisals.

Antique Liquidators — 503 Westlake N. (622-2740). Old English furniture received every 10 days, priced low for quick turnover.

Antiques & Art Associates — 2113 3rd (624-4378). Furinture, china, glass, prints, and books.

Third Hand Shop — 11 W. McGraw (284-3011). Brass beds, roll-top desks, stained glass, oak tables, wicker, and oak furniture.

Trust House Antiques — 4105 E. Madison (325-9977). English and American furniture.

Washington Art Galleries — 3311 Rainier S. (725-2002). European furniture, art glass, and paintings.

Wm. Davis & Co. — 1300 5th (622-0518). Antiques, reproductions, and modern furniture. Interior design service available to buyers.

Rosen-Colgren Gallery — 1207 Pine (623-3230). Rugs, porcelain, and period furniture.

Gasoline Alley — 6501 20th N.E. (524-1606). Disneyana, vintage toys.

Mariko Tada, Inc. — 609 Union (624-7667). Oriental ceramics, jade, ntesuke.

Pandora's Castle — 2026 N.W. Market (782-5717). 17th Century to WWII objects.

Furniture Spa — 7557 15th N.W. (784-0011). Strippping and old furniture for sale.

Books

As much as we'd like to list every bookstore in the area in hopes of making them so happy they'd all stock up on this book, we've decided to list only the specialized stores. Suffice it to say that most large department stores have book sections, and there are numerous others scattered around shopping centers and in the downtown area.

The Book Project — 1502 E. Olive. (324-9086). The best friend in town for small presses, experimental writers, poets, etc. Also publishes newsletter on small presses, and keeps an eye out for the next T.S. Eliot.

A Different Drummer — 420 Broadway E. (324-0525). Magazines, including foreign, general books, used, and science fiction.

Comstock's Bindery & Bookshop — 7903 Rainier S. (725-9531). Rare, Americana, paperbacks, maps, and comic books.

Beatty Book Store — 1925 3rd (624-2366). Large selection of remaindered art books, used books, and paperbacks.

Elliott Bay Book Co. — 1st S. & S. Main (624-6600). One of the best trade bookstores in Seattle. They have a sixth-sense on what to stock.

Fillipi Book & Record Shop — 1351 E. Olive Way (682-4266). Old books, magazines, phonograph records.

Fouray Book Store — 1306 1st (622-6840). The best technical bookstore in town, and one of the best on the West Coast. New, used, and rare.

Quest Bookshop of Seattle — 717 Broadway E. (323-4281). Far Eastern philosophies, meditation, occult, etc.

Shorey's Bookstore — 110 Union (624-0221); 119 S. Jackson (622-8720). An institution among Seattle's old-used-rare booksellers. Whole rooms of books in categories for the intense browser along with all the latest in paperback and hardcover books. Not even Shorey's knows all the books resting on jammed shelves in room after room. It's worth taking your own look.

Tower Books — 20 Mercer (283-6333). Open until midnight every night of the year. Large selection of paperbacks and hardbacks at discount prices.

University Bookstore — 4326 University Way N.E. (634-3400). One of the largest bookstores in the nation with text and trade books stocked, plus clothing, posters, sporting goods, cameras, etc.

Flowers

These downtown shops are members of the Florists' Transworld Delivery (FTD) association.

Alpha Flora — 814 2nd (623-4287)

Crissey — 5th & University (624-6661); 2100 5th (622-1100)

Rosaia Bros. — 2334 6th (622-2858)

Chas. E. Sullivan — 2221 3rd (624-1300)

Furriers

Most of the department stores and men's and women's stores already listed deal in furs. The following stores specialize in fur.

Alaska-Arctic Furs — 5th & Pike (622-6116)

Gordon's Custom Furriers — 1008 Western (623-4274)

Artur Jonas Fur Designer — 1426 5th Ave. Bldg. (622-4807)

Trippy Apparel & Furs — 517 Olive Way (624-0481)

John J. Trippy — 515 Pine (622-5779)

Jewelry

Seattle has hundreds of jewelry stores, but here is a sample of places where you can have jewelry custom designed or buy hand-made items.

Leo Azose & Son — 2018 3rd (622-5323)
Robin's Jewelers — 220 1st S. (622-4337)
Daniel Louis at Nordstrom — 1501 5th (623-2277)
Fox's Gem Shop — 1341 5th (623-2528)
Philip Monroe Jeweler — 527 Pine (624-1531)
Porter and Jensen — 4501 University Way N.E. (632-4050)

Outdoor Recreation

Seattle is within sight of some of the best hiking, climbing, skiing, fishing, and kayaking spots in North America. To quote a defunct TV show, "No brag, just fact." In fact, a short time ago, there were at least 200,000 backpackers in the area, according to one store. Most have annual sales, but be prepared to camp on the sidewalk if you want first grab at these events: SNIAGRAB, 3-day sale held in early Sept. at Seattle Center, sponsored by Osborn & Ulland. Recreational Equipment Inc., camping sale in April, ski sale in Oct. Eddie Bauer, annual sale in early Sept.

Athletic Supply — 901 Harrison (623-8972). Complete equipment for all sports, individuals, and teams.
Eddie Bauer — 5th & Union (622-2766); Bellevue Square (453-0450). The elite of the outdoor recreation stores in the area. A fly fisherman's headquarters as well as hunters and campers. Famous for down clothing and high quality outdoor gear of all types. Expedition outfitter.
Early Winters — 300 Queen Anne N. (284-4979). All types of outdoor gear and tents of their own design. Gor-Tex rain wear.
Fiorini Sport — University Village (523-9610). Skiing, hiking, sports clothing and equipment.
Harris Conley — 1304 2nd (624-8361). A highly rated golfer's shop.
MSR — 631 S. 96th (762-0210). Mountain Safety Research, Inc. specializes in climbing gear and stoves.
North Face — 4560 University Way N.E. (633-4431). Specialists in backpacking clothing and equipment.
Osborn & Ulland — 2nd & Seneca (624-6954). One of the best shops for outfitting skiers and tennis players. Branches at Northgate, Southcenter, and Bellevue.
Recreational Equipment Inc. — 1525 11th (323-8333). The "Co-op," so named because it is a cooperative that pays you back an average of 10 per cent on your year's total purchases. Emphasis here is on backpacking, mountaineering, kayak-

ing and bicycling. Heavy emphasis on conservation. Expedition outfitter.

The Mountain Shop — 10700 5th N.E. (363-3667). Specializes in winter sports equipment but also has stock of hiking gear, tennis equipment, and water skis.

Warshal's — 1st & Madison (624-7300). Specializes in fishing and hunting equipment with a complete photographic department that wheels and deals in new and used cameras and accessories; for the amateur and pro.

Thrifty Places to Shop

Seattle, like many cities, offers numerous opportunities for the canny money managers and thrifty shoppers to buy food, clothing, and sports equipment at significant savings. Some of the places operate all year. Others, such as Sniagrab (bargains spelled backwards) by Osborn & Ulland open and close on one weekend. The Children's Orthopedic Hospital Guilds also host one gigantic rummage sale at the Seattle Center Exhibition Hall once a year. Watch the newspapers for news of these and similar events. Not so well known are the out-of-the-way sample shops, consignment resale emporiums, and used clothing outlets operated by charity organizations as a fund-raising activity. Irregulars and seconds are also offered at factory outlet stores, principally in this area for outdoor wear — ski jackets and the like. For more complete information and many more bargain places to shop, see *Seattle's Super Shopper — The Guide to More than 350 Places to Buy Practically Everything for Less,* which includes thrifty places to shop in Tacoma.

Organized according to activity, the following outlets will aid cash-strapped families to extend their buying power.

Clothing and Other

Factory Outlets — During the manufacture of clothing, small irregularities sometimes slip through and are caught by quality control. Since these off-quality items cannot be sold through normal channels, they are sold at reduced prices at a factory outlet — sometimes in the basement of the manufacturing facility.

Fabrik Seconds Shop — 321 Broadway E. (329-2110). Seconds, complete sets, or open stock, of stoneware.

Pacific Trail Sportswear — 1310 Mercer (622-4561). Seconds and samples of ski jackets, sport jackets and apparel, and tennis wear.

Sportcaster Co., Inc. — 160 S. Jackson (624-2214). Basement outlet with huge stock of irregular and sample ski and sporting apparel, backpacks, sweaters, and remnants of materials used in manufacturing apparel.

Sears, Roebuck & Co. — 1st S. & S. Lander (344-4830). Bargain basement has a constant turnover of clothing of all kinds, household goods, draperies, appliances, etc. with some minor flaw that prevents their being sold at regular price or discontinued items from their catalogs.

Fell & Co., Inc. — 360 Upland Dr. (575-8383). Features Levi's products of all kinds for men, women, and children.

Kusak Cut Glass Works — 1303 Rainier S. (324-2931). Once-a-year sale around the end of October of their beautiful crystal pieces that don't quite measure up to their high standards.

Sample Shops — These outlets sell brand new, first quality clothing discounted by a third to a quarter from normal retail prices. Samples have been hauled around to stores by salesmen and represent the newest styling for the coming season. However, unless you are an average size, you may not find a fit in the sample shops because samples emphasize differences in colors and styling and come in limited size ranges.

Dorothy's — Suite 212, Olympic National Bldg, 920 2nd, entrance on Madison (622-0253). Overstocks and closeouts, junior, misses, and women's sizes. Sportwear, long and short dresses.

Kay's Sample Shop — 218 Terminal Sales Bldg., 1st & Virginia (682-0298). Salesmen's samples of Leslie Fay, Vera, and Lady Manhattan blouses, skirts, and dresses, sizes 7/8 and 9/10.

Nordstrom's — 1501 5th (628-2111). Clothing Rack downstairs at downtown store with broken stock of bargains that changes daily. Shoe Rack, also at downtown store, offers broken sizes and styles at cut prices for try-them-on-yourself fitting.

pic-A-dilly — Has 10 outlets throughout the area. Features name brand overruns of misses and juniors clothing sizes 3-16. Huge stock with rapid turnover.

Punch 'n Judy — 413 15th Ave. E. (324-4409). Children's
    sportswear, outerwear; infant through size 14.

Sample Shop Etc. — 7836 S.E. 28th, Mercer Island (232-6080).
    Salesmen's samples of shirts, ties, slacks, sweaters, and
    leisure suits plus women's clothing.

Consignment Shops — Used clothing sold in consignment
shops will usually be of better quality and newer fashion than
used clothing in charity resale shops because the owner receives
part of the sales price. Thus, a person is motivated to turn over
clothing before it is out of style or worn badly. Prices will
likewise tend to range higher than for donated clothing.

Chrysalis — 123 116th S.E., Bellevue (454-6388). New and used
    better quality clothing.

The Cracker Barrell — 2251 140th N.E. (Evans Plaza), Bellevue
    (641-3855). Bellevue's original consignment shop; men's,
    women's, children's clothing, jewelry, accessories.

Clothes Closet — 4137 California S.W. (938-2110). Men's,
    women's and children's clothing; purses, books, and
    jewelry.

Dark Horse — 11810 N.E. 8th, Bellevue (454-0990). Men's and
    women's fashions.

Dreamland — 619 Broadway E. (329-8044). 1940's and older
    clothing, jewelry, lamps and furniture. Rather than con-
    signment, owner buys outright.

Mary's pop-ins— 2123 Queen Anne N. (282-5151). Consign-
    ment, men's and women's clothing. No children's wear.

Mouse Closet — 521 156th S.E., Bellevue (641-0531). Children,
    maternity, handcrafted fashions.

Pandora's Boutique — 10867 N.E. 2nd Pl., Bellevue (455-3883).
    Men's, women's and children's clothing and accessories.

Redress — 513 156th, Bellevue (746-7984). Clothing, purses,
    accessories, and Hawaiian styles, too.

Tree House — 15742 Redmond Way (885-1145). Clothing for all
    ages and some marked-down new clothing.

Charity Resale Shops — Collect donations of clothing and
some other household miscellany for resale, usually to raise
funds for a specific charity.

Bargain Fair — 4401 Wallingford N. (632-9452). Clothing plus
    small items, such as dishes, jewelry, and knicknacks.
    Assistance League of Seattle.

Children's Orthopedic Hospital Friendly Exchange — Gigantic

rummage sale once a year in October in Display Hall at the Seattle Center.

Children's Orthopedic Corner Cupboard — 4560 University Village Plaza N.E. (634-5400). Specialty antiques — donated to hospital, appraised, and priced for sale.

Children's Orthopedic Thrift Shop — 2026 3rd (622-7609). Furniture, cameras, china, clothing; all in excellent condition.

Cloud 9 — 6518 Roosevelt Way N.E. (524-4440). Shop maintained by St. Stephens Episcopal Church. Top-rated women's and men's clothing, china, housewares, and small appliances.

Council of Jewish Women's Thrift Shop — 1501 Pike Pl. (682-2697). Clothing of all kinds, some furniture and small appliances.

Emmy's Attic — 7418 S.E. 24th, Mercer Island (232-6561). Antiques and collectibles consigned; clothing donated. Emmanuel Episcopal Church sponsors.

Goodwill Shopping Center — Rainier S & S. Dearborn (329-1000). Largest Goodwill store in the world plus a museum. Old style fashion shows. Rehabilitated donations for house and clothing.

Hadassah Nearly New Shop — 414 Broadway E. (325-4974). Recommended for appliances, clothes, and jewelry; also stocks housewares and books. Donated by Hadassah.

High Hopes — 6814 Roosevelt Way N.E. (524-3399). Operated by the King County Unit of the American Cancer Society. Small furniture and appliances, toys, and clothing.

Overlake Service League Thrift Shop — Bellevue Square (454-6424). Men's, women's, and children's clothing. Small furniture, knicknacks, and household goods.

R Shoppe — 5435 Ballard N.W. (783-4230). Donations by Ryther Guilds of Ryther Child Center. Clothing, books, linens, housewares.

Salvation Army Thrift Stores — 1010 4th S., main store (624-0200); antique store (622-9117). Eight other stores in the Seattle area.

St. Vincent de Paul — 1001 Fairview N. (623-1492). Wide variety of items including clothing. Two other stores in Seattle area.

Trinkets and Treasures — 517 15th E. (325-5942). Good clothes, antiques, collectibles, and furniture. Maintained by Church of the Epiphany.

Value Village Thrift Store — 12548 Lake City Way N.E. (365-8232); 2929 27th S. (723-5000). Donations from Northwest Center for the Mentally Retarded. Furniture, clothing, etc. Three other stores.

The Wise Penny — 4744 University Way N.E. (524-8585). Donations from Junior League of Seattle. One of the best for children's clothing; also men's and women's clothing and accessories. Small furniture.

Damaged Goods and Liquidators

Goods damaged during shipping will often be sold as a lot to satisfy insurance claims. Most of the goods are undamaged or damaged so slightly as to be imperceptible. Food, furniture, and general merchandise are offered by outlets specializing in obtaining and selling damaged goods. Offerings vary widely, depending on shipments.

AAA Liquidating — 19945 1st S. (824-3033). Mostly new merchandise, factory overruns, and close-outs. Clothing, radios, jewelry, general merchandise.

Molin & Offer — 1770 4th S. (682-6740). Groceries, furniture, appliances, general merchandise.

Pacific Iron & Metal's Browsville 2230 4th S. (628-6256). Building materials, fiberglass, paint, housewares, toys, etc.

Fabrics

Discount fabrics, bolt ends, irregulars, and damaged goods are offered in numerous stores to cut cost for the home seamstress:

Pacific Iron's Fabric World — 2230 4th S. (628-6237). Eight other branches.

Hancock Fabrics — 6034 Empire Way S. (723-6859), 3922 S.W. Alaska (932-1110), 8728 Holman Rd. N.W. (783-2434), 17171 Bothell Way N.E. (363-7767); 125 S.W. 148th, Burien (242-5095); 15625 N.E. 8th, Bellevue (6412970)

Plenty of Textiles — 2909 N.E. Blakely (524-4383)

Calico Corners — 210 105th N.E., Bellevue (455-2510). Seconds of upholstery, drapery, & slipcover fabrics.

Outdated Bakery Goods

When bakery goods, including bread, are not sold during their first day, they are returned to the bakery and sold at a thrift outlet store for a reduced price. Sometimes, overruns or bread slightly damaged in packaging is sold fresh — at reduced prices. The following list of outdated bakery goods outlets permits shopping at a convenient place regardless of where you live:

Ruth Ashbrook Bakery — 1407 11th; also Center Bldg., Redmond

Best Pies — 1000 Mercer

Continental Baking Co. (Wonder Bread) — 1924 S. Jackson, 14701 15th N.E.

Gai's Bakery — 2006 S. Weller, 97th & Aurora N; 23009 Military Rd. S., Kent; 13817 N.E. 20th, Bellevue

Langendorf Bakery — 2901 6th S., Hwy. 99 S. & S. 200th

Oroweat Bakery — 1604 N. 34th, 3425 S. 146th; 134th N.E. & N.E. Bellevue-Redmond Rd., Bellevue; 125 Diagonal Way S.W., Everett

Roos' — 1534 Pike Pl.

Van de Kamp's — 3666 Stone Way N., 11454 16th S.W.

Co-op Stores

These store-front food cooperatives permit members to buy foods at low cost in exchange for various amounts of labor or a small "loan" fee is paid monthly by members until a set amount is paid into the co-op. Senior citizens are exempt from the fee at most stores. Stores also sell to nonmembers but at higher prices. Often the stores emphasize natural foods. Call the individual co-op for their current policies.

Bulk Commodities Exchange — 1423 Western (447-9516)

Phinney Street Co-op — 400 N. 43rd (633-2354).

Puget Consumers Co-op — 6504 20th N.E. (525-1450); 10718 N.E. 68th, Kirkland (828-4621)

Auctions

Touch your left ear lobe, flick an eyebrow, blink rapidly three times or whatever you do to let the auctioneer know you're bidding, and take advantage of the numerous auctions in the Seattle area. Here's a sample of the auctions, ranging from country to city to government-sponsored.

Butterfield & Butterfield — P.O. Box 3702, Bellevue, 98009 (455-9831). Specializes in fine furnishings, art objects, paintings, Oriental rugs; estate dispositions.

Bushell's Auction House — 2006 2nd (622-5833). Home furnishings, antiques, estates. Sales on Tuesdays.

Seattle Auction Service — (525-3456). Furniture, appliances, antiques.

U.S. Customs Service — An auction is held each year in November of goods unclaimed or confiscated, ranging from Christmas decorations to clothing to jewelry. Call 246-8805 for information and catalog, which will be sent two weeks in advance of the sale.

Police Department — Every two or three months, depending on the amount of goods received, the Seattle Police Department holds an auction of stolen items or unclaimed lost-and-found goods. Many bikes end up in this auction. For information, watch the local newspapers or call the police department's public information office (625-2051).

General Services Administration — This is a humdinger of an auction, always conducted with sealed bids by mail. You can buy everything from 16 tons of bolts, useless car batteries and x-ray film to automobiles, boats, tractors, and even an occasional Coast Guard cutter measuring 350 feet or longer. The list of items for sale is more fun to peruse than a Sears catalog. To be placed on the mailing list, call or write the GSA Property Management and Disposal Service, 15th & C S.W., Auburn 98002 (833-6500).

We report with regret and a touch of anger the passing of local auctions by the Post Office and Greyhound. Both have ceased their auctions of unclaimed property in Seattle, and now send those goods to San Francisco to be disposed of in public auctions. Unfair!

Two institutional auctions also should be noted: *Pacific Search,* a natural-history magazine published in Seattle, holds a fund-raising auction each November and auctions off experiences with notable people in the Northwest. For information and a catalog, *Pacific Search,* 222 Dexter N., Seattle, 98109 (682-5044).

The other major auction is PONCHO, a black-tie affair held each fall to raise money for the arts in Seattle. Everything from a meal cooked by the symphony conductor to a $100,000 home is auctioned off. Proceeds are divided among various artistic organizations in the city. Information: PONCHO 1906 42nd E. (322-3440).

RESTAURANTS

A Selective Guide to Dining

IF ONE of the surest signs of prosperity is the growth of restaurants, then Seattle must be going through a very prosperous period. Restaurants and cafes open almost daily, and many survive the first few critical months. The days of a restaurant opening being accorded the same fanfare one expects from the arrival of the King Tut exhibit seem gone forever.

We have selected restaurants that appear to be established well enough to still be with us when the guide is revised again next year, and have based our selection on those either we are personally familiar with or have been recommended by people whose judgment we respect.

We have yet to see a rating system, other than by expense, that is an adequate means of telling readers where to eat. Service changes from day to day, and we do not care to make up readers' minds for them. If you are a member of the group that must have a clever review to quote over dinner, we're sorry. We do not care to arm customers with a set of prejudices beforehand, and we personally resent being told which sauce is lacking what ingredient or some other such trivia. Experts, almost always self-appointed, seem more intent on displaying their erudition than dispensing information.

So consider this a suggestion list only. We are well aware we have left out some perfectly acceptable places that are popular, even "in" places, and one can complain with some justification that we've lumped the mundane with the excellent. To these and other culinary crimes we plead guilty. But we do not plead guilty to listing places in which we've had poor experience.

Remember, we have listed about 100 places to eat. There are easily another 100 perfectly acceptable ones to discover yourself, too many for us to attempt to check out. If we did, we would be undergoing treatment for the gout or jogging around Green Lake to run off the bulges.

Ethnic

Austrian — The Austrian

Bolivian — Copacabana

Jewish — B & B Delicatessen, Matzoh Momma

Chinese — Atlas, Chinese Gourmet, Harbin Mandarin (North China), Tien Tsin (also Korean), Tai Tung, Yangtze Szechwan Restaurant

Czechoslovakian — Labuznik

French — Brasserie Pittsbourg, City Loan Pavilion, Crepe de Paris, Le Pigalle, Le Tastevin, Marcel's Pastry Plant, Mirabeau, The Other Place

German — Bavarian Haus, Schnitzel House

Italian — Domani, Gasperetti's Roma Cafe, Italian Spaghetti House and Pizzeria, Italo's Casa Roma, Le Bistro, Old Spaghetti Factory

Japanese — Asuka, Benihana of Tokyo, Bush Garden Sukiyaki, Mikado Restaurant

Mexican — Aurora's of Mexico, Campos, Casa Lupita, Guadalajara Cafes, Juan's, Pablo's E'Special

Filipino — Alex's

Mid-Eastern, Greek — Lebanon, The Phoenecia, Continental Pastry Shop, Adriatica

Irish — Jake O'Shaughnessey's

Indonesian — Java Restaurant

Scandinavian — Norseman Cafe, Vaersgo

Russian — Russian Samovar

Polynesian — Trader Vic's

Vietnamese — Viet Nam Restaurant, Cafe Loc

Brunch

Here's a list of places that either specialize in brunch or at least serve up a better-than-average late breakfast. Also watch newspapers and billboards for places that offer specials on Husky and Seahawk football days, including charter bus to and from the game.

The Gasworks, 2501 N. Northlake Way

Crepe de Paris, 1333 Rainier Square, 1927 43rd E.

Sea Galley Restaurants
Stuart's at Shilshole, 6135 Seaview N.W.
Great American Food & Beverage Co., 3119 Eastlake E.
John Franco's Hidden Harbor, 1500 Westlake N.
Rosellini's Four-10, 4th & Wall
Lion O'Reilly's & B.J. Monkeyshine's, 132 Broadway E.
Green Lake Grill, 7200 E. Green Lake Dr. N.
Golden Tides, 6017 Seaview N.W.
Deluxe 2, 5401 26th N.E.
Alaska Junction, 4548 California S.W.
The Blue Max, 7299 Perimeter Rd. S.
Hugo's Rotisserie, Hyatt House, Sea-Tac
Washington Plaza Lobby Restaurant, 5th & Westlake
Henry's Off Broadway, 1705 E. Olive Way
Pablo's E'Special, 14 Roy
Mulligan's Old Place, University Village
Latitude 47, 1232 Westlake N.

Breakfast

Some of our concerned readers were good enough to ask us
to include their favorite breakfast spots. They are:

El Gaucho, 624 Olive Way
13 Coins, 125 Boren N.
Mrs. Malia's, 802 2nd

Fish 'n Chips

These restaurants offer the best fish and chips, according to
a *Seattle Times* restaurant reviewer.

Maximilien, Pike Place Market
Frederick & Nelson, 5th & Pine
Sourdough Restaurant, Pier 57
Spud Fish & Chips, 2666 Alki S.W.; 6860 E. Green Lake Way N.
Totem House Fish & Chips, 3058 N.W. 54th
O'Banion's Tavern & Restaurant, 5220 Rossevelt Way N.E.
Skipper's Seafood 'N Chowder House, 613 Broadway E.*
Ivar's Acres of Clams, Pier 54
Ivar's Seafood Bars
Elliott Bay Fish & Oyster Co., Pier 56
Vintage 24, 24th floor Bank of California Building, 900 4th
Burgermaster Drive-Ins

Braille Menus

A growing number of restaurants in Seattle have produced menus for the blind. A recent survey showed that these eateries offered this thoughtful service:

Restaurants in Seattle Center's Center House
Columbia Cafe
Turkey House
International House of Pancakes
VIPs Restaurants
The Bon's Market Place and Cascade Room
The Space Needle
Top of the Pier
Lucky's Restaurant
Horatio's
Tally Ho
La Paloma
Clinkerdagger, Bickerstaff & Pett's

View Restaurants

Although restaurants that advertise their "atmosphere" sometimes try to sell that instead of good food, still there is a demand for places to eat that also have a view, especially for entertaining out-of-town guests. Here are a few listed according to what you will see.

City Skyline — Beach Broiler, 1936 Harbor S.W.; The Cloud Room, Camlin Hotel, 8th & Pine; Top of The Hilton, 6th & University.

Lake Union — Latitude 47, 1232 Westlake N.; Franco's Hidden Harbor, 1500 Westlake N.; Canlis, 2576 Aurora N.; Ivar's Salmon House, 401 N.E. Northlake Way; The Gasworks, 2501 Northlake Way; Hungry Turtle, 2501 Fairview E.; The America's Cup, 1900 N. Northlake Way.

Puget Sound & Olympics — Quesnel's 4703 Beach Drive S.W., Ray's Boathouse, 6049 Seaview N.W.; Mirabeau, Sea-First Bldg. 46th floor; Quinn's, Shilshole Bay; Captain's Table, 333 Elliott W.; The Galley, Pier 57; Elliott Bay Fish & Oyster Co., Pier 56; Hiram's 5300 34th N.W. (view of the locks); Stuart's at Shilshole, 4135 Seaview N.W.; Edgewater Inn, Pier 67; Mirabeau, 4th & Madison.

Everywhere — Space Needle, Seattle Center

Alphabetical Listing

Symbols: AE-American Express; VISA; CB-Carte Blanche; DC-Diners Club;MC-Master Charge.

Adriatica — 1107 Dexter Ave. N. Devotees of the French restaurant, Chez Paul, still arrive outside this restored Victorian house and look disoriented. But the new restaurant is as good as the old, and the food from Mediterranean nations has caught on in Seattle. Dinner only. 5:30-10 p.m. Tues.-Thurs; till 11 p.m. Fri. & Sat. Major cards (285-5000). Expensive.

Alex's — Pike Place Market. A small cafe, but probably the only one in Seattle serving Filipino foods, and the prices are low.

America's Cup — Mariners Square, 1900 N. Northlake Way. The second in Peter Huwiler's growing chain (Huwiler's in University Village is the first), and one of the most popular spots in the University area. Specializes in not really specializing—dishes from North America, Australia, and various European nations. Also known for the careful attention given to preparing garden-fresh vegetables. Lunch 11 a.m.-3 p.m. Mon.-Sat., Sun. Brunch 9:30-2:30. Dinner 4:30-10:30 Sun.-Thurs., to 11:30 Fri. & Sat. Cocktail lounge and piano bar. Major credit cards. Reservations recommended (633-0161). Moderate.

Andy's Diner — 2963 4th S. A converted railroad-car restaurant specializing in steaks; a popular lunch spot. Full bar. Mon.-Sat. 11:30 a.m.-11 p.m.; closed Sun. Reservations accepted (624-4097). VISA, MC, AE. Moderate.

Asuka — Lobby of Park Place Building, 6th & Seneca. When this Japanese restaurant opened, with its beautiful views across the Freeway Park and contemporary mixed with traditional Japanese furnishings, everyone first talked about its beauty, then its food. The order could be reversed because the food holds its own with the view. Lunch: Mon.-Fri. 11:30 a.m.-1:45 p.m. Dinner: Mon.-Thurs. 5:30-10 p.m.; Fri & Sat, to 10:30 p.m. Reservations advisable (682-8050). VISA, MC, AE.

Atlas Chinese Restaurant — 424 Maynard S. Many insist this cafe serves the best Chinese food in Seattle, and if not the best, certainly one of the best selections. Serves dinners only and is closed on Mon. No bar, no credit cards. Reservations (623-0913).

The Austrian — 2357 10th E. A split-level restaurant with the top floor a fiine-dining salon with antique furnishings. The lower level is Bavarian wine cellar decor, with strolling musicians. Excellent Austrian food. Hours: Lunch 11-2; dinner 5-11. Open every day. Reservations recommended (322-8028). Moderate.

B & B Delicatessen — 414 Olive Way. Lobby of Times Square Bldg. Kosher-styled menu dinners served from 5 p.m. Comfortable, clean surroundings while you snack on items such as gefilte fish or knishes. Beer and wine. Mon.-Sat. 9 a.m.-9:30 p.m. Reservations accepted (622-4575). VISA, MC. Inexpensive.

Benihana of Tokyo — 1200 5th. Located in the IBM Building Plaza. Japanese cuisine with steaks prepared at your table by flamboyant, young cooks who whirl and twirl knives faster than a gunslinger. Cocktails and lounge entertainment. Mon.-Fri. 11:30 a.m.-2 p.m.; Sun.-Thurs. 5:30-10 p.m.; Fri.-Sat. until 11 p.m. Reservations required Fri. & Sat. nights (682-4686). AE, VISA, DC, CB, MC. Moderate.

Boondock's, Sundecker's & Greenthumb's — 611 Broadway E. As the name seems to imply, plants abound in this restaurant lending an atmosphere of intimacy and warmth. Varied wine list and a 33-page modestly priced menu ranging from snacks to complete dinners. Weekdays 11 a.m.-3 a.m.; weekends 9 a.m.-4 a.m.; Sun. until 2 a.m. Reservations for 12-plus only (323-7272) so expect a long wait. VISA, MC, AE. Moderate.

Brasserie Pittsbourg — 602 1st. One of Seattle's most famous restaurants, and deservedly so. Excellent and imaginative. French provincial luncheon and dinner served in an 1893-vintage building — molded tin ceiling, marble countertops, and tile floor. Full bar. Mon.-Sat. 11:30 a.m.-2:30 p.m.; 5:30-10:30 p.m.; closed Sun. Reservations advisable (623-4167). VISA, MC, AE. Expensive.

The Broadway — 314 Broadway E. One of those restaurants that could baffle patrons with beauty, instead of good food and service, but doesn't have to. The menu isn't extensive but what is offered is first-rate and doesn't occupy time that could be spent admiring the interior design. A stand-up bar reminiscent of older cities that were never affected by Seattle's Blue (and dumb) Laws, lots of potted plants, canopies, mirrors, and tile floors. Lunch 11:30-4 p.m. Mon.-Fri., noon-4 p.m. Sat. Dinner 5:30-10:30 p.m. Mon.-Thurs til 11:30 p.m. Fri & Sat., 5-10 p.m. Sun. Full bar. Reservations recommended (323-1990). VISA, MC, AE.

Bruccio's — Pier 52. Seafood and steak menu with an outside fish bar. Enjoy a cocktail at the bar while waiting for your ferry — remote control TV's scan the ferry dock for you. Sun.-Thurs. 11 a.m.-10 p.m.; Fri-Sat. 11 a.m.-11 p.m. Reservations advised (682-3652). VISA, AE, MC. Moderate.

Bush Garden Sukiyaki — 614 Maynard S. Japanese decor and cuisine. Dining is a pleasant, calm experience at low tables with geisha service. Cocktails. Mon.-Sun 5:45-10 p.m. Reservations necessary (682-6830). VISA, MC, AE. Moderate.

The Butcher Restaurant — 5701 6th S. Specialty is steaks, prime rib, and salad bar, with a variety of seafood and continental dishes. The Greenhouse Terrace is a popular part of the place, and the bar has a lengthy happy hour each work day. Lunch served Mon.-Fri.; dinner daily. Reservations recommended. (763-2215). All major credit cards. Moderate. Also at 300 12th N.E., Bellevue (455-3930).

The Canal — Foot of 24th Ave. N.W. After decades of having only a tavern and a refreshment stand at the entrance of the Ballard Locks, now we have an explosion of good restaurants. This used to be a boat-building shed and has been turned into a popular restaurant with graphics, weavings, and other bits of tasteful camouflage to conceal the building's past. The menu is mainly beef and chicken plus a good seafood selection. Lunch 11-3 p.m., dinner 5-11 p.m. Mon.-Thurs. and 5-midnight Fri. & Sat. Closed Sun. Full bar. Major cards. Reservations (783-1964).

Canlis — 2576 Aurora N. One of Seattle's most formal and expensive restaurants. Overlooking Lake Union. Excellent service, seafood and steaks from the charcoal broiler. Of special note are the shish kebabs and Caesar salad prepared at your table. Cocktails, piano bar nightly from 7:30 p.m.-1a.m. Mon.-Sat. 5:30 p.m.-11 p.m. Reservations recommended (283-3313). AE, VISA, CB, MC. Expensive.

Casa Lupita — 1823 Eastlake E. (325-7350); 437 108th N.E., Bellevue (453-9795). Mexican cuisine ranging from Mexican Bean Soup to Steak a la Chicana. Full bar. Lunch and dinner Mon.-Thurs. 11 a.m.-9 p.m.; Fri.-Sat. dinner until 11 p.m.; Sun. until 10 p.m. Reservations accepted. VISA, MC. Inexpensive.

Charlie's — 217 Broadway E. A period piece; 1930's-style Hollywood decor with Gary Cooper and Merle Oberon, among others, on the wildly floral walls while songs — most of which are so bad that they're nostalgic and that makes them good — resound throughout the joint. But the menu isn't 1930's at all. It is very up-to-date with adequate prices (that means they charge enough but don't get carried away with the profit motive). The menu lists more than 60 selections with 6 dinner specialties served only after 5 p.m. Examples are a baby rack of lamb, with the *Times'* columnist John Hinterberger described as "tender as a rabbit's handshake." Full bar, Mon.-Fri. 11:30 a.m.-3 a.m.; Sat. 10 a.m.-3 a.m.; Sun. 9 a.m.-1 a.m. All bank cards. Reservation accepted (323-2535).

Chinese Gourmet — 364 Roy. Like so many family-operated Chinese restaurants, this one is unpretentious, friendly, and the food superb and of such generous portions you will almost always take some home. A good place to start or finish a visit to the Seattle Center. Hours: Tues.-Thurs. 11:30 a.m.-11:30 p.m., Fri til 1 a.m., Sat., 2 p.m.-1 a.m., Sun., 2 p.m.-10 p.m. Full bar. Major credit cards. Reservations (285-9919 or 282-6616).

Clinkerdagger, Bickerstaff and Petts Public House — 205th & Aurora, Edmonds. An informal, new trend, restaurant with English pub decor, friendly waitresses costumed as English wenches, and pewter table settings. The food is not traditional English, it is excellent. Varied menu including Quiche Lorraine, steaks, and seafood. Cocktails and wine. Mon.-Sat. 11:30 a.m.-2 p.m.; Mon.-Thurs 5:30-10 p.m.; Fri.-Sat. 11:30 a.m.-2 p.m.; Sun. 4:30-9 p.m. Reservations advised (775-2561). VISA, MC, AE.

Continental Restaurant and Pastry Shop — 4549 University Way N.E. Featuring Greek cuisine in a combination of restaurant, pastry shop and delicatessen. An inexpensive way to sample a variety of Greek dishes. Wine. Seven days, 9 a.m.-11 p.m. (623-4700). AE, VISA, MC, DC. Inexpensive.

Copacabana Cafe — Pike Place Market. Founded several years ago by a refugee from one of Bolivia's periodic revolutions, the Copacabana has long been an institution at the markets. Probably the only place in the area specializing in Bolivian cooking, and all at reasonable prices. Lunch 11:30-4 p.m., Mon.-Sat. Dinner on Fri. only 5:30-10 p.m. Beer and wine. No credit cards. No reservations (622-6359).

Crepe de Paris — 1333 Rainier Square. The old country French charm of the original Crepe de Paris was lost in the move to new quarters, and the intimate atmosphere replaced with a noisy room, but the menu still is superb and includes onion soup, 30 varieties of crepes plus 11 dessert crepes as well as a few noncrepe dishes. Beer and wine. Mon.-Thurs 11 a.m.-11 p.m.; Fri.-Sat. 8 to midnight. Closed Sun. Reservations for parties of 8 or more (623-4111). VISA, MC. Moderate. Another Crepe de Paris at 1927 43rd E. (329-6620).

Daniel's Broiler — 200 Lake Washington Blvd. Aged steaks, rack of lamb chops, veal and fresh salmon are among specialties. Restaurant overlooks Lake Washington and boat dock. Dinner Tues.-Sun. 5 to midnight. Reservations recommended. All major credit cards. Valet parking. (329-4191). Expensive.

Domani — 604 Bellevue Way N.E., Bellevue. Excellent northern Italian food with cannelloni a house specialty and French dishes as a bonus, some of which (filet de porc "Nicoise" and filet de veau aux "Champignons") are for two. Lunch from 11:30 a.m.-2:30 p.m. Mon.-Fri.; dinner from 5-10 p.m. Mon.-Thurs. til 11 p.m. Fri.-Sat. Lounge is open to legal closing. Reservations accepted (454-4405). MC, VISA, AE. Moderate.

Drake's Salad Bar — 915 4th. Located in YMCA Bldg. Fresh healthy foods, a relaxing atmosphere. Features salads, soups, and sandwiches. Open 7 days 7 a.m.-7 p.m. (583-0966). Inexpensive.

El Gaucho — 624 Olive Way. Conventional menu moderately to expensively priced specializing in meat preparation. Popular lunch spot. Mon.-Sat. 11 a.m.-4 a.m., Sun. 10 a.m.-11 p.m. Features a multi-course Hunt Breakfast from midnight to 4 a.m. Strolling guitarist. Long wine list. Reservations advised (682-3202). Full bar. AE, VISA, MC.

Emmett Watson's Oyster Bar — A tiny place in the Pike Place Markets (behind the Soames-Dunn Bldg.) with lots of fresh oysters, even if you might have to stand while you eat them. A pleasant courtyard is part of the attraction. (622-7721).

F.X. McRory's Steak, Chop & Oyster House — Occidental S. & S. King. A vast restaurant across from the Kingdome. Proprietors are Timothy Firnstahl and Michael McHugh, who also operate Jake O'Shaughnessey's. Named for a restaurant opened in 1915 in New York, McRory's will seat 350 usually noisy patrons, parties, and pro-sports fans in 11,000 square feet of space. It features a well-stocked bar, premium meat, and an oyster bar with marble counters, oysters in the shell on ice, and a condiment bar where patrons can make their own sauce. Cocktails, beer & wine. VISA, MC, AE. Expensive. No reservations.

Franco's Hidden Harbor — 1500 Westlake N. Dining on a Lake Union boat dock amid yachts. Excellent seafood dishes. Casual, friendly service and prices trending up. Hours: Mon.-Sat. 11 a.m.-11 p.m. Sunday brunch. Full bar (282-0501). VISA, MC, AE, DC. Expensive.

The Frederick & Nelson Restaurant — Eighth floor, Frederick & Nelson, 5th & Pine. One of the few restaurants in Seattle that will remind one of those grand old restaurants in San Francisco, Denver, and New York. It is a vast, high-ceilinged room with table after table, each with sparkling white linen and heavy silver. Even the salad is served in silver bowls on a mongrammed silver plate. The lunches are more popular with regulars than dinners, and their chicken and beef pot pies bear no relationship to those bachelors buy frozen at the supermarket. It formerly was called a tea room, but the addition of a full bar rendered that name obsolete. Lunch from 11 a.m. daily; dinner 4:30-7:30 Mon. & Fri.; Sun. noon-4 p.m. All charge cards. Reservations (682-5500).

Gasperetti's Roma Cafe — 220 4th S. Favorite hang-out of local politicians and former athletes. Excellent Italian food served by a friendly staff. Popular after-the-Dome-show stop. Wine cellar and full bar. Mon.-Fri 11 a.m.-10:30 p.m.; Sat. til midnight. Reservations not accepted (623-5932). VISA, MC, AE. Moderate.

Golden Tides — 6017 Seaview N.W. Located on Shilshole Bay, a fast-paced night club restaurant with varied menu, both in dishes and prices. Sandwich bar and disco every night 9:30 p.m.-2 a.m. Sunday dinners are quiet and leisurely with no live music. Sun. 10 a.m.-8 p.m.; Mon.-Sat. 11:30 a.m.-3 p.m.; 5:30-9 p.m. Reservations advised (784-7100). VISA, MC, AE. Moderate.

The Goose — 5th & University. A nostalgic place with marble table tops, mahogany booths, and continental cuisine. Nightly entertainment. Lunch Mon.-Sat. 11:30-3. Dinner Mon.-Thurs. 5-11 p.m. Fri.-Sat. 5-12. Reservations recommended. (682-3066). Major credit cards. Expensive.

Great American Food & Beverage Co.'s Conglomerate — 3119 Eastlake E. A conglomeration of good food, luxurious 1890's decor complete with museum quality antiques, and waiters and waitresses who provide continual entertainment with their singing and costumes. No reservations except for parties of 6 or more, birthdays, and anniversaries. A feature for 6 or more is the Fabulous Plank Feast served on a long board laden with food. Full bar. Sun.-Thurs 11 a.m.-11 p.m.; Fri.-Sat. til 1 a.m. (323-8855). VISA, MC, AE. Moderate.

Greenstreets — 2040 Westlake N. Features chicken, spareribs, wide variety of burgers, salads, omelets, and sandwiches.

View of Lake Union. Open daily for lunch and dinner. (285-2040). VISA, MC. Inexpensive.

Guadalajara Cafe — 1429 4th. Downstairs at the corner of 4th & Pike (entrance on the 4th Ave. side), one of the best Mexican restaurants in Seattle. Cafes by the same name, same ownership, at 1718 N. 45th in the University District (632-7858), and 15400 N.E. 20th, Bellevue (641-0828). All inexpensive. Beer and wine. Hours: (downtown) Mon.-Thurs. 11 a.m.-10 p.m.; Fri. & Sat. til-midnight. (U. Dist.) Mon.-Sat. 11:30 a.m.-9 p.m. Reservations not necessary (622-8722). VISA Inexpensive.

Henry's Off Broadway — 1705 E. Olive Way. One of the popular places for those who like to see and be seen at the proper places, and enjoy quality food and drink while there. Large and airy with marble-topped tables and bar, fresh flowers, and lots of plants; rack of lamb Dijon and abalone doré amandine, among the house specialties. Lunch 11 a.m.-2 p.m.; dinner 5:30-11 p.m. weekdays, 5-10 p.m. Sun. Full bar, major credit cards, reservations recommended (329-8063). Moderate.

Hiram's at the Locks — 5300 34th N.E. — A delightfully unpretentious place right on the Ballard Locks in an industrial-architecture building covered with corrugated steel painted factory green. Predominately seafood menu, small wine list, and a house dressing of honey and lime. Plus that great view over the locks. Lunch 11:30 a.m.-3 p.m. Mon.-Fri.; dinner 5-10:30 p.m. daily and a bit later on Fri. & Sat. Reservations advised (784-1733) Moderate.

Hungry Turtle — 2501 Fairview E. Feed the ducks from the glassed-in deck of this Lake Union restaurant. Moderately priced meat and seafood menu, piano bar in cocktail lounge — 5 p.m.-1 a.m. Lunch and dinner Mon.-Thurs. 11 a.m.-11:30 p.m.; Fri.-Sat. 11 til 12:30 a.m.; Sun. noon-10 p.m. Reservations recommended (329-6333). VISA, MC, AE, DC. Moderate.

Italian Spaghetti House & Pizzeria — 9824 Lake City Way N.E. Specialty is stuffed lasagne and cannelloni alla Romano, and of course, spaghetti and pizza. Beer and wine. Mon.-Sat. 4:30 p.m.-1:30 a.m.; Sun. til 10 p.m. Reservations recommended for parties of 6 or more (523-2667). VISA, MC. Inexpensive.

Italo Casa Romana — 6400 Empire Way S. Some call this the best Italian restaurant in Seattle. Followers of Italian cuisine will find Calzone here. Cocktails. Mon.-Thurs. 11 a.m.-10:30 p.m.; Fri.-Sat. 11 a.m.-11:30 p.m.; Sun 4-10 p.m. Reservations suggested for 8 or more (722-0449). VISA, MC. Inexpensive.

Ivar's — This seafood group is one of Seattle's most popular under the same ownership. *Acres of Clams* — Pier 54, foot of Madison. Weekdays 11 a.m.-11 p.m. Sidewalk fish bar open until 2 a.m. for ferry and foot traffic (624-6852). *Captain's Table* — 333 Elliott W. Seafood with live entertainment and dancing from 9 p.m.-2 a.m. Hours: 11 a.m.-1 a.m. Mon.-Sat. til 11 p.m. Sun. Cocktails. Lunch reservations only (284-7040). VISA, AE, MC. *Ivar's Indian Salmon House* — 401 N.E. Northlake, under the freeway bridge on Lake Union. Alder-smoker salmon in Indian longhouse decor. No reservations accepted (632-0767). Lunch 11:30 a.m.-2 p.m. Mon.-Fri.; dinner: 5-10 p.m. every night. AE, VISA, MC. Salmon House take-out fish bar open Sun.-Thurs. 11 a.m.-11 p.m.; Fri.-Sat. til 1 a.m.; no credit cards. All moderate. *Ivar's Smith Tower Cafe* —2nd & Yesler (624-1777). Ivar's newest. Ivar also bought out a chain of local seafood bars which serve the same delicious food for which he is famous.

Jake O'Shaughnessey's — 100 Mercer, in the Hansen Baking Company complex near the Seattle Center. This is one of the places for people to be "seen" but the food, drinks, and service are superb. Jake's dispenses what must be the most expensive brandy in the land; Ragnaud's, $3,600 a case, $45 a shot. Their bartender also sings opera or Irish, and if you don't see a local celebrity, it will be a surprise. 1890 decor, menu features prime rib roasted in a casing of salt for 8 hours, stews, and alder-cooked salmon. Cocktails, beer, and wine. Mon.-Sat. 5-11 p.m.; Sun. 5-10 p.m. No reservations accepted (285-1897). VISA, MC, AE. Moderate.

Java Restaurant — 8929 Roosevelt Way N.E. Seattle's only Indonesian restaurant. Dishes range from delicately seasoned pork sate to highly spiced rigsttafel. Simple decor. No liquor. Dinners only: 4-10 p.m. Closed Tues. Reservations accepted (522-5282). No credit cards. Inexpensive.

Jonah and the Whale — Bellevue Holiday Inn, 11211 Main. Jonah offers one of the outstanding dining experiences in the area serving salads, seafood, fowl, and beef. One word, elegant, says it all for this top restaurant. Lunch is from 11:30 a.m.-2 p.m.; dinner from 6-10:30 p.m. Mon.-Fri. and 6-11 p.m. on Sat. Closed Sun. Lounge entertainment nightly. Reservations are required. (455-5242). All major credit cards. Expensive.

Knight's Diner — 5717 4th S. Dining in an old Pullman car amid Seattle's industrial and manufacturing district. Brisk lunch trade and dinners featuring steaks or ground beef and including deep dish apple pie made on the premises. Mon.-Fri. 6

a.m.-8 p.m. Dinner reservations accepted for large groups only (762-9532). No credit cards. Moderate to inexpensive.

Labuznik — 1924 1st. A few years ago we often visited the Prague Restaurant and admired both the food and the art that was displayed (this was before the gallery explosion). Then the Prague went away, but Peter Cipra, the owner, promised he would return as soon as possible with a new one. He has, and his Labuznik is another winner. Unfortunately, he has been talking about selling out and following other pursuits. We hope he doesn't. A small menu of Czechoslovakian food such as svichova followed by sacher torte or Pala cinky for dessert. Mon.-Sat. 11:30 a.m.-11 p.m. Full bar, major credit cards. Reservations recommended (682-1624). Moderate.

Lakeside Restaurant – 2501 N. Northlake Way. Mirrored, tri-level with a view overlooking Lake Union and boat docks. Limited but good menu of steaks, seafoods, eggs, and sandwiches. Cocktails. Mon.-Sat. 11:30 a.m.-midnight; Sun. brunch 10 a.m.-3p.m. with special children's price. Reservations accepted (632-8941). VISA, MC, AE. Moderate.

Latitude 47 — 1232 Westlake. Informal restaurant on Lake Union specializing in seafood and prime rib; special salads. Full bar — entertainment and dancing 7 days. Mon.-Fri. 11 a.m.-2 a.m.; Sat. from 5 p.m.; Sunday brunch buffet 10 a.m.-3 p.m., dinner to 11 p.m. Reservations advised (284-1047). VISA, DC, MC, AE. Moderate.

Le Bistro — 93-A Pike. A limited number of Italian dishes prepared carefully that include tortellini, fettuccine, cioppino and linguine marinara. Adults only, since it has only a tavern license. Lunch 11:30-3 p.m. Mon.-Sat.; dinner 6-10:30 p.m. Mon.-Sat. 4-9 p.m. Sun. Beer and wine only. Reservations suggested (682-3049).

Le Pigalle — 1104 NE 47th St. Considered by some restaurant regulars as the most consistently fine French restaurant in Seattle. It is a small place — it only seats 48 — and everything is fresh, even the flowers on each table. Specialties include Poulet Normande, Coq au Vin, pork loin in sherry and plum sauce, brandied pepper steak, and braised sweetbreads. Seafood dinners also offered. Lunches Mon.-Fri. 11:30-2:30 p.m.; dinner 5:30-10:30 p.m. Mon.-Sat. Closed Sun. Bank cards accepted. Reservations recommended (525-1525).

Le Tastevin — 501 Queen Anne N. One of Seattle's best and least pretentious French restaurants. Entrees include seafood, veal, steaks, chicken, beef, and lamb ordered with a dinner or a la carte. Complete dinners include soup or salad and a dessert. Excellent wine list and cocktails. Near the Seattle Center and Uptown movie theater, reservations are recommended. Mon.-Fri. 11:30 a.m.-2:30 p.m.; Fri.-Sat. 5 p.m.-11 p.m. (283-0991). VISA, MC.

Mad Anthony's —Commons Building, 1200 112th N.E., Bellevue. A Colonial American-styled inn featuring prime rib cuts and Yorkshire pudding. The lounge features entertainment Tues.-Sat. until closing. Open for dinner only 5-11 p.m. everyday. Reservations accepted (455-1776). VISA, MC, AE. Moderate.

Marcel's Pastry Shop & Tea Room — 1603 14th E. No reservations, no credit cards, no liquor — but one of the best French pastry shops does offer luncheon while seated before a display case of pastry specialties. Mon.-Sat. 11:30 a.m.-5 p.m. (329-7000). Moderate.

Matzoh Momma — 509 15th E. A delicatessen-restaurant, complete with rock music and occasionally live piano, serving kosher Jewish meals and carry-outs of lox, bagels, chicken soup, herring in sour cream, etc. Mon.-Sat. 10:30 a.m.-9 p.m.; Sun 10 a.m.-5 p.m. No reservations or credit cards (324-6262). Moderate.

McCormick's — 4th & Columbia. Menu lists 43 fish entrees, Northwest salmon, Eastern scallops, New England swordfish and steaks. Open for lunch weekdays, every day for dinner. Full bar. Reservations advised (682-3900). All major credit cards.

Merchant's Cafe — 109 Yesler Way. A restoration of Seattle's oldest restaurant with the original 30-foot carved backbar. Continental menu with basement level. Mon.-Thurs. 11:30 a.m.-midnight; Fri.-Sat. until 1 a.m.; cocktails until 2 a.m. on weekends. Entertainment 6-10 p.m. Tues.-Sat. No reservations accepted (624-1515). VISA, MC, AE. Moderate.

Mikado Restaurant — 514 S. Jackson. Authentic Japanese cuisine served in an attractive, modern dining room; also a bay of tatami rooms for privacy. Menu ranges from an excellent sukiyaki to the formal "Kaiseki" dinner (24 hours' notice required). Cocktails. Mon.-Sat 5:30-10 p.m. Reservations advised (622-5206). VISA, AE MC. Moderate.

Mirabeau Restaurant — 4th & Madison. A spectacular view from the 46th floor of the Seattle-First National Bank Bldg. Continental menu, predominantly French. Wine list, cocktail bar. Expensive but the elevator ride is free. Mon.-Fri. 11:30

a.m.-2:30 p.m. for lunch; Mon.-Sat. 5:30-10:30 p.m. for dinner. Reservations advised (624-4550). VISA, MC, AE.

Mrs. Malia's — 802 2nd Ave. Started as a very successful operation called The Snug, but success forced it into a second, larger place and gave the impetus for a larger menu for the lunch crowd, which is indeed always a crowd. The high-ceilinged restaurant opens for breakfast at 7 a.m. and things don't slow up until after the lunch hour is long past. Mrs. Malia's has its own bakery and serves such delicacies as Bolognese chicken breasts, seafood pies, and always fresh-baked bread. Breakfast 7-11 a.m., lunch 11-5:30 p.m., Mon.-Sat.; dinner 5:30-9 p.m. Mon.-Thurs., to 11 p.m. Fri. & Sat. Closed Sun. Full bar, lounge, chamber music with dinner on weekends. Major credit cards. Reservations suggested (624-3287).

Norseman Cafe — 2301 N.W. Market. Chalet-like building with Norwegian decor and menu in the heart of Seattle's Scandinavian district. Cafeteria-style service featuring open-faced Danish sandwiches, Norwegian meatballs, and other delights. Variety of pastries baked on the premises. No alcohol. Mon.-Sat. 8:30 a.m.-5 p.m. No reservations necessary (783-5080). No credit cards. Moderate.

Old Spaghetti Factory — Elliott & Broad. Gay 90's feeling in a renovated brick warehouse near the waterfront. Spaghetti dinners with a variety of sauces served in generous portions while seated at unmatched wooden tables or inside a restored streetcar. Full bar. Mon.-Thurs. 5-10 p.m.; Fri.-Sat. til midnight; Sun. 4-10 p.m. No reservations or credit cards accepted (623-3520). Moderate.

The Other Place — 319 Union. French cuisine with emphasis on fresh game and trout. Game birds are from a farm on nearby Vashon Island. The restaurant is highly rated by local gourmets. Excellent wine list. Mon.-Sat. 11 a.m.-midnight; closed Sun. Reservations advised (623-7340). AE, VISA, MC. Expensive.

Pablo's E'Special — 14 Roy. One of Seattle's newest restaurants paying tribute to the lively dishes from Mexico, Pablo's immediately became a popular place for those who want a little variety and zip in their diets. Contrary to popular belief, all Mexican food doesn't burn a hole in your cheeks — some dishes are quite subtle in their flavor — and Pablo's has a little of each. As with all Mexican food, the price is reasonable and the interior decor attractive. Full bar and lounge. Dinners only from 5 p.m. onward. Major credit cards. No reservations (284-7770).

The Phoenecia — 4725 California. A Lebanese restaurant owned and operated by Hussein Khazaal. It is a family-operated restaurant catering to the family trade in an informal dining room with a scattering of beaten brass and small rugs used as wall hangings. They offer at least 16 dinners plus a wide variety of finger foods, pastries, seafood, African curries, and several vegetarian plates. Shish kebab is, of course, a staple of the menu, but there are others, such as the cous cous, a lamb shank simmered in a sauce of peppery vegetables. Desserts range from pastries stuffed with cheese to spicy mincemeat. Open noon-11 p.m. Tues.-Sat.; 4-11 p.m. Sundays. No alcoholic beverages. Reservations not required (935-8993).

Quinn's Fishmarket & Bar — 7001 N.W. Shilshole Bay Marine. A view of the yachts bobbing in the marina plus the Sound and mountains. A good seafood selection plus steaks. Cocktails, dancing, & entertainment until 2 a.m. Mon.-Sat. 11 a.m.-11:30 p.m.; Sun 4-10 p.m. Reservations recommended (784-4070). VISA, MC, AE. Moderate.

Ray's Boathouse — 6049 Seaview N.W. A popular, lively place on the Sound near Shilshole Bay with a varied menu of good seafood or prime rib. Wine list and full bar. Lunch: Mon.-Fri. 11:30 a.m.-3 p.m. Dinner 6-11 p.m. daily; cocktails until 2 a.m. Reservations almost a must (789-3770). VISA, MC, AE. Moderate.

Red Carpet Restaurant — 1628 5th. An intimate place to dine in the downtown shopping district. Plush, subdued interior with piano bar. Cocktails. Mon.-Sat. 11 a.m.-1 a.m. Reservations accepted (623-5226). VISA, MC, AE. Moderate.

The Red Robin — Eastlake & Fuhrman E., also Northgate Shopping Center, 1600 E. Olive Way, Pacific Plaza Hotel at 4th & Spring. Bills itself as the gourmet burgermaker, and long an established place for graduate students and others on limited budgets. Also now serves pork chops, steaks, fish & chips. Open daily. Call for hours. Inexpensive.

Rosellini's Four-10 — 2515 4th. Presents you with a complete dining experience. Elegant interior, professional waiters, excellent cocktails and wine list, and quality continental cuisine, and the most exclusive take-out service in town. Mon.-Fri. 11 a.m-midnight; Sat.-Sun. 4:30 p.m.-midnight. Reservations advised (624-5464). AE, VISA, MC. Expensive.

Royal Fork Buffet Restaurant — 2205 N. 45th (632-5424). One of 6 buffet places in the chain offering all you can eat for a set price — children under 10 at 19¢ per year. Wide selection of salads and meats; Friday night a variety of seafoods. No liquor. No reservations but normally a fast-moving line. Mon.-Thurs. 11:30-8:30 p.m.; Fri.-Sat. 11:30 a.m.-9:00 p.m.; Sun. noon-8 p.m. Other nearby locations are 16549 Aurora N., 2222 California S.W., 15th & Thomas, 1545 N.W. Market, 10001 Lake City Way N.E. No credit cards. Moderate.

Russian Samovar — 806 E. Roy. A converted house restaurant across from the Harvard Exit theater on Capitol Hill. Leaded-glass windows, interior murals are copies of illustrations from a book of Pushkin fairy tales. A restricted but good menu of American and Russian food. Beer and wine. Lunch: Tues.-Fri. 11:30 a.m.-2 p.m. Dinner: Mon.-Fri 5:30-9 p.m.; Sat.-Sun. 5-9 p.m. No reservations accepted (323-1465). VISA, AE MC. Moderate.

Skipper's Galley — 2223 California S.W. Located in the West Seattle area, Skipper's provides you with a choice of 400 entrees — fresh seafood at its best as well as beef and veal dishes. During the summer months sidewalk tables and checkers are provided. It is so popular that people coming through Seattle by plane often catch a cab to Skipper's, get their meal, then head back to the airport. No liquor. Tues.-Sat. 5-10 p.m., closed Sun. & Mon. Reservations only (937-7445). No credit cards. Moderate.

The Snug — 1414 2nd. Some restaurant owners are interested only in good food, good service, and a steady clientele, and to hell with decor, atmosphere, and the other things that have no effect on the taste of the food. Such a place is The Snug. And they even deliver box lunches to downtown addresses. The menu is of the soup-and-sandwich format with reubens and corned beef, soups too thick to pour, and scrumptious bread and pies freshly baked each day in the mezzanine kitchen. The beverage list runs from the house wine, Almaden, to a long list of teas and soft drinks. Weekdays 8 a.m.-6 p.m., Sat. 11 a.m.-5 p.m. No reservations. Box lunches and downtown delivery available by phoning 682-4303.

Soup and Salad Restaurant — Pike Place Market. Salvation Army decor with a view of the Sound. Omitted from the name is the freshly baked bread served. Inexpensive and fun place to eat while shopping at the Market. No liquor or credit cards. Mon.-Sat. 11:30 a.m.-4 p.m. Inexpensive. Also Soup and Salad After Hours with continental dinners Fri. & Sat. evenings only, from 7 p.m. Reservations necessary (623-5700).

The panoramic splendor of Seattle nestled between mountains and sea slowly unfolds for diners in the revolving Space Needle Restaurant.

Space Needle — Seattle Center grounds. Twirl around Seattle while dining at the 500-foot level. Elaborate menu with prices to match. Cocktails. Breakfast: Mon.-Sat. 7:30-9:30 a.m., Sun. 9 a.m.-2 p.m. Lunch: Mon.-Sat. 11 a.m.-3 p.m. Dinner: Mon.-Sat. 5-11:30 p.m., Sun. 4-10 p.m. Reservations advised (447-3100). Elevator $2 for adults, $1 for children age 6-12. MC, VISA, AE, DC. Westin Hotels. Expensive.

Stuart's at Shilshole — 6135 Seaview N.W. A formal, expensive restaurant with a relatively strict dress code and a view of the large yacht basin thrown in as a bonus. Determinedly nautical in design, the restaurant has boiler-plate interiors similar to being aboard an aircraft carrier with a view and plush appointments. Lunch 11:30 a.m.-3 p.m. Mon.-Fri; dinner 5:30-10:30 p.m. daily; brunch 10:30 a.m.-2:30 p.m. Sat. & Sun. Full bar. Major credit cards. Reservations (784-7974).

Tai Tung Cafe — 659 S. King. A three-generation, family-operated Chinese restaurant with a longstanding reputation for excellent food. Extensive menu with appeal to both the oriental and occidental palate. No liquor. Mon.-Sat. 10 a.m.-3:30 a.m.; Sun. to 1:30 a.m. No reservations (622-7372). No credit cards. Inexpensive.

Thirteen Coins — 125 Boren N. A hard to find spot in the Furniture Mart Building. Posh decor but informal atmosphere serving gigantic portions ranging from corned beef and cabbage to sauteed frog's legs. Full bar. Open 24 hours, 7 days a week. No reservations (682-2513). Also Thirteen Coins Sea-Tac, 18000 Pacific Hwy. S. (243-9500). VISA, MC, DC, AE. Moderate-to-expensive.

Tien Tsin — 1401 N. 45th. A description of the decor of this restaurant in the Wallingford District is unimportant — the food is. An extensive menu featuring authentic Peking style cuisine (no chop suey or egg roll found here) with some Cantonese and Korean dishes. Beer and wine. Tues.-Fri. noon-10 p.m.; Sat.-Sun. 4-11 p.m. Reservations unnecessary (634-0223). VISA, MC. Inexpensive.

The Top of the Pier — Pier 70. A waterfront spot with continental cuisine. Good view of the Sound from the dining room and cocktail lounge. Lunch: Mon.-Sat. 11:30 a.m.-3 p.m. Dinner: Mon.-Thurs. 5-10 p.m.; Fri.-Sat. 5-11 p.m.; Sun. 4-9:30 p.m. Reservations (682-6990). VISA, MC, AE. Moderate.

Trader Vic's — 5th & Westlake, Washington Plaza Hotel. Very pleasant Polynesian and nautical decor, recorded island music, and a Polynesian menu seem to take you to the islands.

The menu is extensive, as well as expensive, and some meats are roasted and smoked in a Chinese oven. Cocktail bar serving regular as well as exotic-looking drinks. Mon.-Sat. 11:30 a.m.-10:45 p.m.; Sun. 5-10 p.m. Reservations advised (624-8520). VISA, MC, AE, DC, CB, Westin Hotels. Expensive.

The Unicorn and The Costermonger — 4550 University Way. Authentic British cuisine in a rustic Tudor setting. Serving the well-known British specialty, steak and kidney pie, or with 24-hour notice, roast pheasant with orange sauce. Imported ales, beer, and wine. Lunch: Mon.-Sat. 11:30 a.m.-2 p.m. Dinner: Mon.-Sun. 5-9 p.m. Reservations for 5 or more (634-1115). VISA Moderate.

Victoria Station — 1880 Fairview E. Railroad cars present an informal setting for USDA choice steaks and self-service salad bar. The cocktail lounge is patterned after a British station waiting room. Full bar. Lunch: Mon.-Sat. 11:30 a.m.-2:30 p.m. Dinner: 5:30-11 p.m. Mon.-Thurs., 5 p.m.-midnight Fri.-Sat.; Sun. 5-10 p.m. Reservations accepted (323-5935). VISA, MC, AE, DC. Moderate.

Viet Nam Restaurant — 914 E. Pike. A small, quiet restaurant serving traditional Vietnamese cuisine. Specialty of the house, Imperial Duck, must be ordered a day in advance. No liquor. Tues.-Fri. 11 a.m.-2 p.m., 5-9 p.m.; Sat. 4-9 p.m.; Sun. 5-9 p.m. Reservations accepted (322-4080). No credit cards. Inexpensive.

The Wharf — Fisherman's Terminal, south end of Ballard Bridge. Seafood is the specialty of this restaurant next to the docks of the nation's largest salmon and halibut fleet. Cocktails and live entertainment. Mon.-Sat. 8 a.m.-12:30 a.m.; Sun. 8 a.m.-9 p.m. Reservations accepted (283-6600). VISA, MC, AE. Moderate.

Yangtze Szechwan Restaurant — 1320 156th N.E., Bellevue. One of the few restaurants in the entire U.S. offering Szchewan-school cooking, this small restaurant nestled among franchised chain restaurants also is one of the most highly rated restaurants in the area. One critic stated flatly it is the best — period. Unlike most Chinese dishes, these are highly seasoned. Hours: Lunch, Tues.-Sat. 11 a.m.-3 p.m.; dinner, Tues.-Sun. 5-10 p.m. except Fri. 5-11 p.m. Reservations (747-2404). VISA, MC, AE. Moderate.

PLACES TO STAY

Overnight Facilities — Deluxe to Open Ground

GRAND HOTELS in Seattle had virtually vanished, with the possible exception of the Washington Plaza, until only recently when the Park Hilton and Seattle Sheraton were built downtown, ending the dominance by Westin's Washington Plaza and the Olympic. The latter was recently turned over to new owners, and at this time is closed for a major remodeling, reopening in 1982.

Seattle is also loaded with flea-bag hotels, some of which have ladies of the night lurking around the corridors. Others look like the place someone would go to shut the windows and turn on the gas. You'll have to search these out for yourself. This is a high-class guide.

Seattle's outdoor orientation and the wild country practically at its doorstep invite campers and recreational vehicles (RVs) from all across the country. Although the most desirable spots are in the hinterland, a few close-in tent spaces and hook-up slots for RVs are available. Most of these are in trailer parks rather than in campgrounds.

NOTE — See Restaurants section for legend of codes identifying credit cards. Quoted prices are for single rooms and are subject to change.

Hotels and Motels

Hotels

Camlin Hotel and Cabanas — 9th at Pine (downtown). 140 units. Color TV, radios, phones. Dining room and coffee shop 6:30 a.m.-11:30 p.m. Cocktails and entertainment. $39-$43. AE, VISA, CB, DC, MC (682-0100).

Edgewater Inn — Pier 67, on waterfront with some balconies over Puget Sound. Air-conditioning, color TV, phones, suites. 230 units. Courtesy cars to all transportation terminals. Dining room and coffee shop 6 a.m.-11 p.m.; Sun. to 10 p.m. Cocktails, entertainment. $37-$44. AE, VISA, CB, DC, MC (624-7000).

Hilton Hotel Downtown — 6th & University. View rooms with air conditioning, color TV, phones, suites. 230 units. Parking garage below. Top restaurant and well-known singles bar. $55-$70. AE, VISA, CB, DC, MC (624-0500).

Park Hilton — 6th & Seneca. Luxurious new addition to the skyline. All amenities, including restaurants and lots of glass and greenery. All major credit cards. $68-$110. (464-1980).

Pacific Plaza — 400 Spring. 170 units. Color TV, phones, 2 restaurants. $36-$41. AE, VISA, DC, MC (623-3900).

University Tower Hotel — N.E. 45th & Brooklyn (University District). 153 units. All corner rooms with views of lakes and mountains. Color TV, some radios, phones. Free parking. Dining room & coffee shop 6:30 a.m.-10 p.m. Cocktails. Transportation to downtown airport, train and bus terminals. $49. AE, VISA, CB, DC, MC (634-2000).

The Warwick — 4th & Lenora. 234 units. Color TV, phones, pool. Coffee shop and dining room featuring special brunch, lunch, and dinner. Lounge with piano entertainment. $55-$75. AE, VISA, CB, DC, MC (625-6700).

Washington Plaza Hotel — 5th at Westlake. 615 units. Tower section (every room with a spectacular view) and the older Benjamin Franklin section (now being turned into a second tower). Some refrigerators. Air conditioning in most units, TV-radio-music, phones, suites, convention facilities, excellent restaurants (Trader Vic's is on the main floor), plush bars, and first-class nightclub entertainment. Pay garage. Dining rooms and coffee shop 6:30 a.m.-1 a.m.; in winter to 11 p.m. $70-$90. AE, VISA, CB, DC, MC (624-7400).

Airport Lodging

Airport Hilton — 17620 Pacific Highway S. 145 units. Opposite Sea-Tac Airport. Air conditioning, color TV, radios, music, phones, pool, wading pool, airport transportation. Dining room and coffee shop 6 a.m.-2 a.m. Cocktails, entertainment. $58. AE, VISA, CB, DC, MC (244-4800).

Holiday Inn of Sea-Tac — 17338 Pacific Highway S. 260 units. Opposite Sea-Tac. Air conditioning, color TV, music, radios, pool, pets allowed. Dining room and coffee shop 6 a.m.-10 p.m. Cocktails, entertainment. $44-$54. AE, VISA, DC, MC (248-1000).

Hyatt Hotel — 17001 Pacific Highway S. 325 units. Adjacent to Sea-Tac. Air conditioning, color TV, radio, music, phones, some refrigerators, suites, pool, sauna, putting green, airport transportation. Dining room and coffee shop 24 hours. Cocktails and entertainment. $48. AE, VISA, CB, MC, DC (244-6000).

Imperial 400 Motel — 17108 Pacific Highway S. 325 units. Adjacent to Sea-Tac. Air conditioning, color TV, radio, music, phones, 5 kitchens $3 extra. Restaurant. Pool, pets permitted. Airport transportation. $30. AE, VISA, CB, DC, MC (244-1230).

Mariott Hotel — S. 176th & 32nd S. Newest and one of the most luxurious hotels in the Seattle area. On a hill overlooking the airport. 506 rooms. All credit cards. $52-$62. (241-2000).

Red Lion Inn — A giant among large Sea-Tac strip hotels, with an even larger new addition. Excellent restaurant. All amenities. $54-$64. All major credit cards. (246-8600).

TraveLodge at Sea-Tac — 2824 S. 188th. 140 units. Opposite Sea-Tac. Air conditioning, color TV, music, phones, pool, coin laundry, airport transportation. Dining room 6:30 a.m.-10 p.m. Cocktails, entertainment, $39. AE, VISA, CB, DC, MC (246-3600).

Vance Airport Inn — 18220 Pacific Highway S. 150 units. Opposite Sea-Tac. Balconies. Air conditioning, color TV, music, phones, some refrigerators, pool, saunas, therapy pool. Airport transportation. Restaurant 6 a.m.-10 p.m. Cocktails. $39. AE, VISA, CB, DC, MC (246-5535).

Other Motor Inns and Motels

Bellevue Holiday Inn — 11211 Main, Bellevue. 180 rooms. Air conditioning, color TV, phones, pool. Coffee shop 6:30 a.m.-10 p.m. Restaurant 6 p.m.-10 p.m., reservations needed. Entertainment in Lounge. Cocktails. Banquet rooms. $46. AE, VISA, CB, MC (455-5240).

Black Angus Motor Inn — 12245 Aurora N. 52 units. Color TV, phones, suites, pool. Restaurant (Black Angus, of course). 7 a.m.-10 p.m. Cocktails, entertainment. $35. AE, VISA, CB, DC, MC (363-3035).

Century House Motor Hotel — 2224 8th. 70 units. Many with balconies. Color TV, phones, a few refrigerators, pool, no pets. Dining room 6:30 a.m.-10 p.m.; Sat. 8 a.m.-11 p.m., closed Sun. $30. AE, VISA, DC, MC (624-6820).

Continental Plaza Motel — 2500 Aurora N. 90 units. Some air conditioning, color TV, radios, some refrigerators, some 2-room units, suites with kitchens $5 extra, pool, pets permitted. Restaurant 7 a.m.-2 p.m.; summer to 9 p.m. only. $40. AE, VISA, DC, MC (284-1900).

Doubletree Inn — In Southcenter Shopping Center, 200 units. Air conditioning, color TV, radio, music, phones, some refrigerators, suites, pool, airport transportation. Dining room, coffee shop, night club, 24 hours. $40-$52. AE, VISA, CB, DC, MC (246-8220).

Greenwood Inn — 625-116th N.E., Bellevue. 183 units. Air conditioning, color TV, phones, pool. Dining room 7 a.m.-3 p.m.; 5-11:30 p.m. Show lounge with Las Vegas style entertainment Tues.-Sun. Cocktails. Banquet rooms, convention rooms for 500. Catering. $41-$43. AE, VISA, CB, DC, MC (455-9444).

Loyal Inn of Seattle — 2301 8th at Denny Way. 89 units. Air conditioning, color TV, music, phones, some refrigerators, near restaurant, sauna, whirlpool. $34. AE, VISA, CB, DC, MC (682-0200).

Ramada Inn — 2140 N. Northgate Way, near Northgate Shopping Center. 136 units. Air conditioning, color TV, music, phones, restaurant nearby, pool, pets permitted. $40. AE, VISA, CB, DC, MC (365-0700).

Sherwood Inn — 400 N.E. 45th near University District. 134 units. Air conditioning, color TV, phones, some refrigerators, suites, pool. Dining room and coffee shop 6:30 a.m.-10 p.m. Cocktails and nightclub entertainment. $42. AE, VISA, CB, DC, MC (634-0100).

Sixth Avenue Motor Hotel — 2000 6th. 168 units. Color TV, radio, phones, dining room and coffee shop 6 a.m.-10 p.m. Cocktails, entertainment. $44. AE, VISA, CB, DC, MC (682-8300).

Thunderbird Motor Inn — 818 112th N.E., Bellevue. 212 units. Air conditioning, color TV, phones, pool. Dining room 7 a.m.-11 p.m., coffee shop 6:30 a.m.-midnight. Cocktails, entertainment. Banquet rooms. $38-$41. AE, VISA, CB, DC, MC (455-1515).

Towne Motor Hotel — 2205 7th. 94 units. Color TV, radio, music, phones, suites, coffee shop 6 a.m.-8 p.m. Cocktails. $41. AE, VISA, CB, DC, MC (622-3434).

TraveLodge Downtown — 2213 8th. 72 units. Some balconies. Color TV, some radios, phones, restaurant nearby. No pets. $34. AE, VISA, CB, DC (624-6300).

TraveLodge by the Space Needle — 6th N. & John. 89 units. Air conditioning, color TV, radio, music, phones, pool, no pets, no restaurant. $39. AE, VISA, CB, DC, MC (623-2600).

Tropics Motor Hotel — 166 Aurora N. 160 units. Air conditioning, color TV, many radios, phones, suites, indoor pool, covered parking. Dining room 7 a.m.-10 p.m., cocktails & entertainment $34. AE, VISA, CB, DC, MC (624-6789).

University Inn — 4140 Roosevelt Way N.E. (University District). 42 units. Some balconies, color TV, phones, 18 kitchens extra. Pool. Coffee shop 6 a.m.-6 p.m. $26. AE, VISA, CB, DC, MC (632-5055).

YMCA — 909 4th. 240 rooms. For students, youths (25 & under), foreign visitors, men, women, and families. Attractive, carpeted rooms, phones, available with color TV/radio, some rooms with private bath. All guests may use physical facilities and participate in resident program activities. Barbershop, tailor, laundry, and restaurant. $16-$18. MC, VISA (382-5000).

Trailer and Tenting Facilities

There are few regular campgrounds in the immediate Seattle area. However, a number of trailer parks with complete hookups welcome overnight guests.

North

Canyon Mobile Park — 3333 228th S.E., Bothell, 98011 (481-3005). Overnighters welcome.

Country Club Mobile Park — 23732 Locust Way, Bothell, 98011 (486-1622). RVs, tents. Adults only.

National Trailer Park — 912 N. 125th, 98133 (362-1408). RVs.

Overland Manor — 1210 N. 152nd, 98133 (363-8558). RVs, tents.

Seattle North KOA — 22910 15th S.E., Bothell, 98011 (486-1972). RVs, tents.

Silver Shores Mobile Home Park — 11621 W. Silver Lake Dr., Everett 98204 (337-8741). RVs, tents. Exit at 128th St. S.W. on I-5 south of Everett.

Trailer Haven — 11724 Aurora N., 98133 (362-4211). RVs.

University Trailer Park — 2200 N.E. 88th, 98115 (525-7828). RVs.

South

Aqua Barn Ranch — 15227 S.E. Renton-Maple Valley Hwy., Renton 98055 (255-4618). RVs, tents.

Burien Trailer Gardens — 14239 Des Moines Way S., 98188
  (243-7888). RVs.
    RVs.
Lakeshore Manor — 11448 Rainier S., 98178 (772-0299). RVs,
  tents.
Orchard Trailer Park — 4011 S. 146th, 98168 (243-1210). RVs.
Rainbow Trailer Haven — 3714 S. 152nd, 98188 (243-3548).
  RVs.
Skyway Mobile Home Park — 13000 Empire Way S., 98178
  (772-4777). RVs.
Willow Vista Trailer Village — 21740 84th S., Kent 98031
  (872-8264). RVs, tents.

East

Seattle Safari — Rt. 1, Box 428F, Snoqualmie 98065 (888-1324).
  RVs, tents. At junction of Hwy. 18 and I-90.
Snoqualmie River Park — P.O. Box 16, Fall City 98024 (222-
  5545). RVs, tents. Hwy. 203 at Fall City.
Trailer Inns — 15531 S.E. Eastgate Way, Bellevue 98006 (747-
  9181). RVs. Exit 11A. Hwy. 405.
Vasa Park Resort — 3560 W. Lake Sammamish Rd., S.E.,
  Bellevue 98008 (746-3260). RVs, tents. Open Apr. 15-Oct.
  15.

King County Park

John MacDonald Memorial Park — Hwy. 203 4½ mi. N. of Fall
  City. RVs, tents.

State Parks

Fay Bainbridge — Ferry to Bainbridge Island; N.E. end of
  island. Tents. (842-3931).
Dash Point — Hwy. 509 5 mi. N.E. of Tacoma. RVs, tents.
  (927-3042).
Saltwater — Hwy. 509 18 mi. S. of Seattle. RVs, tents. Take Des
  Moines exit, I-5.
  For further information concerning State Parks, write the
State Parks & Recreation Commission, P.O. Box 1128, Olympia,
98504. During the summer months call toll free (1-800-562-
8200).

PARKS

Seattle and King County Play Areas

VARIETY expresses one concept of Seattle's wide-ranging Parks and Recreation System. From David Denny's first five-acre park donation, now a grassy lawn near the center of the city, Seattle's parks today encompass nearly 4,774 acres spread from one end of the city to the other.

Multiple facilities are operated by the Seattle Parks and Recreation Department. See Sports and Recreation section for swimming pools and tennis courts. For more information call 625-4671. A folder in two colors showing the location of each of the park facilities may be obtained free by writing to Seattle Parks, 100 Dexter Ave. N., Seattle, WA 98009.

Picnic Reservations — Shelter sites may be reserved year-round at these parks: Carkeek, Discovery, Seward, Woodland, Lincoln, and Gas Works. Fee is $5 per group of 50 (625-4671).

Overnight Park Facilities

Red Barn Ranch — 17601 Moneysmith Rd., Auburn (854-3690). Open to groups by reservation only for day or overnight use. Facilities on the 40-acre ranch include horseback riding, heated indoor/outdoor swimming pool, tennis and basketball courts, meeting hall, arts and crafts room, bunkhouse with restrooms and showers for 60, staff bunkhouse for 11, dining hall, and kitchen. Groups must have adult leadership and a preplanned program.

Camp Long — 35th S.W. & S.W. Dawson (935-0370). Sixty-eight acres open to organized groups for camping and wilderness skills programs; call the camp or Parks Dept. for children's camping programs.

Community Centers

Along with picnicking, flopping in the sun on green grass, swimming at a fresh or salt water beach, and playing softball, tennis, or one-court basketball, your Seattle and King County park systems operate community recreation centers, often in

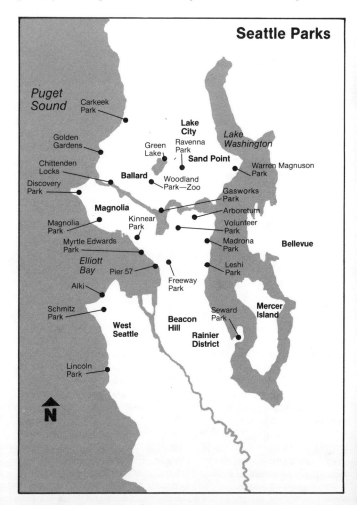

connection with a school building. The range of free and for-fee activities offered will boggle your mind. Formerly called "recreation centers," the Park Departments prefer the new term to emphasize the broader concept of community activities centered at the facilities.

Each of the Seattle centers publishes four seasonal program brochures that describe and schedule programmed activities; plan to get one for your area. Look too at the special centers for arts and crafts at Seward Park, and the Pratt Fine Arts Center, for dance instruction at Madrona Park, and rock climbing at Camp Long. Poncho Theater at Woodland Park and the Bathhouse Theater at Green Lake offer programs for aspiring thespians. Most of the Community Centers offer similar programs, but more ambitious arts and crafts programs may be offered in one than another — or different sports and other activities will be offered in one center and not another. Call the Park Department Information (625-4671) for further information.

Park districts offer a different range of activities, such as track and field meets, overnight camping via bikes or car transportation, canoe trips, and play days.

King County Parks

Outside Seattle the King County Parks Division maintains 61 facilities (at last count) that offer variety — from indoor swimming pools to green grass for quiet contemplation. Since the first King County park opened for public recreation in 1937, the park system has grown until it now encompasses 5,000 acres under the direction of 130 full-time specialists. Park sizes vary from tiny Enatai Beach at ¼ acre just off the south corner of the East Channel bridge on I-90 to 486-acre Marymoor Park in Redmond. A major jump in King county parks resulted from approval in 1968 of Forward Thrust bonds to provide $49 million for purchasing and developing up to 120 new parks, swimming pools, and related facilites. (See Sports and Recreation for pool listings.)

Activities at King County Parks feature do-it-yourself recreation — swimming, launching your boat, sunbathing, and playing ball with friends. Organized activities continue year around with holiday parties, story telling, classes in everything from slimming to crafts, and outings for senior citizens and handicapped children. Sports lessons are offered on a challenging schedule at many facilities.

For complete information on current and upcoming programs, call 344-3982 on weekdays between 8:30 a.m. and 4:30 p.m. Or, write to Department of Community Development, Parks Division, 226 King County Courthouse, Seattle, WA 98104 to receive recreation bulletins regularly.

Other Park Facilities

Bellevue, Mercer Island, Renton, and Kirkland are a few of the surrounding suburbs that also maintain their own independent park and recreation programs. Check with the city hall in each of these surrounding cities for complete information on their recreation programs and facilities.

Special Parks

Among Seattle's parks are special spots — unique to Seattle for one reason or another and treasured by citizens and guests alike. Each offers its own special charm. These are our pick —

Waterfront Park is peopled mostly by Seattleites although visitors to the Elliott Bay docks just north of the ferry terminal also roam around the viewpoints and water access. Seattleites grab for the quiet and serenity near their bustling work location or professional office — only a few steps down University or Union and under the Alaskan Way viaduct to a clear spot with benches and walkways to watch the ever-changing panorama of Elliott Bay with Puget Sound and the Olympics beyond. Gulls circle overhead and cascades of water tumble over the gigantic fountain near the park's northern end. A glass-enclosed public viewing gallery with an outside deck is at the end of Pier 57. The promenade extends to Seattle's waterfront Aquarium (see Aquarium listing in Sightseeing.)

Discovery Park represents a bounty from the military and will be developed gradually in the years ahead. Seattle acquired nearly 400 acres of the property at the northwest corner of Magnolia Bluff from what was Fort Lawton. The land includes 2 miles of beaches, isolated forested ravines, small streams, and open meadows — and plans are to reserve much of it as a nature park. Cars and motorized vehicles are banned from the park except for designated parking areas. To explore its many treasures, you must hoof it along the trails. A half-mile "parcours"

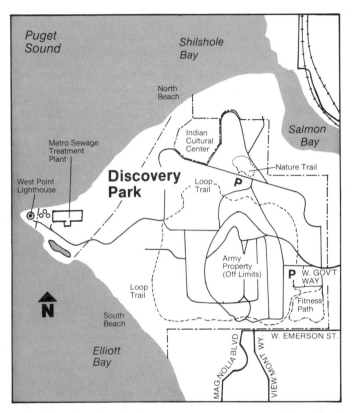

or health path with 15 exercise stations winds through woods of alder and maple. Discovery Park's comparative isolation from the city's noise, dramatic views, varied topography, and expansive natural areas offer the visitor a chance to enjoy a wilderness experience only minutes from Seattle's bustling city center. Included in the multiple-use park is Daybreak Star, an Indian cultural center where you can watch Indian craftsmen at work, plus musicians and dancers. It is near the main gate.

Enter the park from the south at W. Emerson and Perkins Lane. A north gate opens near W. Commodore Way and 40th W. The main gate is at W. Government Way and 36th W. Along the beach area the Coast Guard operates the West Point Light

Station, open 1-4 p.m. weekends and holidays. Discovery Park is open daily from dawn to dark. For more information on the park and times for guided nature walks and programs, call 625-4636. Park headquarters are at 3801 W. Government Way, Seattle, WA 98199.

Woodland Park Zoo — If you haven't been to the Zoo lately, you haven't been to the Zoo. New exhibits are everywhere: a Nocturnal House reverses night and day; the Swamp and Marsh feature scattered ponds and an outdoor aviary filled with ducks, herons, coots and other water birds; gorillas roam through a tropical forest with streams, boulders, natural soils, and ample trees for climbing; Asian monkeys leap through tropical forest islands, scampering across waterfalls to chase fellow simians. The latest dream come true is the African Savanna, a paradise for animals and visitors. Lions, hippos, patas monkeys, giraffes, zebras, springboks, walk-through aviary, land and water birds. A slice of the grasslands of Africa right here in Seattle. Observe animals in natural groupings behaving naturally in naturalistic settings. What could be more natural? Only nature itself, and for those who cannot visit the real savanna, the tropical forests, or other faraway lands, Woodland Park Zoo is the next best thing.

Take your time and enjoy the Zoo. Visitors are not permitted to feed the animals and must stay on the pathways. Call 625-4550 for summer programs and information.

The Zoo opens at 8:30 a.m. every day of the year. Closing time varies from 4-6 p.m. according to the season. Admission: $2.50 adults 18-64; $1 youths 13-17; 50¢ children 6-12, senior citizens, and handicapped; free under 6. Annual Passes are your best bet: $7.50 individual, $15 family (including children and their grandparents). Schools and other groups call 625-4550 for admission fees and tour information.

Gas Works Park gets its name from the remains of a plant for manufacturing heating and lighting gas on the north shore of Lake Union. The rusting black towers added drabness to part of Lake Union's skyline for years. Plans for the park called for retaining the bulbous and odd-looking contraptions. A viewing mound offers visitors an unparalleled view of Seattle's skyline from the north. No need to carry your wristwatch; atop the Great Mound is a huge concrete aggregate and bronze sundial. You stand at a specific spot and your shadow marks the hour. You reach Gas Works Park from Pacific Avenue that follows the water back of the plants and docks that front on the water.

GOTHIC GHOSTS of the GASWORKS

Gothic Ghosts guard Gasworks Park at the north end of Lake Union. Now incorporated into the park's facilities, the outmoded monoliths create a fun atmosphere for kids and the surrounding hills provide one of Seattle's choice kite flying spots.

Since Lake Union is a "working lake," the park affords visitors one of the few opportunities to reach the water of Seattle's most centrally located lake. A series of cement arches from a former railway trestle serve as an entrance. An old boiler house with an overhead maze of pipes remaining is a play barn. A picnic shelter and restrooms are also open; the shelter can be reserved for large groups with 2 weeks' notice. Many of the discarded pumps, large machinery, and equipment pieces are refurbished with bright paint — a park full of recycled industrial equipment that is spooky, grotesque, entertaining, stark, fascinating, historical — and a little sad but full of hope for a new life of fun and play.

Freeway Park — Imagine, if you can, the 8-lane freeway roaring through the heart of Seattle as a natural phenomenon — a deep river canyon, for example. Forget that it once encompassed houses, streets, trees, and lamp posts. With this concrete river canyon effectively splitting the town in half, something

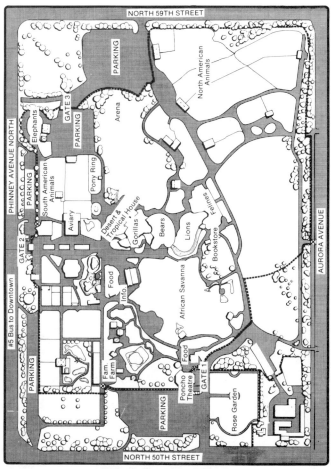

Woodland Park Zoo

was needed to tie the town back together, and to provide a place for people to relax, to eat a brown-bag lunch, to sit beneath trees, and for children to play.

This, in essence, is what went through the minds of the planners who were responsible for Freeway Park. First, they put a big lid over the freeway to create a 5.4 acre platform on which to build the park. They poured tons of concrete, installed miles of pipe, then planted acres of lawn, groundcovers, pathways, plazas, fountains, and waterfalls. Surprisingly, the sound of the waterfalls and fountains plus the screens of trees and shrubs muffle the roar of the freeway only a few feet below.

The park is bordered by 6th Ave. on the west, Spring St. on the south, University St. on the north, and except for a boot-shaped section of pools and lawns, 8th Ave. on the north.

Between Spring and Seneca Streets is a vast "box garden" where big concrete boxes installed at different levels hold plants of various species. From Seneca to University is a concrete canyon with waterfalls of different heights.

Myrtle Edwards and Elliott Bay Park — Two new, adjoining parks run from Pier 71 to Pier 86 with a 1.25 mile pathway for walking or biking along the waterfront. Benches are situated beside the pathway, and there are grassy areas for kite flying. The pathway follows the bulkheaded waterfront until the northern end where it swings past the massive grain elevators blocking the view of Elliott Bay to end at Pier 86, the import car terminal (lemon grove). The Myrtle Edwards Park is at the southern end and has the controversial lumps of stone some consider sculpture.

Seattle Parks Special — Call Metro (447-4800) for information on the parks special routes that touch on the major parks in the city. They run on Sundays and holidays and cost 50¢ for an all-day pass. Buses have logos with "Seattle Parks, North" or "South" on them.

GALLERIES AND MUSEUMS

NW *Arts & Crafts At Their Best*

DURING the past decade Seattle has had an explosion of private galleries, much to the delight of regional artists who had few regional outlets, and patrons who didn't want to go East to buy paintings by a fellow who lived down the street. There are so many now that one wonders if we might not be having too much of a good thing, because galleries have a way of appearing one day then disappearing shortly afterward with the ebb tide of public acceptance.

The following list was accurate at the time it was compiled, but given the high gallery mortality rate, some may be defunct. Call first. Where possible, we have left out those little holes-in-the-wall that call themselves galleries when they actually are places that sell houseplants, bird seed, used books, and an occasional piece of pottery crafted by a niece or son-in-law in an adult-education course.

The other galleries have no need for apologies. They are permitting artists of definite ability and talent to earn enough money to continue their work, and presenting patrons with a wider selection of excellence from which to choose.

Galleries

American Art Gallery — 311½ Occidental S. (447-9477). Specializes in Western art, turn-of-the-century paintings, and sculpture. Hours: 10 a.m.-5:30 p.m. Wed.-Sat.; Noon-5 Sun.

and/or — 1525 10th (324-5880). Exhibits and encourages new art forms, such as video, film, music, and contemporary performance. Workshops, electronic music lessons, arts library. Hours: 11 a.m.-6 p.m. daily.

The Art Gallery — Frederick & Nelson, 5th & Pine (682-

5500, ext. 754). International collection of oils and watercolors; signed and numbered lithographs, etchings and serigraphs; oriental paintings, scrolls, panels and screens. Hours: store hours.

Artists Gallery Northwest — 7814 Greenwood N. (782-0991). Nonprofit cooperative for artists with shows held in malls, fairs, and banks. Hours: daily 11 a.m.-5 p.m.; closed Mon.

Crane Gallery — 1326 6th (622-7185). Antique Asian art emphasizing ceramics. Hours: Mon.-Sat. 10 a.m.-6 p.m.

Davidson — 702 1st (624-7684). Original prints from the 15th to the 20th Century. Tues.-Sat. noon-5 p.m.

East-West Galleries — 102 S. Jackson (583-0030). Post-Expressionist works. Hours: 11 a.m.-6 p.m. Tues.-Sat.

Erica Williams/Anne Johnson Gallery — 317 E. Pine (623-7078). European and Israeli graphics. Hours: Wed.-Sat. 11 a.m.-5 p.m.

Foster/White Gallery — 311½ Occidental S. (622-2833). Contemporary regional painting and sculpture, including Morris Graves and Mark Tobey. Hours: Mon.-Sat. 10 a.m.-5:30 p.m.; Sun. noon-5 p.m.

Francine Seders Gallery — 6701 Greenwood N. (782-0355). Paintings, graphics, sculpture, crafts, and minerals. Hours: Tues.-Sun. 11 a.m.-5 p.m.

Linda Farris Gallery — 322 2nd S. (623-1110). Contemporary paintings and prints. Hours: Tues.-Sat. 11:30 a.m.-5 p.m.; Thurs. evening 5:30-8:30 p.m.; Sun. 1-5 p.m.

Gallery Mack — 123 S. Jackson (623-1414). International and regional artists.

Gordon Woodside Galleries — 1101 Howell (622-7243). Contemporary paintings and sculpture. Hours: daily 11 a.m.-6 p.m.

Gray Gull — Pier 70 (623-2830). Arts, crafts, and contemporary art. Hours: Mon.-Sat. 10 a.m.-9 p.m.; Sun. noon-6 p.m.

Greenwood Gallery — 89 Yesler (682-8900). Contemporary art. Hours: Mon.-Sat. 10 a.m.-5 p.m.

Haines Gallery — 8015 15th N.W. (783-7227). Paintings, sculpture, graphics, and crafts by Northwest artists. Hours: Wed.-Sat. noon-5 p.m.; Sun. 1-5 p.m.

Kiku Gallery of Fine Art — 818 E. Pike (323-1141). Regional and American. Hours: Tues.-Fri 11:30 a.m.-4:30 p.m.; Sat. 10 a.m.-5 p.m.

The Kirsten Gallery — 5320 Roosevelt Way N.E. (522-2011). Contemporary, experimental, Far Eastern mysticism. Hours: Daily 11 a.m.-5 p.m.; Thurs. til 9 p.m.

Legacy Ltd. —71 Marion (624-6350). India, Eskimo, and Aleut art. Hours: Mon.-Sat. 10 a.m.-6 p.m.

The Little Gallery — Frederick & Nelson, 5th & Pine (682-5500). Professional Washington artists and craftsmen. Hours: store hours.

Magnolia Gallery — 3210½ W. McGraw, Magnolia Village (283-1757). Contemporary artists. Hours: Tues.-Sat. 10 a.m.-6 p.m. Closed Mon.

National Art Gallery — Bon Marche, 4th & Pine (344-2121). Contemporary artists, both local and international: Hours: store hours.

NN Gallery — 2421 1st (623-0998). Paintings, sculpture, photography, wall hangings, weaving, batik, and ceramics. Mickery Puppetry Theater during autumn, winter, and spring. Hours: Mon.-Sat. 11:30 a.m.-5 p.m.; Sun. noon-5 p.m.; Fri. 7-9 p.m.

Northwest Craft Center — Seattle Center (624-7563). Hours: June, July, Aug. daily 11 a.m.-6 p.m.; open daily except Mon. rest of the year.

Penryn Gallery — 1920½ 1st (623-0495). Contemporary art. Hours: Tues.-Sat. 10:30 a.m.-5 p.m.

Richard Nash Gallery — 89 Yesler Way (622-1656). Contemporary American prints, ceramics, and glass. Hours: Tues.-Sat. noon-5 p.m.

Silver Image — 92 S. Washington (623-8116). Photographic art, historical and modern. Hours: Tues.-Sat. 11 a.m.-5:30 p.m.; Sun. 1-5 p.m.

Snow Goose Associates — 4220 N.E. 125th (362-3401). Eskimo prints and sculpture from Canadian Arctic; Northwest Coast Indian artwork. Hours: Oct. thru April, Fri.-Sat. 1-5 p.m.

Stillwater Gallery — 1900 Northlake Way (634-1900). Works of Northwest artists and marine art. Hours: Tues.-Fri. 11 a.m.-5 p.m.; Sat.-Sun. 11 a.m.-4 p.m.

Museums

Bellevue Art Museum — 10310 N.E. 4th, Bellevue (454-3322). A new museum representing a goal of the Pacific Northwest Arts and Crafts Association. The museum houses a permanent collection, which is rotated on display; presents traveling and special exhibitions; loaned exhibits; and sells crafts before Christmas in a show. The Bellevue Art Museum School offers classes for adults and children. Admission to the museum is free. Hours: 12-5 p.m. Tues.-Sun.

Coast Guard Museum — Pier 36 (442-5019). Opened in 1977, this is the first museum in the West to explain the work and history of the Coast Guard. Housed in the small, one-story building is a collection of navigational aids, including an octant, chronometer, and magnetic compass. Also on display are ship models, Arctic ivory, and a 4-foot high Fresnel lens made in France for a Puget Sound lighthouse. Nearby is the Puget Sound Vessel Traffic Center, where you can watch Guardsmen monitor ship traffic or on weekends join a guided tour of an ice breaker, cutter, or other ship in port. Hours: Wed. noon-4 p.m.; weekends & holidays 1-5 p.m. Vessel Traffic Center open 8 a.m.-4 p.m. daily. Free.

Fort Lawton Military Museum   Enter the Fort (and Discovery Park) at W. Government Way & 36th W.; the guard will direct you to the museum in the old signal building. The museum was established in late 1976 by the Seattle-King county Military History Society. It has 4 rooms plus a library filled with army mementos from the Civil War to the Vietnam era and photos of Fort Lawton at full strength. Hours: noon-4 p.m., the first 3 weekends of the month. Also available for group tours at other times (281-3060).

Frye Art Museum (Charles and Emma) — 704 Terry (corner of Terry and Cherry), P.O. Box 3005 (622-9250). Works by Edouard Manet, Childe Hassam, Hans Thoma, and other 19th century painters, plus a few 20th century painters such as Andrew Wyeth and Mary Cassatt. The museum also holds frequent contemporary art exhibits and special displays and frequent photographic exhibits. Each year a juried Puget Sound Area Exhibition is sponsored with cash prizes. Guided tours arranged by advance notice. Parking is free in museum lots. Wheelchair entrance at rear; ring buzzer. Free. Hours: Mon.-Sat. 10 a.m.-6 p.m. Closed Thanksgiving and Christmas.

Goodwill Industries Memory Lane Museum — 1400 S. Lane (329-1000). The management thwarted antique hunters, who for years haunted the hangar-like store for bargains, by deciding to hang onto the antiques and display them in a museum within the building. Many of the objects are hanging from the ceiling beams, including coffee mills, sausage grinders, Confederate money, spinning wheels, baby buggies, sabers, grain mallets, high-button shoes, and even a stuffed armadillo. An extensive wardrobe collection is put to use in vintage fashion shows every Wednesday except July, August, and December, at noon in the store and frequently at gatherings around Seattle. Free.

Hours: Mon.-Fri. 11 a.m.-7 p.m.; Sat. 11 a.m.-5 p.m., Sun. 1-4 p.m. Closed major holidays.

Henry Gallery — University of Washington campus, 15th N.E. & N.E. Campus Parkway (543-2280). Originally a public art gallery, the establishment reached museum status with its permanent collection of more than 1,500 works from early 19th and 20th century American and European paintings, prints, and ceramics. Numerous Japanese folk ceramics as well. Some 35 exhibitions are shown each year. Co-sponsors film series, lectures, concerts, poetry readings, workshops, and other special events. Free (some lectures and special events have fees,

WEST SEATTLE LIGHT HOUSE

Christopher Paul Bollen

Standing sentinel at the tip of Alki Beach, the West Seattle Lighthouse, though also open to visitors, continues to aid Puget Sound water traffic with its light and booming foghorn.

however). Hours: Mon.-Sat. 10 a.m.-5 p.m. (Thurs. 10-10), Sun. 1-5 p.m. Closed major holidays.

Klondike Gold Rush National Historical Park — See Walking Tours: Pioneer Square.

Museum of History and Industry — 2161 E. Hamlin (324-1125). The best collection of Seattle's history. The spacious museum depicts its events from founding on a smelly tideflat to today. Dioramas depict the founding and several subsequent events, plus photographs of the founders and their documents. Photographs and artifacts from early years. Yesler Mill, shipyards, Klondike gold rush era, Boeing beginnings. A major collection of marine equipment such as wheels from famous ships, engines, bells, and submarine periscopes. The famous hydroplane, Slo-Mo-Shun IV is also displayed. Boeing's famous B-1 seaplane that delivered the first air mail from Seattle to Victoria hangs from the ceiling. A major doll collection with a fantastic house. Several antique cars, fire engines, and a cable car are in the basement level. A special room is devoted to stuffed animals (including the zoo's late gorilla Bobo) and mounted heads from all over the world. Excellent reference library with extensive photo collection. Special children's events and handicraft classes. "Christmas Around the World" is a special holiday program where various nationalities present their Christmas customs. Free but donations accepted. Hours: Tues.-Fri. 11 a.m.-5 p.m.; Sat. 10 a.m.-5 p.m.; Sun. noon-5 p.m. Closed Mon., Christmas, Thanksgiving, New Years, and Memorial Day. Usually open July 4 if not on Monday. Gift shop just added.

Nordic Heritage Museum — 3014 67th N.W. (789-5707). Features the social and family life of nordic countries and the life of immigrants to the U.S. Annual Nordic Yule Fest and other events held in museum. Hours: 11 a.m.-3 p.m. Wed.; 7-9 p.m. Thurs.; 1-5 p.m. Sat.-Sun.

Postal Museum — Pioneer Square Station, 302 Occidental S. (623-1908). Patron rental boxes, three-wheeled carts, documents dating back to the last century, wooden pens with metal points, 2-cent prepaid envelopes, antique postal scales, postal regulation books, canvas mail pouches, and numerous other items in the growing collection. It is undoubtedly one of the few branch post offices in the country with an attached museum (yes, you can mail a letter there). Free. Hours: Mon.-Fri 9 a.m.-5 p.m. Closed Sat., Sun. and legal holidays.

Seattle Art Museum — Volunteer Park, 14th E. and E. Prospect (447-4710). The museum was established in 1933 through the generosity of Dr. Richard Fuller and his late mother, Mrs. Eugene Fuller. They began the museum's internationally famous collection of art from the Orient with an emphasis on jades, sculptures, ceramics, paintings, screens, and decorative art. In addition, the museum has an outstanding collection of Renaissance and Impressionist paintings. The Samuel H. Kress galleries in the museum feature a ceiling fresco by Giovanni Tiepolo (1696-1770) and the "Venus and Adonis" by Paolo Caliari. The Norman H. Davis collection of ancient Greek coins is accepted as one of the most complete on the West Coast. There also is an extensive collection of Greek pottery and relics from the Aegean Sea dating back to the Bronze and Iron Ages. The regional art collection is one of the largest such collections in the country, and it includes Mark Tobey, Kenneth Callahan, and other Pacific Northwest artists. The Seattle Art Museum is oriented to the community and has free public tours every Wednesday at 12:30 p.m. and every Sunday at 2 p.m.; free film series throughout the year; free chamber music concerts in the 240-seat auditorium; Senior Citizen Day the first Friday of every month (except during summer months); lectures, travelogues, tours, art classes for children, lending services for slides and tours, and an annual architectural tour of outstanding Seattle homes. Hours: Tues.-Sat. 10 a.m.-5 p.m.; Thurs. eve. 7-10 p.m.; Sun. noon-5 p.m. Closed Mon., New Year's Day, Christmas, Thanksgiving, Memorial Day. Closes at 1 p.m. Dec. 24 and 31. Open July 4 if not Monday. Art Museum members, free. Non-members: adults $1; students and senior citizens 50¢. Children free if accompanied by an adult. Every Thursday is free day.

Seattle Art Museum Pavilion — Seattle Center (447-4710). The Seattle Center arm of the museum is used mainly for exhibits of contemporary art, juried exhibits, traveling art shows, regional art, and occasional special exhibits and musical events. Also sells art books, prints, jewelry, and crafts. Adults $1; students and senior citizens 50¢. Free every Thursday. Hours: Tues.-Sat. 10 a.m.-5 p.m.; Thurs. til 9 p.m.; Sun. & some holidays, noon-5 p.m.

Seattle Children's Museum — See Children.

Thomas Burke Memorial Washington State Museum — University of Washington Campus just inside the 17th N.E. and N.E. 45th entrance (543-5590). An outstanding collection of North American Indian culture with artifacts from the Northwest Coast tribes — Bella Coola, Tlingit, Haida, Kwakiutl, and

Nootka. Many masks used by dancers and shamans; spirit boards used in ceremonial dances; carved storage boxes and chests; ceremonial blankets, wool, and cedar bark clothing. The Hall of Anthropology has a collection of fossil plants, a dinosaur footprint, several skulls for the morbid, and an outstanding collection of moths and butterflies. The Hall of Ornithology features a collection of coastal sea-birds, owls, rare and extinct birds, and a push-button system that lets you hear the songs of several varieties of birds. Several exhibits are from the Pacific Islands, including a large collection of tapa cloth from the Tonga Islands and items from Polynesia, Micronesia, and other Pacific Islands. Eskimo and Greek artifacts also are displayed. Free. Hours: Tues.-Sat. 10 a.m.-4:30 p.m.; Thurs. til 9 p.m.; Sun. 1-4:30 p.m. Closed Mon. and legal holidays.

Wing Luke Museum — 414 8th S. (623-5124). This museum to preserve and interpret Chinese culture is named for a former city councilman who died in 1965 when his plane crashed in the Cascades. Permanent exhibits include such diverse items as firecrackers, fans, parasols, herb remedies, unusual foods, and photographs. Special exhibits and classes are offered in brush painting. Lectures and demonstrations of techniques in Origami. Art auctions are held each November to raise funds. Free. Hours: They vary so call first. Usually Tues.-Fri. 11 a.m.-4:30 p.m. and some evenings.

TRANSPORTATION

Getting Around Can Be Fun

SEATTLE is known as the jumping-off city for Alaska, the Arctic, and the Orient (it is closer to Japan than any other major U.S. city). Consequently, the Seattle-Tacoma International Airport and the Port of Seattle have a distinctly international flavor to them with families dressed in parkas and mukluks rubbing shoulders with Orientals and East Indians.

Airlines

These major airlines use Sea-Tac and connect with all other international airlines and have either headquarters or offices there:

Alaska Airlines (433-3100), American (433-3950), Braniff International (623-2390), British Airways (382-9180), Continental Airlines (624-1740), Delta (241-2300), Eastern Airlines (622-1881), Finn Air (223-1033), Mexicana Airlines (623-5228), National Airlines (447-9001), Northwest Orient Airlines (433-3500), Pacific Western Airlines (433-5088), Pan Am (624-2121), Republic (433-6600), Reeve Aleutian (433-5696), Scandinavian Airlines (SAS) (800-421-0850), Thai (241-9400), Trans World, (447-9400), United Airlines (682-3700), Western Airlines (433-4711), Wien Air Alaska (433-5285).

These commuter airlines serve smaller cities in the Northwest: Air Oregon (800-547-9308), Cascade Airways (762-2970), Evergreen International (433-5666), Harbor Airlines (433-5330), Pearson Aircraft (622-6077), San Juan Airlines (624-0215).

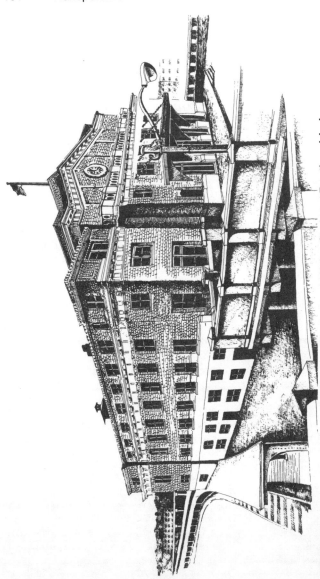

The chuffing of steam engines has ceased to echo in the old Union Station at Fourth and Jackson.

Airport Transportation

Getting to and from Sea-Tac, and parking there, isn't nearly the irritating experience it was before the new multimillion dollar terminal was completed. Now it is a simple matter to drive out, park in the gigantic covered parking lot across from the terminal, and get to the gate as fast as you can walk or ride the automated subway system.

Another alternative is parking your car at one of the numerous outdoor parking lots on Pacific Highway S. near the terminal, all of which provide minibus transportation to the terminal. This is especially recommended if you are going to leave your car overnight or longer since it will cost you about one-fourth as much. The major disadvantage of the private parking lots is that your car will be left outside during your absence.

It is best to call the parking lots, and the airport, for prices on parking. After computing what it will cost, you can compare that against the cost of catching a cab downtown to the Olympic Airline Terminal, 415 Seneca, or the Washington Plaza, 5th & Westlake, and taking the bus to the airport. One-way costs $3.60. A taxicab costs roughly $15 for the same trip. The Suburban Airporter runs from north and east of Lake Washington — cost ranges up to $8.

If you're staying in an airport area hotel, most provide free shuttlebus service to and from the terminal with free phones in the baggage-claim area.

Some phone numbers: Airport Hustlebus Service (343-2070), Sea-Tac Parking Garage (433-5307), Airport Thrifty Parking (246-7565), Airport Dollar Parking (246-5402), Suburban Airporter (455-2355).

AMTRAK

Seattle is served by AMTRAK, and its geographical location makes it a major junction. Seattle catches AMTRAK trains going north and south, and east. A spur AMTRAK route runs to Vancouver, B.C., to connect with the fantastic Canadian passenger train system. The southern route from Seattle heads down the length of Oregon and California. Two choices are available from Seattle to the east: one across the very top of the nation and the other a bit south. The depot is at 3rd & S. Jackson. For information on schedules, prices, and reservations, call 464-1930.

Buses

Metro Transit

Seattle-King County Metro bus system is very good and getting better. It is a county-wide service that covers the entire city of Seattle and schedules runs to all suburban areas, plus routes that go to Tacoma, Enumclaw, Black Diamond, Issaquah, North Bend, Fall City, Carnation, Redmond, and as far east as Skykomish on the Stevens Pass Highway (U.S. Highway 2).

The basic fare is 50¢ anywhere inside the city limits, and an additional 25¢ to other points in King County. You pay as you get on when going toward downtown Seattle, and as you leave the bus headed away from town (to avoid having drivers collect fares in congested areas).

There are a number of plans and fare reductions offered by Metro: On Sundays and holidays a person 16 or older with up to two children, through age 15, pays only one fare.

Senior citizens 65 and older, blind and disabled persons may obtain a $2 monthly pass which allows unlimited rides.

Ticket books with $10 in passes are available at the Metro Customer Assistance Office, 1214 3rd, and a number of banks.

Drivers do not provide change, but if you place a larger amount in the fare box, the driver will on request give you a refund coupon which will be honored at the Customer Assistance Office.

Passes: An all-day pass is sold by drivers on weekends and holidays for $1.25 adults, 60¢ youths 5-15, which gives you a full day's riding privileges. Annual Pass — $209 within city limits, $313.50 in King County for those who ride constantly. Monthly pass $19 and $28.50.

Pets — Well-behaved dogs are welcome, but those appearing to weigh more than 20 pounds will be charged a regular people fare, but no zone fares. Seeing-eye dogs ride free. Cats and other pets must be in a carrier. The driver has the right to refuse a pet boarding, and can force you to remove the pet from the bus, or not let you and your pet enter the bus at all when it is crowded.

It's Free! Metro's Magic Carpet service offers free rides in the downtown area bordered by 6th and the freeway, Battery, the Waterfront and Jackson. The city reimburses Metro for this service, and all you have to do is get on and off and forget about fares. You can board buses from either the front or rear door in this zone, but when the bus leaves it, you'll have to pay the normal 50¢ fare as you disembark.

For other information — routes, schedules — call the 24-hour information number, 447-4800. It is usually busy so you'll have to wait frequently unless you call very early in the morning or the evening. For a detailed map of routes, timetables for each route you're interested in, zone information, and a "Fun Book," which has suggestions of things to do and places to see, call the Consumer Information Office (447-4800), or write Metro Transit, P.O. Box 4325, Seattle, 98104.

Seattle Parks Special — See Parks for information on this special route to Seattle's major parks.

Inter-City

Seattle is served by the two major transcontinental bus lines, Greyhound and Trailways. Greyhound serves other cities and towns in the state; Trailways can operate only between states, which means its busses make no stops until they reach Oregon or Idaho. Information: Greyhound, 8th & Stewart (624-3456); Trailways, 1936 Westlake (624-5955).

Bridges

Mercer Island Floating Bridge — Its real name is the Lacey B. Murrow Floating Bridge, but nobody ever calls it that and probably no more than one percent of the population knows, or cares, who Lacey Murrow was. It was built in 1940 of honeycombed cement to form a mile-long bridge connecting Seattle with Mercer Island. A floating drawspan near the eastern end permits the occasional tug and log boom or exceptionally large boats to pass through. Otherwise, boats go under high-rise sections at either end. It can be a thrill driving across the bridge when a storm is kicking up the lake and throwing water over the side and against cars. It is best to avoid the Mercer Island span during rush hours, because even with a reversible lane giving three lanes of traffic, a bottleneck generally develops both in the morning and night. There has been no toll since 1949.

Evergreen Point Floating Bridge — This newer one lays claim to being the longest floating bridge in the world (1.4 miles). It offers spectacular views of the entire area. It has a two-part span and fountains on each end that occasionally spout. The best news, though, is that the bridge toll has been removed, which causes Seattle grumps to mutter about how easy it is now for out-of-towners to get into town without paying for the privilege.

Hood Canal Floating Bridge — This was the longest saltwater floating bridge in the world, for those impressed with size. It is also the only broken bridge in Puget Sound. It sank in a 1979 winter storm, and a ferry carries people across now. Check with the state ferries for routes and prices while the bridge debate goes on.

Ferries

Alaska Marine Highway System — Better, and more succinctly, known as the Alaska Ferries. This is one of the prime boat trips in North America. The spacious, comfortable ferries are a combination cruise ship and ferry, and offer those who go north to Alaska a more pleasurable and comfortable trip than driving up the Alaska Highway through western Canada. The ferries follow the same route as the elegant cruise ships, and cost considerably less. And you can take your car, camper, motorcycle or bicycle along (at an additional charge, of course).

Every Friday throughout the year the newest ship on the system, the *M.V. Columbia,* departs Pier 48 in Seattle for a trip that ends three days later in Skagway after making stops at Ketchikan, Wrangell, Petersburg, Juneau, and Haines. On the return voyage, it adds Sitka to its itinerary.

Three other Alaska ferries, the *Malaspina, Matanuska* and *Taku,* make the same run from Prince Rupert, B.C., up the Inside Passage to Skagway. They are reached either by catching a British Columbia ferry to Prince Rupert, or by driving there.

Information: Alaska Marine Highway System, Pouch R, Juneau, 99811, or Pier 48, Seattle, 623-1970.

Washington State Ferries — See Sightseeing.

BITS AND ODDMENTS

A Potpourri of Miscellany

Annual Events

Annual events have a way of coming and going, and some make it only as far as the first annual...before fading from the calendars. Those listed here have stood the test of time and should appear again and again.

Watch the newspapers for more detailed information and exact dates. For more information, write to Seattle/King County Convention and Visitors Bureau, 1215 7th, Seattle, 98101.

January

Boat Show — Late in the month, sponsored by Northwest Marine Industries, Kingdome.

February

Chinese New Year Celebration — International District, open houses, parades, exhibits.

March

Public Schools Fine Arts Festival — Seattle Center
Easter Egg Hunt — Seattle Center
Spring Vacation — Fun Forest at Seattle Center open for a week.

April

Fishing season opens third or fourth Sunday in lowland lakes and streams.
African Violet Show — Eames Theater, Pacific Science Center
Seattle Art Museum's Architecture Tour — Capitol Hill homes

May

Folklife Festival — Seattle Center
Inboard Boat Races — Lake Sammamish
Opening Day of Yachting Season — Lakes Washington and
    Union, Ship Canal. See also "Boat Watching"
Seafair Kite Flying Contest — Golden Gardens Park
University District Sidewalk Fair — University Way N.E.
Pacific Northwest Coin Show — Seattle Center
Longacres Race Track opens
Mobile Home Show — Kingdome

June

Burien Arts Festival — Highline High School
Northwest Driftwood Artists Juried Show — Marymoor Park,
    Redmond
Edmonds Art Festival — Edmonds
Fire Festival — Pioneer Square
Scandinavian Midsummer Festival — Vasa Park, Lake
    Sammamish

July

Festival of NW Composers — North Seattle Community Col-
    lege
Fourth of July Fireworks — Various locations
Gilbert & Sullivan Society Concerts — Playhouse
Scottish Highland Games — Highland Stadium, Burien
Pacific Northwest Arts & Crafts Fair — Bellevue
Seafair Grand Parade and Torchlight Parades — Downtown &
    International District.
Pacific Northwest Writers Conference — Seattle or Tacoma

August

Seafair Unlimited Hydroplane Race—Lake Washington
Seattle Begonia Society Show — Northgate Mall
Northwest Inter-Tribal Encampment — Marymoor Park
    Redmond
Gift Show — Seattle Center
King County Fair — Enumclaw
Bumbershoot Festival — Seattle Center
Milk Fund Salmon Derby — Puget Sound
Black Community Festival

September

CHAOS (Capitol Hill Arts on Show)
Seafoodfest — Bergen Place Park, Ballard
Gem and Mineral Show — Seattle Center
Western Washington State Fair — Puyallup
Seattle Symphony season begins — Opera House
Seattle Dahlia Show — Seattle Center
Seafair Salmon Derby — Puget Sound
State Ceramic Show — Seattle Center
Inboard Boat Races — Lake Sammamish

October

Issaquah Salmon Festival
Mushroom Show — Science Center
Haunted Houses — KJR Radio and other organizations
Greek Bazaar — St. Demetrios Greek Orthodox Church, 2100 Boyer E.
Numerous ethnic and religious bazaars Oct.-Dec.

November

Cat Show — Seattle Center
Boy Scout Show — Kingdome

December

Christmas Kaleidoscope — Seattle Center
Christmas Around the World — Museum of History and Industry
Santa Claus Train — Puget Sound Railway Historical Museum near Snoqualmie Falls. Rides at reasonable prices.
Science Circus — Pacific Science Center

Children

Gourmets, social critics, and snobs in general may shun and sneer, but restaurants catering to the family trade exist and the kids love them. If it weren't for them, many mothers would be stuck with a passel of kids in the house for birthdays and special occasions, and families of limited means would have little opportunity to expose their children to restaurant dining.

Not listed here are the hundreds of drive-ins sprinkled around Seattle on main throughfares because they are obvious choices and a listing would be a rehash of the Yellow Pages.

Instead, these restaurants make a production of dining for kids, and the influence of Walt Disney is apparent. If you expect a quiet, sedate dining experience, see our regular restaurant listings. If you want a little razzle-dazzle in your life and you children's lives, read on:

Enchanted Village — 36201 Kit Corner Rd. S., Federal Way (927-4100). Family park with carousel, goats, sheep, fantasy buildings, people in cartoon costumes, rides. One price for all day. Group rates available.

Farrell's Ice Cream Parlors — These are located at Southcenter, 930 N. 130th (just off Aurora N.), Northgate, and 10116 N.E. 8th in Bellevue. They have the dubious distinction of being mentioned in the book, *The Greening of America,* in a rather convoluted attempt to prove that the pioneering spirit is dead in America. Gracious! The gaudy, friendly, noisy eateries are decorated in Gay Nineties style, and kids celebrating their birthdays receive a free sundae along with a drum-banging and the group sing-along "Happy Birthday." Reservations are not accepted. Southcenter (244-1895); North End (364-1891); Northgate (363-1890); Bellevue (454-1895).

The Gasworks Restaurant — See listing in Restaurants for the Sunday brunch special.

Pizza & Pipes — 100 N. 85th (782-0360) and 550 112th N.E. Bellevue (453-1441). A giant pipe organ and silent movie clips provide the sound and sight. Also many varieties of pizza sandwiches, and salad bar. Popular with preteen and teen groups as well as families.

Shakey's Pizza Parlors — These are similar to Farrell's with the obvious difference in menus, and you'll find more older people dining. Numerous locations, two in Seattle and on the outskirts of town: Auburn, Bellevue, Burien, Federal Way Lake City, and Renton. Children under 12 register for the Birthday Club and receive a free small pizza and soft drink. They also receive balloons, trinkets, and lots of attention.

Royal Forks Buffets — See Restaurant listing.

Ivars — See Restaurant listings. Acres of Clams and the Salmon House are best for kids.

The Old Spaghetti Factory — See Restaurant listing.

Other Places for Kids

ACT (A Contemporary theater) — See Theater listing in Entertainment Section.

Arts and Craft Classes — After school, Sat., and summer classes at individual Seattle Parks and Recreation Centers and at the Department's new Pratt Fine Arts Center, 1902 S. Main. For schedules and sign-up call 625-4671.

Bathhouse Theater — See Theater listing.

Daybreak Star Indian Cultural Center — See Sightseeing Section.

Farms — Lake Serene Pony Farm, 3915 Serene Way, Lynnwood (743-2112); ages 3-14, trail riding all year.

Fun Forest — See Seattle Center.

Longacres — Sat. morning workout shows including a training race held on 5 Saturdays during the racing season (226-3131).

Museums — See Galleries and Museum section
Museum of History and Industry
Klondike Gold Rush National Historical Park
Thomas Burke Memorial Museum
Coast Guard Museum

Piccoli Theater — See Theater listing.

Poncho Theater — See Theater Listing.

Red Barn Ranch — Open to groups; see Seattle Park Dept. listing.

Seattle Junior Theatre — 158 Thomas (622-7246). This is recognized as one of the best children's theater organizations in the nation. It holds a series of three productions during the school year in the Opera House and Playhouse. Special performances are scheduled each Christmas holiday as well as Sunday family matinees. Call for schedule and special arrangements for groups.

Tours — See Sightseeing for specific information.
Harbor Tours
Hiram C. Chittenden Locks — Viewing the fish ladder and the operation of the locks is a fun way to spend the afternoon.

Industrial Tours — Almost all the manufacturing plants with tours welcome children. Candy, bakery, and pop plants hand out samples.

Underground Tours — Fun for over-fives to poke around with their flashlights in all those dark corners.

Woodland Park Zoo — See Guided Tours and separate listing in Parks section.

Seattle Children's Museum — 117 Occidental S. (284-2444).

This new museum serves as an educational center for children and families with exhibits that encourage participation: displays on how musical instruments make sounds, how people of many cultures live, and how the handicapped surmount the problems of the "normal" world. Hours: 10 a.m.-3:30 p.m. Mon., Wed., & Sat. Admission, $1 per person; adults must be accompanied by a child.

Seattle Public Libraries — Main Library, 1000 4th (625-4992). The main library and all branches have children's programs the year around which include picture-book time, puppet shows, story telling, films, poetry clubs, talks by authors of children's books, creative dramatics for 4-5 year-olds, and a summer reading club. "Dial-a-Story" for primary age children (625-4584); new stories prepared each Friday. Also available (main branch only) are children's records, 16mm films, and pictures. Sometimes special tours for children are offered. Call libraries for programs and watch for listings in newspapers, particularly the *P-I's 206 Magazine* on Friday and *The Seattle Times' Tempo Magazine,* same day.

King County Library System — Service Center, 300 8th N. (344-7465). Similar to programs offered by the Seattle system. Monthly bulletins available at check-out desks of all branches and listed in newspapers.

Senior Citizens

Seattle supports one of the most progressive city-funded programs to make life more pleasant and useful for persons 65 and over in the United States. The city established the Senior Information Center within the Dept. of Human Resources primarily to reduce the cost of necessities for senior citizens, and the program was met with enthusiasm by the business community.

Following are some of the savings available to senior citizens over 65 residing in Seattle or King County.

Metro Buses — 15¢ a ride anywhere in the county or $2 a month. Passes available at the Seattle Tower, 1214 3rd, call 447-4800 or 625-4834.

Pet Licenses and Taxi Discounts — If your income is less than $7,833 for a single person, or $10,227 for couples, you can get a 60 percent discount on taxi fares and a 50 percent discount on pet licenses. Call 625-4834 for information.

Free Appliance Parts — Free replacement parts for range, water heater, or permanently connected electric heating are available by calling 625-4834 for an application. Your income must be less than that listed above for pet licenses and taxi discounts.

Restaurant Discounts — If you're in the income bracket, (see Pet Licenses for criteria) about 100 restaurants will give you a discount on meals. Call 284-1139 and ask about Golden American program. Card costs $2.

Pacific Science Center — Admission is $1.

Other Discounts — Some pyarmacies, food co-ops (see Shopping), tours, and theaters. Call 625-4834 or the individual business and inquire.

Free Tuition — Seattle Pacific University offers free tuition to senior citizens working toward a degree. The student must sign up for classes that are not filled by regular students. Call Admissions for information (281-2021). University of Washington and other state schools have $5 fee for courses, space available basis.

Mayor's Office for Senior Citizens — 315 Jones Bldg., 1331 3rd (625-4834). Possible discounts on water-sewer-garbage bills, City Light surcharge exemption, reduced bus fare passes, etc.

Tax Exemptions — King County Assessor's Office (County Administration Bldg., 500 4th (344-4120). Possible deferment and exemptions of property taxes.

Chore Services — Bellevue (455-7030): Burien (464-7120); Capital Hill (464-7250); Federal Way (838-9000); Kent (872-6300); Rainier Valley (721-4140).

Food

Low-Cost Meals — Several places offer low-cost meals, including: the Columbia Club (622-7280); Northwest Senior Center (784-2500); Georgetown National Guard Mess Hall (763-0500); East Madison YMCA (325-1400); Calvary Presbyterian Church in Enumclaw (TA5-3820); Sartori School, Renton (255-7931); St. James Lutheran Church, Highline (244-7706); Nisei Veterans Hall (322-1122); Millionaire Club (624-5033).

Meals and low cost staples for the home-bound are available from "Meals on Wheels" (522-7666).

Seattle-King County Nutrition Program for the Elderly (525-8272). Hot meals every weekday for 60 or older in neighborhood centers. Usually open from 10 a.m.-2 p.m., providing recreation, escort service, volunteers. Call for nearby location.

Queen Anne Nutrition Site — 1st W. & Howe (625-4040). Sponsored by Queen Anne churches, Park Dept., and Seattle Mental Health. Hot meals served Thurs. at noon for 60 and over. Reservations must be made by the previous Mon.

S.P.I.C.E. — 313 1st S. (587-3524). Lunch, recreation, and health clinic in some Seattle Public Schools. Cost 75ᶜ for lunch; free health checkups; call for location.

Free food is available by calling 632-1285.

Medical Services

Community Home Health Care — 2633 Eastlake E. (322-0930). Health care services; and sells a directory of services for handicapped and elderly.

FISH (324-3214) — Volunteers provide transportation and help in getting from house to car. Call to see if available in your part of city.

Outreach for Older Adults — 604 3rd (625-2791). Social worker and doctor or nurse will visit homes to evaluate physical and mental condition and recommend needed services. Sliding scale fee, but not mandatory.

Pioneer Square Neighborhood Health Station — 206 3rd (624-6601). Geared to older persons, access to language bank, help with medical problems.

Seattle-King County Dept. of Public Health Geriatric Clinics — Free services for those 60 and over at activity centers and SPICE locations. City, central region (625-2571); north of Ship Canal (363-4765); county, southwest area (244-6400); southeast (288-2620); east of Lake Washington (885-1278).

Hospice of Seattle — 819 Boylston (322-1881). Offers home care for terminally ill.

Programs

Seattle Dept. of Parks and Recreation — 8061 Densmore N. (625-2981). Offers a program of lawn bowling, field trips, concerts, etc.

Day Care Centers — Columbia Lutheran, 405 N. 48th (632-7400); Daybreak, 1111 110th N.E. (454-9063); Mt. St. Vincent, 4831 35th S.W. (937-3700); Northwest, 1414 N.W. 85th (784-8285); University Congregational Church, 4515 16th N.E. (524-2321). Personal care, health screening, social activities.

Senior Centers — King County Senior Services & Centers, 800 Jefferson (447-7805) operates most of these, which provide daytime social activities, arts and crafts, bus trips, etc. Central Area, 500 30th S.; Jefferson House, 800 Jefferson; Northwest, 5249 32nd N.W.; Wallingford, 4649 Sunnyside N.; Greenwood, 525 N. 85th; Lee House, 7515 39th S.; West Seattle, 4217 S.W. Oregon; Tallmadge Hamilton House, 5525-15th N.E.; Shoreline, 835 N.E. 155th. Also Central Openhouse at Central Lutheran Church, 1710 11th (322-7500); The Columbia Club, 424 Columbia (622-6460); The North Shore Senior Center, 9929 N.E. 18th, Bothell (487-2441).

The Lifetime Learning Center — Sacred Heart Catholic Church, 205 2nd N. (283-5523). Offers low cost continuing education.

Volunteer Opportunities

Foster Grandparent Program — 5230 15th N.E. (364-0300). Work with day-care and retarded youngsters 5 days a week for 4 hours. Paid mileage, hourly wage, and meals.

Volunteer Service Office of Seattle Public Schools — Puts persons 55 or older at work directly with students in tutoring or classroom assistance or in libraries (587-6490).

King County Retired Senior Volunteer Program — Finds work opportunities in private and nonprofit agencies (323-2345).

Reassurance Service

Reassurance Telephone Call Service — A free call to seniors living alone to make sure they're all right. Providence Hospital (326-5711); West Seattle Hospital (938-6000).

Postal Alert — Mailmen alert to oldsters living alone (625-4834).

Organizations

Seattle-King Co. Div. on Aging — 400 Yesler Bldg. City (625-4469); county (854-6110). Plans delivery of services to elderly.

Gray Panthers — Good Shepherd Center, 4649 Sunnyside N. (623-4759). Part of a national group working for social change, such as fighting against mandatory retirement, decent housing at reasonable rent, etc.

Japanese American Citizens' League — 316 S. Maynard (682-7364). Represents rights of Japanese-American, with the Issei group dealing with the needs of the elderly.

Nursing Home Ombudsman Program — Jones Bldg., 1331 3rd (625-4834). Helps solve problems faced by residents of skilled and intermediate care nursing homes and their relatives.

Citizens for Improvement of Nursing Homes — 305 N.E. 47th (283-9485). Statewide, attempts to improve quality of care in nursing homes, some patient advocacy.

Homesharing Programs for Seniors — 522 19th E. (329-7303). Matches homeowners with compatible tenants for mutual economic and social benefit.

Foster Families for Older Adults — Works to place clients 62 or over with homeowning seniors or families; seeks those wanting to share their home.

Senior Rights Assistance — 208 Lowman Bldg., 107 Cherry (623-7765). Trained senior citizens offer legal information and assistance in social security, medicare, health insurance, wills, etc.

Social Security Administration — Telephone service for those over 65 (733-9222).

King County Senior Barter Bank — 18220 96th N.E., Bothell (485-6525). A clearing house for those seniors wishing to trade skills with other seniors.

Elderly Citizens' Coalition — 5614 Rainier Ave. S. A political group for low income senior citizens to take their problems to the Legislature.

Senior Services & Centers, Home Repair Division — 1419 23rd (324-7092). Provides free labor for minor home repairs — plumbing, carpentry, electrical work, ramps, and railings. Clients furnish the material.

Northwest Senior Craftsmen — Pier 70 (623-2780). Hand-made items made by senior citizens sold on consignment.

Information

Senior Information Center — (285-3110). Room 315 on the 3rd floor of the Jones Bldg. at 1331 3rd. A place to go to just relax in the lounge and visit or obtain help and information on all services available to senior citizens. Among the things available at the center are: combined Metro I.D. card (with picture) and Senior Citizen I.D. card for discounts, property tax exemption applications, applications for utility credit, and more. Call or visit the center for any information concerning senior citizens.

Senior Services Information & Assistance — 100 W. Roy St. (285-3110). Counseling for over 60's with problems in health care, housing, home maintenance. Workers will visit homes to give information on services and help fill out applications. Can arrange transportation for medical appointments and grocery shopping with 10 days' notice (small fee for transportation).

Red Cross Aid to Aging — 2515 S. Holgate (323-2345). Similar services as above.

Climate

Someday a climatological genius, perhaps the same one who wanted to set off an atomic bomb in the Van Allen Belt, is going to suggest a way to give Seattle more clear weather, and when he does, somebody is going to throw him, charts and graphs and all, into Puget Sound. If there is anything Seattleites don't want, it's someone messing around with the thing they complain the most about.

Mild weather year round makes waterfront living particularily appealing in the Seattle area.

In the winter it rains a lot, and when it isn't raining, it looks like it just did or is going to in a few minutes. In the summer it rains less, but not enough less (is that good writing, or is that good writing?) to satisfy the constant complainers.

True, true. It does rain a lot, and there are weeks when the sun is only a dim memory; something somebody saw last month in Las Vegas or Wenatchee. Yet it seldom gets very cold in Seattle — perhaps a week out of the year with freezing temperatures — nor does it get very hot even in August. The record is 99°F. in 1960.

The weather is one of the favorite, but least effective, tools of that grumpy group that calls itself Lesser Seattle, whose purpose is to discourage immigrants to Seattle. They insist it rains all the time, but the ski buffs know that means yards of snow in the winter. Lesser Seattle says the sun never shines, but to a desert rat that is more soothing than Coppertone. Lesser Seattle says there is so little difference between the seasons one has to watch the calendar to know the month, but who needs blizzards, droughts, and tornadoes? They'd as well give up and admit it: Seattle isn't perfect, but nobody or nothing is. Some places are better than others, and Seattle is one of them.

So here are the statistics, courtesy of the National Oceanic and Atmospheric Administration, compiled from its station at Seattle-Tacoma International Airport. Please bear in mind that these statistics are for the airport only; it does get both colder and hotter in downtown Seattle on occasion. For more information on Pacific Northwest weather, see *Weather of the Pacific Coast* by Walter Rue, also published by The Writing Works, $4.95 in bookstores.

Health

Major Hospitals

Cabrini Hospital — Terry & Madison (682-0500) 225 beds

Children's Orthopedic Hospital & Medical Center — 4800 Sand Point Way N.E. (634-5000) 196 beds, burns center

Group Health Hospital — 201 16th E. (325-9400) 260 beds

King County Harborview Medical Center — 325 9th (223-3000) 250 beds, emergency trauma center

Northwest Hospital — 1551 N. 120th (364-0500) 262 beds, communicative disorders, stroke unit

Overlake Memorial Hospital — 1035 116th N.E., Bellevue (454-4011) 160 beds

Providence Medical Center — 500 17th (326-5555) 333 beds, cardiac center, rehabilitative center

Swedish Hospital & Medical Center — 747 Summit (292-2121) 422 beds, Northwest Kidney Center, Tumor Institute, and Fred Hutchinson Cancer Research Center

University of Washington Hospital — 1959 N.E. Pacific (543-3300) 298 beds, teaching, research, neonatal intensive care, spinal cord injury center

U.S. Govt. Public Health Service Hospital — 1131 14th S. (325-8000) 257 beds

U.S. Govt. Veteran's Hospital — 4435 Beacon S. (762-1010) 354 beds

Virginia Mason Hospital — 925 Seneca (624-1144) 290 beds

Low-Cost Medical Clinics

Asian Community Health Clinic — 2902 Beacon S. (682-5143). Staffed by doctors who speak Cantonese, Mandarin, Japanese, Tagalog, and Ilocano. Physicals, immunization, V.D. test. Tues. 6:30-9:30 p.m.

Country Doctor — 402 15th E. (322-6698). General medical and physician referral.

Fremont Women's Clinic — 6817 Fremont N. (789-0773). Geriatrics and gynecology clinic. Mon.

High Point Community Clinic — 3142 S.W. Holly (935-8150). All services but major surgery and X-ray. $2 fee for low income.

Indian Health Clinic — 1212 S. Judkins (442-5770). Medical, dental, mental, and eye care. Alcohol program. Sliding fee scale.

Pioneer Square Neighborhood Health Station — 206 3rd (624-6601). Geared to elderly but will accept persons in area or low income. Access to Language Bank.

Seattle King County Health Dept. — Public Safety Bldg., 3rd & James (625-2151). Family planning, adult and child health, immunization, VD clinic. Free to ability to pay.

Senior Services & Centers, (447-7805). Various locations in the city; provide foot care, health education and nutrition counseling, and recreational activities for the elderly.

S.P.I.C.E. 144 N.E. 54th (587-3524). Health clinic, meals, and recreation for elderly in various Seattle Public Schools. Noon meals 75¢.

Sydney Miller Clinic (Black Panther) — 169 19th (322-1038). Physicals, prenatal care, minor surgery, sickle cell anemia, food program. Free

Southwest Clinic — 9407 16th S.W. (625-4261).

Southeast Clinic — 5619 Rainier S. (625-2785).

University of Washington Dental School (543-5830) — Long waiting period but low-cost orthodontics and dental care.

Free Legal Clinics

The Young Lawyers Section of the local bar association has set up free legal clinics, 4 thus far with more under consideration. They operate one night each week. They are 7-9 p.m. in the Fremont Clinic, Country Doctor, Southwest Clinic, and Southeast Clinic. See Low Cost Medical Clinics for addresses and telephone numbers. If you are a lawyer and want to help call 622-3150.

Miscellaneous

Northwest Center for the Retarded (285-9140) — Training school for retarded children and adults.

Alcoholics Anonymous — (447-4542).

Cancer Lifeline (447-4542) — 24-hour telephone counseling service.

Community Alcohol Center — 8537 Phinney N. (789-1616). Family counseling, sliding scale fee.

Community Service Officers — Seattle Police Dept., 2018 E. Union (625-4661). City residents — emergency food, shelter, and clothing.

Crisis Clinic — 1530 Eastlake E. (447-3200). Counseling and financial aid for stranded individuals.

Millionair Club (624-5033) — Free breakfasts and dinners.

Tel-Med (285-4000) — Health information in layman's language, 175 three-to-five minute tape recordings.

Schools

Colleges and Universities

Seattle Pacific University — 509 W. Bertona (281-2000).

Seattle University — 12th & E. Columbia (626-5720).

University of Washington — 15th N.E. & N.E. 45th (543-2100).

Community Colleges

Bellevue Community College — 3000 Landerholm Circle S.E., Bellevue (641-0111).

Edmonds Community College — 20000 68th W., Lynnwood (775-4444).

Highline Community College — S. 240th & Pacific Highway S. (878-3710).

Seattle Community College — North; 9600 College Way (634-4400); Central: 1701 Broadway (587-3800); South: 6000 16th S.W. (764-5300).

Shoreline Community College — 16101 Greenwood N. (546-4101).

Other Schools

Antioch University Seattle — 1729 17th (323-2270)

Burnley School of Professional Art — 905 E. Pine (322-0596).

City College — 407 Lyon Bldg., 607 3rd (624-1688).

Cornish School of Allied Arts —710 E. Roy (323-1400).

Golden Gate University — 310 Skinner Bldg., 5th & Union (622-9996).

University of Puget Sound, Seattle Campus — 315 Yesler Way (682-0210).

Spectators along the Montlake Cut enjoy waterside seats as University of Washington and rival school crews race between Lake Washington and Portage Bay for the yachting season Opening Day.

Private and Parochial Schools

The desegregation of public schools, plus a general disenchantment with the quality of public schools, has caused an exodus to private schools in Seattle. Vacancies in nonpublic schools are at a premium in both parochial and private institutions, and new ones spring up almost overnight.

Private — Bush School (K-12), 405 36th E., 98112 (322-7978); Evergreen/Gifted (preschool-7), 15201 Meridian N., 98133 (364-2650); Lakeside School (5-12), 14050 1st N.E., 98125 (365-6161); Seattle Seguin (learning & language disabilities only), 225 N. 70th, 98188 (789-1070); University Preparatory Academy (7-12), 8015 27th N.E. (525-2714); Warren Reading Foundation (1-12), 4261 Roosevelt Way N.E., 98105 (632-6666).

Parochial — Superintendent of Catholic Schools (for all Catholic schools); Catholic Archdiocese of Seattle, 907 Terry, 98104 (622-8880); Hope Lutheran (preschool-9), 4446 42nd S.W., 98116 (935-8500); Seattle Christian (preschool-12), 19639 28th S., 98188 (824-1310).

Adult Education

Seattle has gone on an adult-education boom during the past few years. All colleges and universities in the city offer a staggering number of courses, from belly dancing to some of the more obscure folk dances to the classics. Public schools and community centers also offer evening adult education classes for noncredit. For information, call each of the schools listed above or your neighborhood high school or community center.

Sister Cities

In the good name of brotherly love, Seattle has "adopted" six sister cities. There were seven, but Dawson City, Yukon, showed a distinct disinterest in the program, so the old gold-rush town was dropped from the roster.

The sister cities now are Bergen, Norway; Tashkent, U.S.S.R.; Beer Sheva, Israel; Mazatlan, Mexico; Kobe, Japan; and Nantes, France.

Foreign Visitors

In its role as a major Pacific seaport and a port of entry for Scandinavian countries via the polar flights, Seattle offers a number of services for foreign visitors and businessmen, each designed to break down the language and cultural barriers.

Language Bank — This volunteer group is composed of people who speak various foreign languages, and someone is available on a 24-hour basis. It is sponsored by the Seattle Altrusa Club, and the phone number is 622-4250.

Seattle Americans-at-Home Program — This program is operated jointly with the U.S. Travel Service and makes it possible for visitors from foreign countries to visit Seattle-area families in their homes. Visitors may find information about the program in their home countries from embassies, travel services, and other travel-oriented organizations. They fill out a form giving pertinent information, and they are met at the Seattle-Tacoma International Airport by multi-lingual receptionists of the "Operation Welcome" program who arrange the final transportation to the Seattle home. Information: 447-7273, which is the Seattle/King County Convention and Visitors Bureau.

Seattle Banks with Foreign Departments — These banks offer complete banking service for foreign visitors and businessmen, handling everything from investment to monetary exchange: Bank of California, 900 4th (587-6100); Bank of Tokyo, Ltd., 1111 3rd (382-6000); Canadian Imperial Bank of Commerce, 801 2nd (223-7954); Pacific National Bank of Washington, 1215 4th (292-3111); Peoples National Bank of Washington, P.O. Box 70, (344-2300); Rainier National Bank, 1100 2nd (621-4111); Seattle-First National Bank, 4th and Madison (583-3131); Seattle Trust & Savings Bank, 804 2nd (223-2000); Taiyo Kobe Bank, Ltd., 900 4th (682-2312).

Foreign Consuls in Seattle — Austria, 2126 Sea-First Bldg. (624-3450); Belgium, 1415 5th (623-5005); Bolivian, 13933 S.E. 60th, Bellevue (641-9865); Britain, 1216 Norton Bldg. (622-9253); Canada, 412 Plaza 600 Bldg. (447-3804); Chile, 616 Joshua Green Bldg. (623-1675); Costa Rica, 1822 N.W. 46th (632-3373); Denmark, 2900 Bank of California Center (223-1820); Ecuador, 322 Boylston E. (324-4151); Finland, 515 Union (682-1959); France, 707 E. Harrison (323-6870); Germany, 1617 IBM Bldg. (682-4312); Guatemala, 914 2nd (624-5920); Honduras & Nicaragua, 1218 3rd (623-4493); Iceland, 5610 20th N.W. (783-4100); Italy, Exchange Bldg. (623-4656); Japan, Rainier Tower Bldg. (682-9107); Korea, 2033 6th (682-0132); Mexico, 1402 3rd (682-3634); The Netherlands, 10 Wall (623-5300); Panama, 222 Williams S., Renton (255-0186); Peru, 18511 58th N.E. (488-1187); Philippines, 810 3rd (624-7703); Sweden,

The *Preston*, a sternwheeler operated by the U.S. Corps of Engineers, picks up floating logs and debris to keep lake and waterway passages clear.

1020 Joseph Vance Bldg. (622-5640); Switzerland, 5304 3rd S. (762-1223).

Professional Baby Sitters

Best Sitters, Inc. (682-2556). 24-hour service, children & elderly. Motels-hotels.
James Baby Sitters (283-9500) — 2609 3rd N.
Seattle Baby Sitting Service (325-4321) — 10600 Main, Bellevue.
Downtown Seattle — See Shopping section for drop-in sitting services.
Day Care Referral (721-4110)

Home Repairs

Home Owners Club of Seattle — 1202 Harrison (622-3500). One of the few such clubs that have been a success, it was organized to give homeowners more time enjoying themselves and less fiddling around the house making repairs. For $25 a year a homeowner can call to report a problem, from yard work to new construction, and the club will see that the work is done at a fair price. They keep a list of fully investigated contractors, and a representative of the club may visit your home to consult with you on the work needed and possible cost. Join and you will have time to enjoy the activities listed in *The Seattle GuideBook.*

Libraries

Seattle Public Library

Main Library, 1000 4th (625-4952), quick information on any subject (625-2665). The Main Library offers a wide variety of research materials for scholars, including rare manuscripts, historical photographs, and rare books. Meeting rooms are available for groups, and the library maintains an extensive music and film rental library. Call for information on tours of the bindery and other behind-the-scenes activities.

Municipal Reference Library — 307 Municipal Bldg. (625-2853). Open weekdays as a reference service to city and county employees as well as persons interested in local government.

Other libraries are housed in the colleges and universities, all of which may be used by the public. Of particular interest to historians is the University of Washington library and its Special Collections section with one of the best libraries on the Pacific Northwest, Alaska, and the Arctic in existence.

King County Library System

Headquarters, 300 8th N. (344-7465). County-wide the system conducts a wide variety of programs for the public of all ages. A sample month's program for various branches would include films, a winemaking workshop, visits by the Seattle Repertory Theater's "Rep 'n Rap" troupe talking about a new play and performing excerpts from it, a talk by a policeman on home security, autograph parties for authors, and a talk on home canning and freezing by a county extension officer. The system also offers numerous children's programs (see For Children). The modern-architecture branches are located in Algona, Bellevue, Black Diamond, Bothell, Boulevard Park, Burien, Burton, Carnation, Des Moines, Duvall, Fall City. Federal Way, Forest Park, Foster, Issaquah, Kenmore, Kent, Kirkland, Lake Hills, Lester, Maple Valley, McMicken, Mercer Island, Newport Way, North Bend, Pacific, Park Lane, Preston, Redmond, Redondo, Richmond Beach, Shoreline, Skykomish, Skyway, Snoqualmie, South Park Courts, Valley Ridge, Vashon, Vista, and White Center. Bookmobiles run on a scheduled basis to smaller communities and rural areas.

Singles Groups

There are more than 50 organizations sponsoring activities, lecture series, and consultation services available for single adults. These are in addition to — and separate from — the computer dating firms, escort services, and other businesses that capitalize on loneliness. Most of this partial listing are sponsored by churches or similarly legitimate and serious organizations.

All City Jewish Singles — Largest Jewish group in area (232-7115). Recreational and cultural.

Association of Formerly Married Catholics — Meetings Sun. at 7:30 p.m. in the F.R.E.D. house, Broadway E. & E. Roanoke (767-6372).

Chancellor Club — For single Catholics 21-40. Meetings second Wed. each month at 6727 Greenwood N. (782-6281).

Chareso Club — For unmarried Catholics over 35, (624-7735).

Couriers — For singles 21-35. Meetings each Sun. in the Inn of University Presbyterian Church, N.E. 47th & 16th N.E. Sponsors small group activities (524-7300).

Divorce Lifeline — Meetings with speakers covering a wide range of subjects for the divorced. First Wed. each month at First Presbyterian Church, 8th & Madison (624-2959).

Federation of Single Adult Groups (FOSAG) — 217 9th N., Seattle, 98109 (623-8632). A nonprofit corporation founded in 1967 to exchange and circulate information of interest to single adult groups and individuals — not a single-adult social club.

FOCAS (Fellowship of Christian Adult Singles) — Chapters throughout the Greater Seattle area meeting Sun. mornings at 9 a.m. FOCAS sponsors Pacific Northwest Christian Singles Convention each spring, retreats, tours, banquets, and various seminars. For information call 525-7995.

Parents With Partners, Inc. — Activities for single parents and their children. Call 271-2538 for information on chapters in Seattle area.

Puget Sound Singles — Dances 1st and 3rd Fri. of each month at Carpenters Hall, 2512 2nd (485-7020 or 282-7149)

Single Adult Members (SAM) — 1415 N.E. 43rd, Seattle, 98105 (784-5450). Potluck dinner, third Sunday each month at Univ. Unitarian Temple.

Singletonians, Inc. — For those age 30 to 55. P.O. Box 30051, Seattle, 98103 (525-4158).

Solo Center — 6514 35th N.E. (522-7656). A home-style (but nonresidential) resource providing a social support system for adults in transition due to separation, divorce, widowing, changing lifestyle, new location, and never-married. Rap sessions, classes, programs, information, and referral services plus drop-in socializing are available almost every evening. Nonprofit, nondenominational, operated mainly by volunteers.

Solo Center/East — N.E. 8th & 108th N.E., Bellevue. Similar program as Seattle organization. Drop-in program Mon., Wed., and Fri.

South End Singles — Crestview Center, 16200 42nd S. Monthly

newsletter, weekly events and special trips (282-9481).

Unaffiliated Single Adult Group (USAG) — New member meetings on 3rd Mon. of each month (775-6728 or 282-0824).

Widowed Lifeline — Meetings 4th Tues. each month at 7:30 p.m. at 564 N.E. Ravenna, (527-2266).

Publications

Seattle is one of the few large cities with two major daily newspapers under different ownership and printed in separate plants. But, so far, the city has not supported an underground or counter-culture newspaper. They've tried, but they've all folded for lack of advertising and reader support. The rowdiest newspaper remaining in Seattle is the *University of Washington Daily,* which occasionally spurs a conservative or fundamentalist legislator to rise up and roar that he objects to public funds being used to support a college paper that prints naughty words.

Counting all the neighborhood shopping guides and newspapers that print only classified ads, there probably are in excess of 100 making the rounds. Here's a list of the main periodicals.

Seattle Post-Intelligencer — 6th & Wall (628-8000). The morning paper, owned by the Hearst Corp., is noted for its feature approach to the news, its columnist, Emmett Watson, the *New York Times* news service, and its broad coverage of entertainment news. The Friday paper has *206 Magazine,* a complete entertainment-recreation guide, the Sunday paper includes *Parade* magazine for national coverage of gossip, offbeat items, and features and *Northwest* magazine, the staff-produced local feature magazine with special issues on recreation recommendations. Cartoons include Beetle Bailey, Blondie, B.C., and Steve Canyon.

The Seattle Times — Fairview N. & John (622-0300). The afternoon and Sunday morning paper, considerably larger of the two dailies, is owned by the Blethen family of Seattle, with 49.5% of voting stock held by Knight-Ridder Newspapers. Four staff-produced weekly supplements: *Tempo,* arts & entertainment, each Friday, and the rotogravure full-color *Pacific,* and *TV Showtime* every Sunday. *The Times* has won two Pulitzer prizes. Dick Moody, *Times* Troubleshooter, Eric Lacitis, Walt Evans, Rick Anderson, and John Hinterberger are among popular columnists. Peanuts, Doonesbury, and Wizard of Id lead the comics lineup.

Daily Journal of Commerce — 83 Columbia (622-8272). The *Wall Street Journal* of Seattle, minus the feature stories and interviews. The *Journal* reports all the important contracts, bond sales, and other business news.

Argus — 2312 3rd (682-1212). This is variously listed as a magazine and newspaper. In the past it was lively, iconoclastic, always opinionated, and refreshing. Lately, however, it has become a bit more bland.

Enetai — 1932 1st (625-0513 or 0517). A tabloid newspaper published twice monthly for riders of the Washington State Ferries and sold on newsstands around Puget Sound. The paper has articles on travel, history, personalities, and towns, all related to Puget Sound. It also has one of the toughest crossword puzzles available, correspondents from the major destinations of the ferries, and the most complete calendar of events from the cities around the Sound.

Fishermen's News — Fishermen's Terminal (282-7545). A respected publication devoted entirely to commercial fishing and politics behind it.

Fishing and Hunting News — 511 Eastlake E. (624-3845). It is exactly what its title says, and the coverage is thorough.

Marine Digest — National Bldg. (682-2484). News and features about shipping in the Northwest with reports from each port district.

Marple's Business Newsletter — Colman Building (622-0155). A report on Pacific Northwest business every two weeks. By subscription only.

Nor'westing — 105 4th S. Edmonds (776-1990). A pleasure boating magazine; news and feature stories.

Pacific Banker & Business — 1 Yesler Way (623-1888).

Pacific Northwest — 222 Dexter N. (682-2704). Magazine about man and nature in the Northwest. Features on plants, animals, and fish of the region; also environmental problems, book reviews, news digest, calendar of events.

Puget Soundings — 1803 42nd E. (324-3638). Published by the Junior League of Seattle, Inc., the slick magazine has essays, word and photo, on local issues including schools, civic projects, the environment, and arts.

Seattle Guide — Pioneer Bldg. (682-5960). A free weekly listing of entertainment, sightseeing, and restaurant information. Available in restaurants, hotels, and information centers around town.

Signpost — See Hiking.

Soundings Northwest — P.O. Box 1062, Bellevue, 98009. A guide to FM Radio and an arts calendar. Available by subscription or at record, radio, and bookstores.

Sunset Magazine — Tower Bldg. (682-3993). Publishes a Northwest edition with travel and gardening information for the regional audience.

The Weekly — 1932 1st (623-3700). Founded by David Brewster, an alumnus of *Seattle Magazine* and *Argus,* this tabloid offers in-depth coverage of local and regional politics, arts, and some business. Complete guide to entertainment and recreation with a great deal of space devoted to restaurants and shopping.

Up the Down Sidewalks

Some of the sidewalks are so steep between 1st and 3rd that cleats were cast in the concrete. Actually, steps would have been better. And if you're going downhill, you're in danger of getting started on a trot that won't be able to stop until you're teetering precariously on the curb with taxis whipping past.

But there's a way around this, so simple that many people never think of it. You use elevators and escalators. Suppose, for example, you arrive in town on the Bainbridge or Bremerton ferry and you have to get up to 5th. You cross Alaskan Way on the overpass and end up on 1st at Marion. Cross 1st, enter the Exchange Building, go up the escalator to the 2nd Avenue level, cross it and go into the next building. Proceed. All buildings on the hillsides have street levels marked on elevator buttons.

This won't keep you completely dry when you're walking in the rain, but it will put less of a strain on your lungs and anti-perspirant.

Public Restrooms

Hardly any. It takes imagination, gall, desperation, and determination to find public restrooms in Seattle. Apparently the only truly public ones are in the Pike Place Market and Freeway Park, although there is frequent talk about building them in some of the mall areas, such as Westlake Mall. There is also talk of restoring the elegant one in Pioneer Square beneath the pergola. Some of the large department stores have them for the convenience of their customers, but unless you've been there before you've got to waste frantic moments asking a clerk where they are cloistered. But don't blame the city government or the stores; security, both personal and for the fixtures, is difficult with the high incidence of vandalism, today's equivalent of the old "Kilroy was here" signs. Tips: stroll into a bar or restaurant that doesn't have a maitre d'. Walk into a good hotel. But never look like what you're there for. After a few such trips, you'll have the best places spotted, and you might even become friends with the owners of the establishments.

City and County

Beating City Hall

First, call the Citizens Service Bureau (625-2482), which will take your complaint and send a copy to the appropriate department head, who must report back within 20 working days with either a resolution or good excuse why the problem is impossible to solve.

If that doesn't work, try the Seattle-King County Ombudsman in the County Courthouse (625-4211). The office has the staff to investigate corruption and governmental abuse and is an independent agency answering to no politicians.

If your problem is only a little one or you need advice not available at those two offices, try the "little City Halls" (Community Service Centers). These offices provide information, accept utility bill payments, issue pet licenses, register voters, and assist in neighborhood programs. They are: Ballard, 5349 Ballard N.W. (625-5035); Central, 2315 S. Jackson (625-4167); Fremont, 3410 Fremont N. (632-1285); Greenwood, 8541 Greenwood N. (625-4388); Lake City, 12707 30th N.E. (362-2825); Southeast, 3808 S. Edmunds (625-2785); Southwest, 9407 16th S.W. (625-4261); South Park, 8201 10th S. (767-3650); University, 4720 University Way N.E. (625-2048).

Going To Court

Some people make a hobby of attending trials in the various courts in Seattle, which isn't a bad way to spend a slow afternoon. One way to participate within the safety of numbers is to sign up through the Rainier Community Action Center (725-2010) or call the various courts for information on cases being tried. Municipal Courts (625-2755); Superior Cour (583-4610) or call the various courts for information on cases being tried. Municipal Courts (625-2755); Superior Court (583-4610, after 11 a.m.), and U.S. District Court (442-5648).

City and County Council Committee Meetings

For information on these, call Seattle City Council (625-2469). County Council (344-2500).

Private Clubs

There are numerous private and fraternal clubs, including the Elks, Moose, American Legion and other national organizations. Some of those listed below have reciprocal guest arrangements with other clubs across the country. The major ones are:

Washington Athletic Club, 1325 6th (622-7900)
Rainier Club, 4th & Marion (622-6848)
College Club, 5th & Madison (622-0624)
University Club, 1004 Boren (622-1132)

Some Things Newcomers Should Know

Voting — You must be at least 18 years old and a U.S. citizen. There are no residency requirements, but you must have registered to vote at least 30 days before any election. Information: King County Voter Registration Dept., 553 King County Bldg., 5th & James, 98104 (344-5282).

Taxes — There is no state personal income tax, rather it is taken impersonally when you buy any non-food item, at the rate of 5.4 percent. State law limits property taxes to one percent of the true and fair value, but special levies for schools, cities, counties, road districts, etc., can be tacked onto this — and are.

Business and occupation (B & O) taxes are levied on gross income or receipts, state taxes range from .0466 to 1.06 percent, and city taxes are 0.1 percent. Gasoline tax is 9 cents a gallon for state and 4 cents federal. Motor vehicle taxes are $13.50 for a new-car purchase plus a 2 percent excise tax, and each following year the basic fee is $10 plus 2 percent of the vehicle's depreciated value. When bringing a car into the state, you must have a car inspection, $10 and a $13.50 transfer fee plus a 2 percent excise tax on the depreciated value of the car. License plates expire on a staggered basis now. Be warned, however, that the wheels of the Dept. of Motor Vehicles turn slowly and that it takes up to three months for titles on cars to be transferred. Also, getting information from the department is usually an exercise in futility. Driver's license costs $3 for the examina-

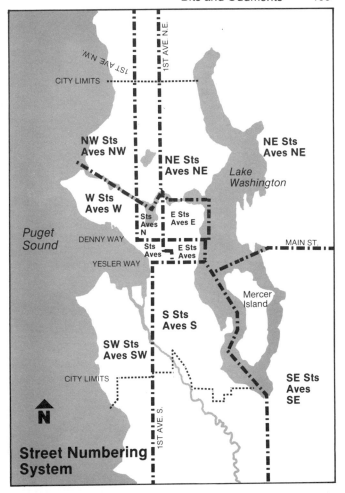

Street Numbering System

tion plus $7 for the license that is good for two years and costs $7 for renewal.

Utilities — You will most likely have to pay a deposit when you start a new service with Pacific Northwest Bell, City Light, Washington Natural Gas Co., the Water Dept., and for garbage collection. The rates vary according to the service you want and arrangements you had with utilities at your former address.

Ferries carrying passengers and cars from the busy waterfront to the Kitsap Peninsula and Puget Sound Islands are a vital transportation link in the Seattle area.

TELEPHONE NUMBERS

A Handy Guide to Services

Useful Telephone Numbers

Abortion Referral Service,
  634-3460
Aircraft Accidents & Low
  Flying Complaints,
  767-2747
Alaska Travel Bureau,
  624-1477
Alcohol Hotline, 722-3700
Alcoholics Anonymous,
  323-3606
Alcoholism Info. & Referral
  Center, 623-8380
  N. End, 367-2700
  S.W., 242-3506
American Cancer Society,
  283-1152
American Civil Liberties
  Union, 624-2180
Animal Birth Control Clinic,
  624-5419
Animal Control Service,
  625-4721
Arboretum Foundation,
  325-4510
Army Corps of Engineers,
  764-3742
Audubon Society, 622-6695
Audubon "hotline," 455-9722
Auto. Club of Wash. (AAA),
  292-5353

Auto Impound, 625-2061
Auto Licenses, 344-4000
Auto Recall, 800-424-9393
Auto Theft, 625-2501
Avalanche Report
    Snoqualmie Pass,
    422-SNOW
  Mt. Baker, 1-599-2714

Better Business Bureau,
  622-8066
Bicycle Hotline, 522-BIKE
Birth Control Information,
  625-2865
Birth & Death Records,
  625-2075
Boat Numbering Info.,
  784-8282

Canadian Govt. Office of
  Tourism, 447-3811
Cancer Lifeline, 447-4542
Carpool, 625-4500
Cascade Ski Report, 634-0200
Census Bureau, 442-7080
Chamber of Commerce,
  447-7200
Charitable sales Permits,
  625-2606
CIA, 442-0824

Citizen's Serv. Bur. (info. & complaints), 625-2482
City Council Info., 625-2469
City Light, 625-3000
City Parks Info., 625-4671
Coast Guard, 442-7363
Community Information Line, 447-3200
Community Crime Prevention Program, 625-4724
Congressmen
    Mike Lowry, 442-7170
    Joel Pritchard, 442-4220
Consular Corps, 682-4312
Consumer Complaints & Inquiries, 625-2712
Consumer Credit Counseling Serv., 682-3290
ConsumerLine, 464-6811
Consumer Taped Info., 464-6372
Consumer Products Safety Com., 442-5276
Consumer Protection (State), 464-6684
Cooperative Extension Service, 344-2686
Cooperative Extension Taped Information, 344-7984
County Council Info., 344-2500
Crisis Clinic, 447-3222
Crystal Mt. Report, 634-3771
Customs Service, 442-4678

Daughters of the American Revolution, 323-0600
Day Care Referral Serv., 721-4110
Dentist, 24-hr. answering serv., 935-7779
Dial-A-Bible Store, 725-2200
Dial-A-Prayer, 725-2200
Dial-A-Story, 625-4858
Doctor, 24-hr. answering

serv., 622-6900
Driver's License
    Bellevue, 455-7119
    Downtown, (Renewals only), 464-5846
    North, 364-2830
    Greenwood, 545-6755
    Renton Highlands, 255-4412
    South, 764-4137
Drug Abuse
    Drug Enforcement Adm., 442-5443
    Open Door Clinic, 524-7404
    Addiction Services, 622-7090

Elder Citizen's Coalition, 624-1774
Emergency Shelters (SeaHaven Hostels) 624-8012
Employment Security Dept., 464-7212
English Speaking Union, 524-5100
Environmental Protection Agency, 442-1200
EPA's Noise Program, 442-1253
Evergreen Safety Council, 622-1670

FBI, 622-0460
FCC, 442-7653
Federal Energy Office, 442-7285
Federal Information Center, 442-0570
Federal Job Information Center, 442-4365
Ferries, Sched. Info., 464-6400
Fire, 911
Flood Control, 344-3874
Food & Drug Adm., 442-5300

Food Stamps, 455-7058
Forest Fire Reports,
   1-800-562-6010
Friends of the Earth, 633-1661

Gamblers Anonymous,
   624-8080
Garbage Dump Info.,
   625-2325
Govt. Printing Office
   Bookstore, 442-4270
Gray Line Tours, 343-2000
Gun Permits, 625-2071

Handicapped Services Unit,
   625-4701
Highway Conditions Report,
   464-6010 (winter only)
Highway Dept. Info.,
   764-4097
Historic Preservation
   344-7503
Human Rights Com.,
   464-6500

Immigration, 442-5956
Insurance Com., Consumer
   Info., 464-6290
IRS, 442-1040

Keep Washington Green
   Assoc., 543-2750
King County
   County Executive,
      344-4040
   Elections Div., 344-2565
   Library System,
      344-7465
   Parks, 344-4232
   Veterans Aid, 344-2656
   Youth Service Dept.,
      323-9500
King County Medical Society,
   285-0221

Language Bank, 622-4250
Lawyer Referral Serv.,
   623-2988
League of Women Voters,
   329-4848
Legal Services Centers,
   464-5911
Liquor Control Bd., 464-6860
Lost Pets Hotline, 283-7387

Marriage Licenses, 344-3933
Medic One, 911
Medic One Contribution,
   223-3341
Medicare, 763-9222
Metro Info., 447-4800
Metro Lost & Found,
   447-4822
Missing Persons, 625-2882
Municipal League, 622-8333

Narcotics Section, 625-4471
Nat. Council on Aging,
   623-1987
Nat. Forest & Nat. Park
   Info. 442-0170
   Report, 442-7669
Nat. Org. for Women,
   523-2111
Northwest Ski Report,
   634-0071
Nursing Home Ombudsman,
   625-4834

Ombudsman, (City) 625-4211
   or 344-3452
Open Door Clinic, 524-7404
Organ Donor Information
   Center, 624-1444

Pacific Science Center,
   624-3724
Parking Meters (defective),
   625-2694
Passports, 442-7941
Peace Corps, 442-5490
Pet Licenses, 625-2591

Phenomena Research,
  722-3000
Pioneer Assoc., 325-0888
Planned Parenthood,
  447-2350
Poison Control Center,
  634-5252
Police, 911
Population Dynamics,
  632-5030
Postal Info., 442-7850
Public Defender, 344-3462

Rape Relief, 632-7273
Rat & Insect Control,
  625-2763
Recycling Info.,
  1-800-732-9253
Rubber Tree, 633-4750
Runners' Hotline, 522-7787
  324-6537 nite

SCORE, 442-4518
Seafair, 623-7100
Seattle Arts Com., 625-4223
Seattle Center, 625-4234
Seattle Design Com.,
  625-4501
Seattle Div. on Aging,
  625-4711
Seattle Harbor Tours,
  623-1445
Seattle/King Co. Convention
  & Visitors Bur., 447-7273
Seattle Public Library,
  625-4952
  Quick Info., 625-2665
Senators
  Henry M. Jackson,
  442-7476
Senior Citizen's Info.,
  625-4834
Senior Citizen's
  Serv.-Mainstay, 285-3110
Sierra Club, 632-6157
Small Bus. Adm.. 442-5534

Soc. Sec. Adm., 763-9222
Space Needle, 682-5656
State Dept. of Ecology,
  885-1900
State Game Dept., 464-7764
State Parks Info.,
  1-800-562-8200 (summer
  only)
State Patrol (Seattle,
  Bellevue, Mercer Isl.),
  455-7700
  Suburban, 464-6610

Tax Information
  Bus. Tax, 625-2194
  Employment Sec. Tax,
  442-1040
  Internal Rev., 442-1040
  Real Estate Tax
  Statement, 344-3850
  Sales Tax (excise),
  464-6827
Tel-Law, 382-0860
Tel-Med, 285-4000
Time, 844-1111
Transit Info., 447-4800
Travel Immunization,
  625-2158
Traveler's Aid Soc., 447-3888

Underground Tours
  Info., 682-1511
  Reserv., 682-4646
Unemployment Ins.,
  464-6080

VD Clinic, 625-2134
Veterans Adm., 624-7200
Veterans Hosp., 762-1010
Veterinary, 24-hr. answering
  serv., 284-9500
Visitng Nurse Assoc.,
  282-9800
VISTA, 442-5490
Voters Reg. Info., 344-5282

Wash. Environmental
    Council, 632-1483
Wash. State Employment
    Office, 464-7600
Wash. State Health Facilities
    (Complaint Info.), 284-6477
Wash. State Heart Assoc.,
    285-2415
Water, Sewer & Garbage
    Bills, 625-5000
Weather Forecast, 662-1111
Weather Serv. Recording,
    285-3710

Whale Hotline,
    1-800-562-8832
Wild Bird Clinic, 824-6249 or
    (emerg.) 246-4808
Woodland Park Zoo
    Recording, 782-5045

YMCA Hotline, 447-3202
Youth Serv. Center, 323-9500

Zero Pop. Growth, 633-4750
Zip Code Info., 442-5605

Phone 'N Games

About Health

**If your child says there's a shark in the Ballard pool and he
hasn't see "Jaws,"**
    Animal Control, 625-4721
If the raisins in your cereal are doing the Australian crawl,
    Food and Drug Adm., 442-5300
For thrifty medical shopping,
    Tel-Med, 285-4000; ask to hear tape No. 19.
For the shot that is felt around the world,
    Travel Immunization, 625-2158
If your doctor prescribes snake's eyes or bat wings,
    King County Medical Society, 285-0221
To defuse the population bomb,
    Rubber Tree, 633-4750
If your frame is getting bottom heavy,
    TOPS. 255-1927
Need help from above?
    Dial-A-Prayer, 725-2200
If your tooth aches before breakfast,
    Dentist, 24-hour answering service, 935-7779
For a pain that aspirin won't cure at 2 a.m.,
    Doctor, 24-hour answering service, 622-6900
To sidetrack a mainliner,
    Narcotics Section, 625-4471

If you have a crick in your sacroliac,
   Assoc. of Wash Chiropractors, 241-2668
If your dog attracts a crowd,
   Animal Birth Control Clinic, 624-5419

About Safety

If Snoopy and the Red Baron buzz your house,
   Aircraft Accidents & Low Flying Complaints, 767-2747
If you're lost in the people-mover at Sea-Tac,
   Traveler's Aid Society, 447-3888
If your safety razor wasn't,
   Consumer Products Safety Commission, 442-5276

About Environment

To find out if Chicken Little is right,
   Weather Forecast, 662-1111
If you want to save a wild river,
   Friends of the Earth, 633-1661
When you can't see the Sea-First Building at high noon,
   Environmental Protection Agency, 442-1200
If your neighbor's furniture is floating past your window,
   Flood Control, 344-3874
Was it a pileated woodpecker or a tommy gun?
   Audubon Society, 622-6695
To find out what's dining on your azaleas,
   Arboretum Foundation, 325-4510

About Public Services

If the last elevator ride gave you a nose bleed,
   Elevator Permits & Inspections, 625-2540
If you lost your VW bug in a chuckhole,
   Street Maintenance, 625-2725; after 5 p.m. 625-4327
If your neighbor is raising hogs,
   Zone Code Information, 625-4518
If your boat becomes a submarine
   Coast Guard, 442-7343
For a tender passage,
   Ballard Bridge, 282-9525
The lifetime guarantee just died.
   Consumer Complaints & Inquiries, 464-6684
To set up your own sweatshop,
   Minor's Work Permits, 464-6800

To report W.W. III,
  Defense Civil Preparedness, 486-0721
To prove you exist,...or did,
  Birth & Death Records, 625-2075
For a list of jobs for somebody else,
  Employment Security Dept., 464-7697
To create a ripple in the air waves,
  FCC, 442-7653
If you've perfected perpetual motion,
  Federal Energy Office, 442-7260
If you want to reroute the Columbia River alongside I-90,
  Army Corps of Engineers, 764-3742
**If your dog went out to make a mess on the neighbor's lawn
  and didn't come back,**
  Animal Control Service, 344-3907
To zip up your mail,
  Zip Code Information, 442-5605
**To find out how long it will take a Christmas card to get
  across town,**
  Postal Information, 442-7850
To find out if Rough Riders are eligible for VA loans,
  Veterans Administration, 624-7200
To find out how much vacation you have left,
  Unemployment Insurance, 464-6080
If you find Bigfoot,
  State Game Dept., 464-7764
If your neighbor's plant just ate your fence,
  State Dept. of Ecology, 885-1900
If you're sleeping alone and something nibbles your ear,
  Rat & Insect Control, 625-2763
If your spouse — and bank account— are missing,
  Missing Persons, 625-2882
If you lost your seat on the bus,
  Metro Lost & Found, 447-4822
If your beer tastes like water,
  Liquor Control Board Office, 464-6070
If you really can't get there from here,
  Highway Dept. Information, 764-4097

About Money

Does 83% compounded monthly sound a mite steep?
  Consumer Protection, 464-6684

To find out how rich you'll be when you retire,
Social Security Adm., 763-9222
If even the loan sharks turn you down,
Seattle Credit Bureau, 626-5575

About Cars

To get rid of your neighbor's junk heap,
Auto Impounds, 625-2061
If your neighbor got yours first,
Auto Theft, 625-2501
To hit the road to Lilliwaup
Automobile Club of Washington, 292-5353

About Homes

If Ma Bell won't talk to you,
Telephone Repairs, 611
If you don't want your outhouse torn down,
Landmarks Preservation Board, 625-4501
If your gas range develops reverse thrusters,
Washington Natural Gas, 622-6100

About the Law

If you want to make it legal and end a friendship,
Marriage Licenses, 344-3933
When a fellow really needs a friend,
Public Defender, 344-3462
If Perry Mason is too busy for your case,
Lawyer Referral Service, 623-2988
To learn if your mother-in-law is deductible,
Internal Revenue Service, 442-1040

If You're Curious

To see the city from above,
Space Needle, 682-5656
To see the city from below,
Underground Tours, 682-1511
But if you don't want to burn your bridges or draft cards,
Passports, 442-7941
For the business boys in the white hats,
Better Business Bureau, 622-8066
To be a female chauvinist,
National Organization for Women, 632-8547
If little green men land on your patio and it isn't Halloween,
Phenomena Research, 722-3000

INDEX

(First number denotes main entry)

DOWNTOWN LOCATION
GUIDE

1. Washington Plaza Hotel
2. Visitors' Bureau
3. The Bon
4. Monorail Terminal
5. Frederick & Nelson
6. Medical-Dental Bldg.
7. Pike Place Market
8. J.C. Penney
9. Nordstrom
10. Seattle Aquarium
11. Waterfront Park
12. Post Office
13. Hilton Hotel
14. Rainier Tower
15. Olympic Hotel
16. Financial Center
17. Metro Office
18. Arcade Plaza
19. Seattle Tower
20. IBM Bldg.
21. YWCA
22. Federal Courthouse
23. Public Library
24. Sea-First Bldg.
25. Federal Reserve Bank
26. Bank of California Bldg.
27. YMCA
28. Federal Bldg.
29. Federal Office Bldg.
30. Norton Bldg.
31. Chamber of Commerce
32. Seattle Municipal Bldg.
33. Public Safety Bldg.
34. King County Administration Bldg.
35. King County Courthouse
36. Smith Tower
37. Occidental Park
38. AMTRAK Station
39. Klondike Gold Rush Park
40. Grand Central Arcade